P9-CCL-209

A NEW OWNER'S
GUIDE TO
CAIRN TERRIERS

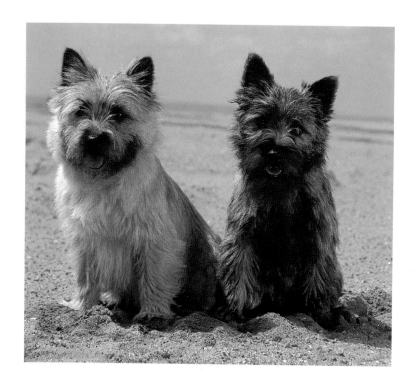

JG-166

Overleaf: Cairn Terriers owned by Michele Potenza.

Opposite page: Adult Cairn Terrier owned by Eleanor Buesing.

The Publisher wishes to acknowledge the owners of the dogs in this book, including: Pat Broyles, Michael Bruggeman, Eleanor Buesing, Ruth Deavers, Susan DeWitt, Carolyn Harrand, Myrtle Hawley, Louise Hooper, Kathy Norris Kompare, Suzane LaMarana, Marly Lucier, John Miksa, Sandra Murray, Frank Palmieri, Danelle Potenza, Michele Potenza, Ursula Schafer, Geraldine and Kathleen Sedora, Dianna Sibley, Susie Snellgrove, Denzel Spencer, Kathy Engel Stabler, Bill Taylor, Mr. and Mrs. G. Wallace, Karen Zarobinski, Dayle Ziesmer

The author acknowledges the contribution of Judy Iby to the following chapters: Health Care, Identification and Finding the Lost Dog, Traveling with Your Dog, and Behavior and Canine Communication.

A NEW OWNER'S GUIDE TO
CAIRN TERRIERS

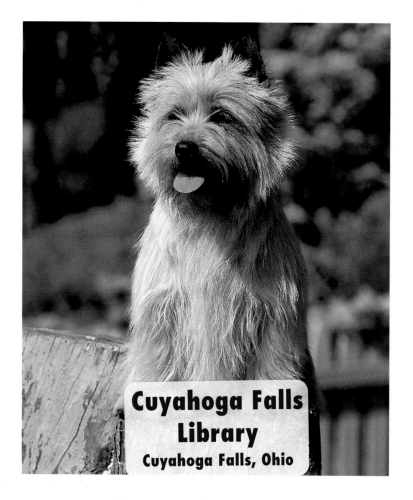

**Cuyahoga Falls
Library**
Cuyahoga Falls, Ohio

SANDRA MURRAY

T.F.H. Publications, Inc.
One TFH Plaza
Third and Union Avenues
Neptune City, NJ 07753

Copyright © 2004 by T.F.H. Publications, Inc.

All rights reserved. No part of this publication may be reproduced, stored, or transmitted in any form, or by any means electronic, mechanical or otherwise, without written permission from T.F.H. Publications, except where permitted by law. Requests for permission or further information should be directed to the above address.

This book has been published with the intent to provide accurate and authoritative information in regard to the subject matter within. While every precaution has been taken in preparation of this book, the publisher and author assume no responsibility for errors or omissions. Neither is any liability assumed for damages resulting from the use of the information herein.

If you purchased this book without a cover you should be aware that this book is stolen. It was reported as unsold and destroyed to the publisher and neither the author nor the publisher has received any payment for this "stripped book."

Library of Congress Cataloging-in-Publication Data
Murray, Sandra.
A new owner's guide to Cairn terriers / Sandra Murray.
p. cm.
ISBN 0-7938-2815-5 (alk. paper)
1. Cairn terrier. I. Title.
SF429.C3M87 2004
636.755—dc22
2003023044

www.tfh.com

ABOUT THE AUTHOR

Sandra Murray and her husband, Michael, have exhibited and bred show dogs for over 30 years, beginning with Irish Setters in 1968. When their two preschool children wanted a smaller dog that was easier for them to handle, the resulting search led to Cairn Terriers. With their very first Cairn, purchased in 1979, the Murrays were hooked on this irresistible breed.

Their Cairncroft Kennel was established in 1982 and has utilized both domestic and imported breeding stock from the UK and Scandinavia in creating dogs capable of excelling in both conformation and performance competition. While juggling the demands of raising children, earning a post-graduate degree, and teaching college courses, Sandra has piloted nearly 20 Cairncroft-bred dogs to their championships. Now able to focus more time on her dogs, Sandra's breeding and showing schedule has intensified. She has also contributed many articles on Cairn Terrier related topics to dog magazines and has judged Specialty Sweepstakes.

Sandra serves on The Cairn Terrier Club of America's Board of Governors and on its Education Committee. She is a charter member of the Cairn Terrier Club of Denver, the Rocky Mountain Terrier Association, and the Rocky Mountain Goal Diggers Earthdog Club.

Contents

2004 Edition

Independent, intelligent, and playful, Cairns are noted for being "easy keepers."

Ch. Ohioville-Glenmore Lucky Duck owes his look to the Cairn Terriers in his bloodline.

Choose a Cairn puppy that is alert and active, with bright eyes and a shiny coat.

The Cairn Terrier's loving and happy disposition makes him an ideal family pet.

Cairn Terriers excel in agility.

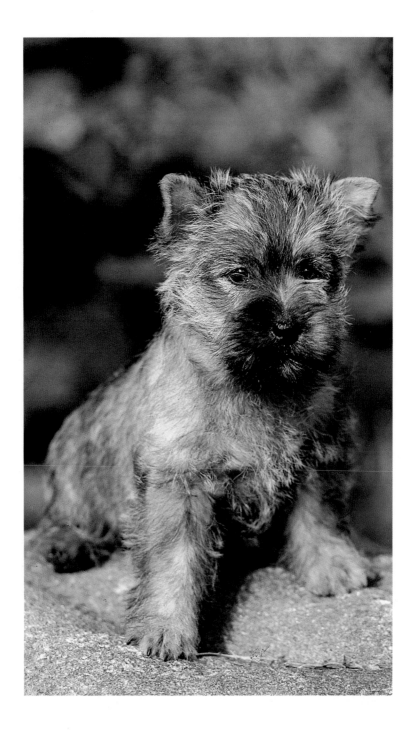

HISTORY of the Cairn Terrier

J ust how different are the genes of a Shih Tzu from the genes of a Great Dane? Those two breeds seem opposite in appearance, so their genes must be quite different, right? Actually, less than a one-percent difference exists in the genetic makeup between the heavy-coated dynamo of the Toy Group, the Shih Tzu, and the smooth-coated giant of the Working Group, the Great Dane. How can this be? Every single breed of dog that is registered with the American Kennel Club (AKC), which is over 100, descends from *Canis lupus*, the wolf.

HUMAN-DIRECTED DEVELOPMENT OF TRUE DOGS

Beginning thousands of years ago, humans began using wolves, probably captured as pups, to help them hunt for food. Later, humans would specifically breed animals that possessed the abilities and dispositions to most efficiently accomplish the main purposes in life for early man—to eat and not be eaten.

Although it may seem unlikely when looking at the little Cairn Terrier, the domesticated dogs of today all share the wolf as their common ancestor.

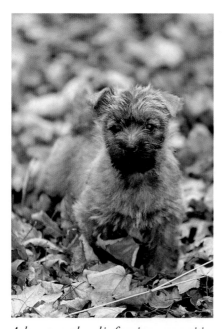

As humans gathered in farming communities and towns, they needed dogs that could hunt the vermin that destroyed their crops and food stores. These dogs became known as terriers, derived from the Latin word "terra," meaning earth, which is where these energetic diggers went after their prey.

These prehistoric hunters selected wolves with temperaments best suited for cooperative hunting relationships and with juvenile or adolescent personalities. Why? Such animals would be far less aggressive, far less likely to make a human their meal (instead of the intended antelope), and much more likely to accept a human as their "alpha," or pack leader. Also, and very importantly, only young wolves bark. Mature adult wolves growl, whine, snarl, yip, and howl, but do not bark. However, that adolescent trait of barking proved most valuable to early humans, so they selectively kept and bred those wolves that retained that trait. A canine that lived in or near human settlements could warn of approaching danger with loud barking, which was the key to survival. A group of early hunters could easily follow the sound of their barking wolf-dogs to quickly locate prey, and then use their canine partners to dispatch this next meal for the clan. Obviously, the reward for the wolf-dogs was a much steadier food supply than a wild pack of wolves could ever hope to have. Humans had what no wolf pack did—a variety of man-made weapons—so they could kill much more efficiently and consistently than wolves. These first semi-domesticated canids found life with humans to have definite bonuses!

The symbiotic relationship between human and canid flourished over the millennia. In addition to needing varied types of hunting dogs, humans required canine partners to help with livestock and other farm work when agricultural societies developed. Such selective breeding practices resulted in true dogs—dogs of a variety of types and sizes. Thus, the various breeds of dog began to appear.

EVOLUTION OF TERRIERS, ESPECIALLY CAIRN TERRIERS

As humans gathered in farming communities, towns, and cities, they needed dogs that possessed a passion for pursuing and killing rodents and other vermin attracted by the ready food sources where people congregated. For reasons unknown, the majority of dogs specifically bred to kill vermin came from Britain. They became known as terriers, derived from the Latin word, *terra*, meaning earth, which is exactly where these energetic diggers went after their prey. An utter fearlessness in pursuing fox, badger, or wild cat into their dens distinguished this group of dogs from others. The earliest recorded mention of terriers occurred in *The Boke of St. Albans* (1486) by Dame Juliana Berners, which listed the variety of dogs found in England, including the terrier. In 1576, Abraham Fleming wrote the first book in English that dealt entirely with dogs, aptly titled *Of Englifhe Dogges*. Fleming described terriers as "a perfect smelling group," referring to terriers' keen nose in locating their

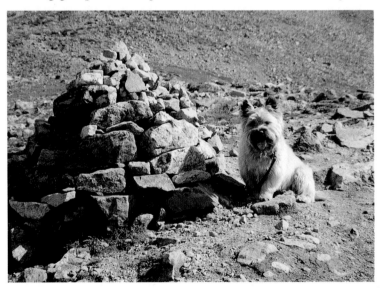

This Cairn Terrier stands next to the breed's namesake, a rock cairn. Farmers of the harsh Scottish Highlands once depended on the fearless and tenacious Cairn to bolt out fox, badgers, and otters from among the rock piles that marked their territories.

quarry. John Lesley gave us a glimpse into the general appearance and work of a terrier in his book, *Historie of Scotland* (1561), in which he described the terrier as "creeping into subterraneous burrows, routs out foxes, badgers, martens, and wild cats from their lurking places and dens. He, if he at any time finds the passage too narrow, opens himself a way with his feet and that with so great labour that he frequently perishes through his own exertions."

In addition to such terrier tenacity, Oliver Goldsmith, in 1774, added the following preference for "voice," that true dog trait of barking: "The terrier is a small kind of hound, with rough hair, made use of to force the fox and badger out of their holes; or rather to give notice *by their barking* in what part of their kennel the fox or badger resides, when the sportsmen intend to dig them out."

Only recently has modern technology enabled working terriers to wear a position-locating collar or beeper to aid their owners in finding them below ground. For centuries, a good, loud bark was the only clue as to where to dig for the terrier and his quarry.

By the 19th century, engravings and paintings were showing long- and short-legged terriers with rough and smooth coats. A book published in Edinburgh in 1829 describes "the rough haired Scotch," as well as other types of terriers. The author Thomas Brown went on to describe this dog as "generally low in stature, seldom more than 12 or 14 inches in height, with a strong, muscular body and short, stout legs; his ears small...his scent is extremely acute." Brown was describing the Old Scotch Terrier, the progenitor of separate breeds like the Cairn Terrier, Scottish Terrier, Dandie Dinmont Terrier, and West Highland White Terrier. Such dogs originated in the harsh environments of the western Highlands of Scotland and on the offshore Western Islands, particularly the Isle of Skye.

Of the separate breeds (West Highland White, Scottish Terrier, Skye Terrier, and Dandie Dinmont) that developed from the Old Scotch Terrier, the Cairn Terrier is most similar in conformation. These fearless hunters of the Highlands specialized in bolting fox, badger, and otter from among the rocks; hence, their eventual name. Cairn Terriers were so popular that King James of England and Scotland sent 6 of them as a gift to France prior to his death in 1625, nearly 400 years ago. Several Scottish families have records of the dogs owned by their ancestors dating back 200 years. The better known of these families are the Macdonalds of Waternish, the Drynoch strains of the MacLeods, and the Mackinnons of Kilbride—all from the Isle of Skye.

The crofters or farmers of Scotland also had a great need for dogs bred from these kennels, with packs often owned by a tod hunter— "tod" meaning fox in Gaelic. The tod hunter rented out his skills and his pack to the crofter to locate the den of the fox that was destroying his chickens and geese. Bold, tenacious Cairns would confront the foxes in their dens with such fierce fury that the foxes would bolt for the outside, only to meet their death at the hands of the tod hunter. In some cases, the Cairns themselves killed the fox, badger, or otter that they had been sent to ground to battle. In the course of such fierce fights, it was not uncommon for the Cairns to be severely wounded or killed because the dogs never, *ever* gave ground to their quarry. Interestingly, barn cats had the responsibility of decreasing the population of rats and mice on the Scottish crofts. In previous centuries, Cairns were used exclusively on large vermin.

An early 19th century painting de-picted Scottish lairds in kilts, hunting otter while clambering over a boulder field and accompanied by a pack of terriers, distinctly Cairn in appearance. Otter were considered vermin by the land-owners because of the large number of salmon and trout they consumed from rivers and streams. Notably, the men were on foot, because the terrain was too rough for horses to traverse.

As the 19th century passed into the early 20th, confusion reigned regarding the

In 1912, The Kennel Club in England approved four championship shows for the Cairn Terrier, and the breed was off and running. Cairns became popular pets and show dogs throughout Britain, which led to their eventual importation into the US.

Cairn's name; his origin on the Isle of Skye caused him to be known as a Skye Terrier, which conflicted with an already established terrier breed of that name. At times he was also called the Scotch Terrier, again raising conflict with the developing breed of the Scottish Terrier. At the turn of the 20th century in Britain, Cairn-like dogs were entered in dog shows as Shorthaired Skye Terriers or Prick-eared Skye Terriers. Because there was already a breed club registered with The Kennel Club for the Skye Terrier, breeders of that terrier objected strongly. The controversy came to a head in 1910 when pioneer Cairn Terrier breeders Mrs. Campbell and Miss Hawke entered their Cairns in classes for Skye Terriers. The Kennel Club of England met to resolve the issue and decreed that all Shorthaired Skyes would be transferred to the new register for Cairn Terriers without a fee until July 1, 1910. By 1912, four championship shows were approved for Cairn Terriers, and the breed was off and running. Cairns became popular pets and show dogs throughout Britain, which led to many being imported into the United States. In fact, well into the 1930s, the vast majority of champions from the United States were imported from England. Although most of our current Cairn champions were born in the United States, some breeders still bring fresh infusions of bloodstock from the UK and even Scandinavia.

The Cairn Terrier in America

The degree of excellence of any breed depends upon the skill and dedication of its breeders and how well those breeders educate the judges who will evaluate the breed in the show ring. Cairn Terriers have been blessed with a group of aficionados who devoted much of their lives to producing consistently excellent dogs. The Cairn Terrier Club of America (CTCA) continues to hold several seminars each year for new Cairn Terrier judges to educate them in the history, correct conformation, movement, and temperament of the Cairn.

Concentrating on the last 20 years, several kennels have contributed greatly to the breed.

Wolfpit, *Lydia Coleman Hutchinson, Middletown, MD*

Lydia Hutchinson continues the kennel established by her parents, the late Taylor and Esther Coleman, with great success. The influence of their foundation sire, Ch. Cairnwoods Quince,

The Cairn Terrier was given official recognition by the American Kennel Club as a member of the Terrier Group in 1938.

is still in evidence in the Wolfpit Cairns. The most recent standard bearer of this line is Ch. Caledonian Berry of Wolfpit, a multiple Best in Show winner, as well as a top producer, and his son, Ch. Caledonian Buck of Wolfpit. Wolfpit has bred over a hundred champions. Mrs. Hutchinson is also an active AKC judge and has served as vice-president and president of the Cairn Terrier Club of America.

Redcoat, Jack and Karen Smith, Fallbrook, CA

Utilizing a combination of English and American bloodstock, the Smiths have bred many champions while also devoting their energies to the CTCA, judging, and the Great Western Terrier Association. Their most recent import, Ch. Cairngold Captain Jack, has proved to be an influential sire with many champion offspring.

Cairmar, Betty and Joe Marcum, Alvarado, TX

Although not as active a breeder as in years past, Mrs. Marcum has contributed greatly to the development of the modern Cairn Terrier in the US. Cairmar has also bred over a hundred champions, some of the most famous being Ch. Cairmar Fancy Dresser, Ch. Cairmar Scot Free, and Ch. Cairmar Cowardly Lion.

Copperglen, Chuck and Carol Ackerson, Manchester, MO

Copperglen has produced a long line of beautifully-headed, harsh-coated Cairns that are very "typey." A few of the more outstanding dogs from this kennel are Ch. Copperglen Fame N Fortune (a national specialty Best of Breed winner), Ch. Copperglen Foxtrot, and Ch. Copperglen Windwalker.

Ragtime, Kathleen Spelman, Monrovia, CA

While remaining a very small kennel, Ragtime has produced some lovely dogs that continue to influence the future direction our breed. Noteworthy are Ch. Ragtime's Ain't She Sweet and her daughters, Ch. Ragtime's Christmas Carol and Ch. Ragtime's Christmas Holly.

Terriwood, Tom and Karin Godwin, Bothell, WA

Terriwood based their breeding program on descendents of Ch. Cairmar Fancy Dresser, but has since blended this bloodstock with other US and English-bred dogs. The Godwins have achieved tremendous success in both showing and breeding in a relatively short period of time. A few of their top winners are Ch. Terriwoods Best Dressed, Ch. Terriwoods Mighty Legacy, Ch. Terriwoods Black Tie (top-winning Cairn for three years in a row), and Ch. Ranic's Summer Star at Terriwood.

Ch. Cairncroft Night Hawk, owned by Michael Bruggeman and Sandra Murray.

Foxairn, *Sanderson and Peggy McIlwaine, Ann Arbor, MI*

A kennel noted for both Wire Fox Terriers and Cairn Terriers, Foxairn was home to two outstanding winners and producers: Ch. Cairnlea's Robson and Ch. Foxairn Tinman. A "Tinman" daughter, Ch. Foxairn Kaliope, has also been a top winner. Foxairn has been most successful in combining the best of British and American bloodstock.

Ohioville, *Ellie and Ralph Buesing, New Paltz, NY*

Ohioville consistently brings out winning Cairns with ring presence and wonderful harsh coats. Some of their top representatives are Ch. Ohioville Hooper, Ch. Ohioville Rooster, Ch. Ohioville Crow, and Ch. Tweedsmuir Ohioville Hudson.

Joywoods, *Larry and Barbara McNamee, Milwaukee, OR*

The standard bearer for this kennel that has had an incredibly strong influence on the breed during the past decade is Ch. Joywoods Donovan. Among his outstanding offspring from Joywood are Ch. Joywoods Rob Roy and Ch. Joywoods Jumpin' Jack Flash.

Goosedown, *Pat and Bill Hassey, Bend, OR*

Ch. Goosedown's Tailor Made was not only the top-winning Cairn for two years in a row, but he also continues as an influential sire of many champion offspring for Goosedown, as well as other kennels.

Cairncroft, *Sandra and Michael Murray, Woodland Park, CO*

Combining the best of British, American, and now Scandinavian bloodstock, Cairncroft has produced two national sweepstakes winners, Ch. Cairncroft Iron Horse and Ch. Cairncroft Quite A Miracle. Several dogs from this kennel have ranked within the top five nationally with their breeder/owner/handler: Ch. Cairncroft Jubilee, Ch. Cairncroft Night Hawk, and Ch. Cairncroft Quite A Miracle. All of the dogs live as companions in the house with the family.

Marquee, *Rebecca Stamps, Trenton, TX*

Basing her brood bitches on stock purchased from Copperglen Cairns, Becky now is crossing those champion, specialty-winning bitches with a stud dog imported from Denmark. This dog, Ch. Robinson Crusoe Quite Macho, is co-owned with Cairncroft Kennel and is already making an impact on the breed with his strong rear propulsion and ground-covering movement.

Obviously, this is only a sample of the many dedicated Cairn Terrier breeders who have influenced and will continue to influence the future of this breed. Our Cairns have never enjoyed such wide and deep good quality nationwide. The next decade will prove most exciting as new, young dogs have their turn to leave a legacy behind in their own offspring.

CHARACTERISTICS of the Cairn Terrier

All puppies are adorable, but the puppy you choose will grow up to exhibit traits that have been carefully linebred into his breed for centuries. Therefore, always go back to the history of the breed you have chosen to determine its characteristics, functions, and personality. Although training can moderate some of those inherent behaviors, no one is going to erase 500 years or more of intensive selective breeding. So how does breed history apply to the Cairn Terrier?

Remember that Cairns lived to hunt in packs, accompanied by their humans. Those two important facts impact the character and temperament of a Cairn. First of all, the Cairn comes loaded with energy and intelligence. To hunt all day in the cold, wet, rocky terrain of Scotland required energy and stamina. Scottish crofters and gamekeepers depended on the Cairn's keen nose and intelligence to independently locate and kill the quarry or rout it from its rocky den for a human to kill. Because of their small size, pack members

The puppy you choose will grow up to exhibit traits that have been carefully linebred into his breed for centuries. By researching the breed's history, you can determine its characteristics, functions, and personality.

cooperated in the corporate hunt to bring down prey much larger than the Cairn himself. Therefore, most Cairns are not aggressive toward other dogs if they are socialized and trained properly. In fact, Cairns that harbor antipathy for each other often become amiable enough companions if they hunt together frequently. That age-old urge to cooperate in the field does indeed bond canine friendships.

Although Cairns did not necessarily need humans to direct them in a hunt, they certainly enjoyed having their companionship. Unlike herding dogs that stayed outside to mind the flocks, Cairns generally lived inside the crofter's hut, sharing the warmth of the hearth with the family. This need for close human contact has remained a dominant characteristic of the Cairn Terrier. Kennel dogs do not develop the full Cairn personality that housedogs possess. Cairns raised in close companionship with humans respond much better to subtle cues from their owners, show an exuberant love of life, and rejoice in the simplest of activities. Therefore, many reputable breeders will not sell a puppy or even an adult dog to a family whose members are away from home all day. Prospective

Cairn Terriers have proven to be one of the most adaptable breeds, thriving equally as well in an apartment as on rural acreage.

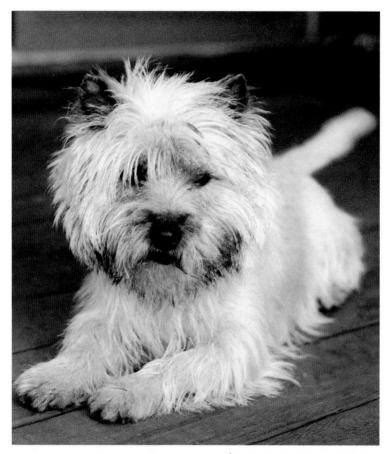

Although devoted pets, Cairns are extremely independent, so their owners need to be mentally one step ahead of their dogs in order to convince them that obeying a command is going to be worth their while.

buyers must provide puppy day care, which means coming home at lunchtime to feed and exercise their Cairn or providing a trusted friend or neighbor who will responsibly provide the socialization and outdoor exercise that the dog needs during the day.

Personality

Although Cairn Terriers show affection, their love is not of the demanding, constantly needing-to-be-touched sort. When a Cairn "runs low" on love, he returns to his humans for "filling up" and then merrily trots off. Many Cairns simply want to be

The Cairn Terrier's great intelligence, energetic personality, and sense of humor makes him a wonderful companion for people of all ages.

near their owners. Because they have proven to be such faithful, happy companions, many people involved in the breed can never settle for just one Cairn. Male Cairn Terriers, in particular, seem to be especially devoted to their owners and tend to be more affectionate than the females, who can sometimes be a bit independent.

Cairn Terriers have proven to be one of the most adaptable breeds, thriving equally as well in an apartment as on a rural acreage. As long as he receives the necessary exercise and mental stimulation to satisfy his energetic personality and active intelligence, the Cairn thrives. Unlike some breeds, the Cairn Terrier is not a "one man" or even a "one family" dog. The Cairn simply and purely loves people! He may have a favorite member of the family, but he tries to spread his love to everyone around him.

It is often thought that Cairns must have a built-in kid gene because the vast majority of the breed absolutely adores children— whether they've been raised with children or not. Cairns are sturdy enough to enjoy childish roughness and small enough for children

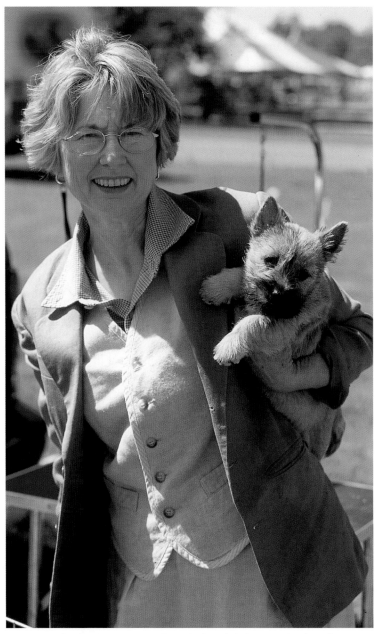

The motto for the Cairn Terrier from the breed club in Scotland is "the greatest little pal in the world."

to handle. Of course, until a child is old enough to responsibly handle a dog, an adult should always supervise any interactions. Unfortunately, many good dogs have transformed into biters because of parents' lack of supervision, thus forcing dogs to protect themselves the only way they know how.

BREED ATTRIBUTES

The Cairn's ability to work independently comes to the fore in his attitude toward obedience. Slavish devotion to obey an owner's every command may describe a Border Collie, but not a Cairn Terrier! Cairns are very intelligent and have a great sense of humor, so Cairn owners need to be mentally one step ahead of their dogs and prove to them that obeying a command is going to be worth their while. That same intelligence and sense of humor make the Cairn Terrier a natural for games of all kinds. When happy or pleased with himself, a Cairn "grins" by squinting up his eyes, pulling his mouth back at the corners, and loosely laying his ears back on his head, all while his body wriggles with joy and his tail wags merrily. No one knows how to squeeze more joy out of life than a Cairn Terrier! This trait makes them great companions for their humans. In fact, the motto for the Cairn Terrier from the breed club in Scotland is "the greatest little pal in the world!"

STANDARD for the Cairn Terrier

The current breed standard for the Cairn Terrier has remained essentially the same since it was adopted by the Cairn Terrier Club of America in 1937 and approved by the AKC on May 10, 1938. Instead of revising the standard itself, the Board of Governors of the CTCA published a booklet called *Interpretation, Clarification, and Amplification of the Cairn Terrier Standard,* which includes very helpful drawings to aid in understanding how a Cairn should look and move. For more information, check out the CTCA's web site at *www.cairnterrier.org.*

STANDARD AND CLARIFICATION COMMENTS

General Appearance—That of an active, game, hardy, small working terrier of the short-legged class; very free in its movements, strongly but not heavily built, standing well forward on its forelegs, deep in the ribs, well coupled with strong hindquarters and

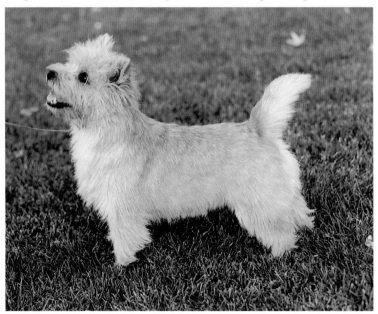

A standard is a blueprint by which breeders can endeavor to create the ideal of the breed.

presenting a well-proportioned build with a medium length of back, having a hard, weather-resisting coat; head shorter and wider than any other terrier and well furnished with hair giving a general foxy expression.

Clarification: This first sentence describes the essential picture of "a big dog in a small package." The Cairn is of the short-legged terriers, but a working terrier, not so low to the ground as to have a "weasley" look yet not too high on leg as to appear "up on stilts." The word "medium" is the key word throughout this standard. Not a short-back, square-looking terrier, but a terrier with enough length of back to be able to twist and turn in and out of holes and among rocks with quick movements is ideal.

Author's Comments: Both the Cairn Terrier and the West Highland White Terrier fall more accurately into the category of "medium-legged" rather than "short-legged." The Cairn does not possess the short legs of a Scottie or a Dandie Dinmont Terrier, nor does he have the longer legs of a Welsh or a Lakeland Terrier. Every aspect of the Cairn's body and personality should proclaim a bold, strong, yet lithe and agile working terrier with an emphasis on "working."

Head:

Skull—Broad in proportion to length with a decided stop and well furnished with hair on top of the head, which may be somewhat softer than the body coat. *Muzzle*—Strong but not too long or heavy. *Teeth*—Large, mouth neither overshot nor undershot. *Nose*—Black. *Eyes*—Set wide apart, rather sunken, with shaggy eyebrows, medium in size, hazel or dark hazel in color, depending on body color, with a keen terrier expression. *Ears*—Small, pointed, well carried erectly, set wide apart on the side of the head. Free from long hairs.

Clarification: The head is very broad and short. The muzzle shorter than the length of skull. The ideal proportion of muzzle to skull is four to five. The muzzle is full but not heavy, yet broad enough to hold a full set of large, strong teeth. Heads may go to extremes and be too heavily boned, appearing coarse and too fine or "snipey." Please note the standard does not call for a foxy head—only for a foxy expression (smart, alert, cunning), which is lost if the head is coarse or overdone.

Large, strong teeth are important. There should be six incisors upper and lower. The bite is either level or scissors—not overshot or undershot. The nose black only. The preferred eye color should

The general appearance of a Cairn Terrier is that of an active, hardy, small working terrier.

The Cairn's very broad and short head is quite unique among the Terrier Group, as is his smart and cunning expression.

be dark hazel (not black), and eyes should be medium in size, oval in shape, and wide set, giving a "devilish" look to the Cairn. Ears are small, wide set, properly placed on the sides of the head, but carried upright.

Author's Comments: The Cairn's head is quite unique among the terriers, so his structure and that true Cairn expression are most important and not easy to maintain in one's breeding program.

Many breeders prefer a true scissors bite. "Dark hazel" eye color, in modern parlance, means a rich, dark brown.

Tail—In proportion to head, well furnished with hair but not feathery. Carried gaily but must not curl over back. Set on at back level.

Clarification: Length of tail should equal height of ears. A standing Cairn should be able to have a ruler parallel to the ground from the tail's tip to the ear's tip. The tail is set high, at back level, but the ideal tail carriage is not necessarily vertical and should never be curled over the back. A Cairn going around the ring and carrying his tail at one or two o'clock is fine.

Body—Well muscled, strong, active body with well-sprung, deep ribs, coupled to strong hindquarters, with a level back of medium length, giving an impression of strength and activity without heaviness.

Clarification: A firmly put together body with a heart (or egg) shaped rib cage, not barrel ribs or slab sided is correct. Level back is desired. A good topline is a combination of proper placement of the bone structure, as well as correct angulation.

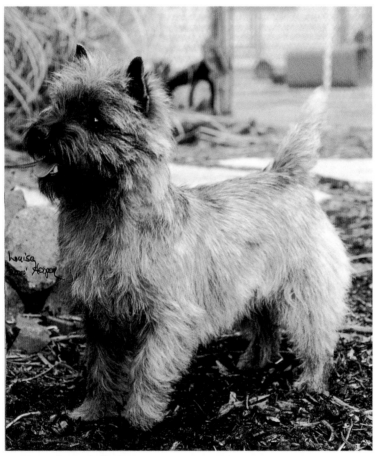

With a well-muscled body, deep ribs, and strong hindquarters, the Cairn gives the impression of strength and activity without heaviness.

Shoulders, Legs and Feet—A sloping shoulder, medium length of leg, good but not too heavy bone; forelegs should not be out at elbows, and be perfectly straight, but forefeet may be slightly turned out. Forefeet larger than hind feet. Legs must be covered with hard hair. Pads should be thick and strong and dog should stand well up on its feet.

Clarification: There should be some overhang in the front; the pro sternum should be fairly prominent with the front legs well back in under the withers. Front legs are straight and well muscled without a tendency of a fiddle-front, but front feet may turn out slightly for digging purposes. However, this does not mean "east-west" front feet. Front feet are larger than back feet (again for digging purposes) with good depth in the pad and strong pasterns, never down on the pasterns. Feet should be tight—with no indication toward a splayed foot. Nails must be kept short.

Hindquarters: bend of stifle should be in proportion to shoulder layback to allow for a smooth, even gait. Hindquarters muscled

The Cairn Terrier has a hard and weather-resistant double coat, which should be the same length all over the body.

According to the standard, the Cairn may be any color except white.

with straight hocks. Cow hocks and open hocks should be severely penalized. Gait: should move freely and easily with reach in front and drive in rear on a loose lead. When viewed from the front, the legs should be straight and show reach. Any tendency toward winging or paddling should be penalized—as should crabbing. When viewed from the rear, the gait should show drive with the hocks parallel to each other and not too close together.

Author's Comments: Originators of nearly all of the breed standards were horse people who clearly understood what proper movement looked like and what was required physiologically in the dog to produce that proper movement. Most of today's dog breeders do not "ride to hounds," so they must spend many hours of study and observation to identify correct movement. Then even more work goes into actually being able to produce dogs with such movement. To further complicate matters, correct movement in a Chow, for example, is not correct movement for a Cairn Terrier. However, a common denominator does exist for all those breeds that had to traverse miles of rough terrain as efficiently as possible—the Cairn included. That phrase, "freely and easily" says it all, if one pictures a dog that reaches far in front and drives off a powerful rear with the hind leg extending back an equal distance to the reach in front. During this free and easy movement, the topline of the Cairn should remain relatively level with no wasted bouncing up and down motion.

Coat—Hard and weather-resistant. Must be double-coated with profuse harsh outer coat and short, soft, close furry undercoat.

Clarification: This hard, double coat is most important in the Cairn, as it was designed to keep cold and water from penetrating the skin. The profuse coat should be thick and a minimum of two inches in length. It should be the same length all over the body. Any appearance of the "jacketed" or "sculptured" look of the more stylized terriers should be severely penalized.

Color—May be of any color except white. Dark ears, muzzle and tail tip are desirable.

Clarification: Any color except white is permissible; however, any markings resembling the old black and tan terrier

The ideal Cairn Terrier should be of balanced proportions and appear neither leggy nor too low to the ground, and neither too short nor too long in body.

(Doberman-type markings) or parti-colored markings are highly objectionable and should not be allowed. Dark points—muzzle, ears, tail—are desirable.

Ideal Size—Involves the weight, the height at the withers and the length of the body. Weight for bitches, 13 pounds; for dogs, 14 pounds. Height at the withers—bitches, 9 $1/2$ inches; dogs, 10 inches. Length of body from 14 $1/4$ to 15 inches from the front of the chest to back of hindquarters. The dog must be of balanced proportions and appear neither leggy nor too low to ground; and neither too short nor too long in body. Weight and measurements are for mature dogs at two years of age. Older dogs may weigh slightly in excess and growing dogs may be under these weights and measurements.

Clarification: While the weight and height limits are important, it should be stressed that the overall balance of the dog is most important. A well-boned, properly coated dog may appear larger than a light-boned, short-coated dog. A slightly under or oversized dog of obvious quality is preferable to a proper sized dog lacking the desired attributes.

Author's Comments: Besides stressing the overall balance and proportions of a Cairn, one needs to remember that this is a rectangular-shaped dog, able to turn about in a narrow den. He must not be so small as to prove inept in fighting his quarry nor so large as to not be able to speedily work his prey in a nine- to ten-inch diameter den entrance and tunnel.

Condition—Dogs should be shown in good hard flesh, well muscled and neither too fat or thin. Should be in full good coat with plenty of head furnishings, be clean, combed, brushed and tidied up on ears, tail, feet and general outline. Should move freely and easily on a loose lead, should not cringe on being handled, should stand up on their toes and show with marked terrier characteristics.

Clarification: A Cairn should not be too heavy in body or in weight. They are not chunky little dogs and should have a little extra length of loin to be agile. In feeling behind the rib cage along the sides of the dog, a very slight depression is good in the loin area. Not that you want to feel the hip bones, but you do want to feel the ribs and you want some leanness through the body. Cairns are not as heavy boned as the Westie or Scottie.

Author's Comments: What both the standard and the clarification are describing is a long distance runner, not a weight lifter. The Cairn, although certainly strong and tough, has a lithe athlete's body that can twist, turn, double back, and leap—all with grace and agility and incredible endurance.

FAULTS

1. *Skull*—Too narrow in skull.

2. *Muzzle*—Too long and heavy a foreface; mouth overshot or undershot.

3. *Eyes*—Too large, prominent, yellow, and ringed are all objectionable.

4. *Ears*—Too large, round at points, set too close together, set too high on the head; heavily covered with hair.

5. *Legs and Feet*—Too light or too heavy bone. Crooked forelegs or

The Cairn Terrier has often been described as "a big dog in a small package."

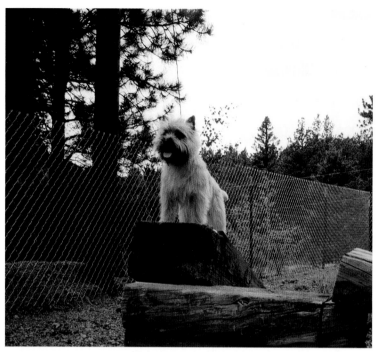

Strong and tough, the Cairn has a lithe, athletic body and incredible endurance.

out at elbow. Thin, ferrety feet; feet let down on the heel or too open and spread. Too high or too low on the leg.

6. *Body* —Too short back and compact a body, hampering quickness of movement and turning ability. Too long, weedy and snaky a body, giving an impression of weakness. Tail set on too low. Back not level.

7. *Coat* —Open coats, blousy coats, too short or dead coats, lack of sufficient undercoat, lack of head furnishings, lack of hard hair on the legs. Silkiness or curliness. A slight wave permissible.

8. *Nose* —Flesh or light-colored nose.

9. *Color* —White on chest, feet or other parts of body.

Approved May 10, 1938

SELECTING Your Cairn Terrier

The price of a purebred dog is minuscule in comparison to the total lifetime costs of dog food, veterinary bills, toys, crates, grooming equipment, bedding, etc. Shopping for the lowest priced puppy or buying the first available puppy is both risky and costly in the long run. Where does one begin, then, to look for a healthy, well-socialized, and well-bred Cairn Terrier puppy?

The obvious sources to avoid are puppy mills and ads in the paper. Kennels that raise multiple breeds for sale or have more than three or four litters a year immediately become suspect as puppy mills. Such kennels operate strictly from the profit motive, meaning they don't perform the necessary genetic testing of their breeding stock to ensure healthy puppies. These kennels view their dogs as livestock. Although the dogs may be kept clean and well fed (and many are not!), they are deprived of human contact and affection. How can you possibly predict the personality that your puppy will develop if his parents have never received the necessary love and attention?

Many Cairn Terriers sold through classified ads in the local paper come from "backyard" breeders; for example, families that may have wanted their children to experience raising puppies or thought their Cairn was so cute that she should have a litter. Unfortunately, these are not sound reasons for breeding a dog. Consequently, serious health and conformation problems may appear in such litters, with the future costs of these problems to be borne by the unsuspecting puppy buyer.

Many wonderful Cairns have found homes through Cairn rescue volunteers, but these often abused or neglected dogs require extraordinarily patient people with a great deal of time and love to devote to their second-hand dogs. Rescue Cairn Terriers are not always the best choice for some families. Fortunately, Cairn Terriers are not as common as other breeds, so they are seldom found in shelters. Also, reputable breeders work extremely hard to match Cairns with their prospective owners so that the dogs do not end up in shelters.

PICKING A HEALTHY PUPPY

Remember the wording of the Cairn Terrier standard? It calls for an "active, game, hardy, working terrier" with very specific

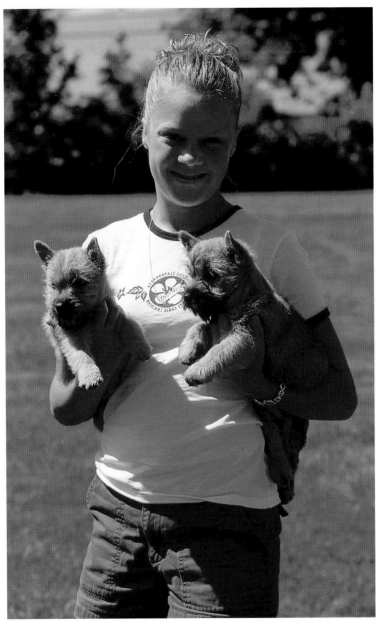

The purchase of any puppy is an important step, because the well-cared-for dog will live with you for many years. Be sure to thoroughly research the breed before bringing a Cairn Terrier home.

Rely upon recommendations from national kennel clubs or local breed clubs when looking for a reputable breeder.

descriptions of how a Cairn should be built and move. Why? If a Cairn is built properly, he will remain active and free from bone- and joint-related diseases well into old age—and Cairns live a long time! Therefore, anyone wanting a truly typey, sound, healthy puppy that has been properly socialized with people needs to contact a reputable Cairn Terrier breeder. The Cairn Terrier Club of America (CTCA) maintains a web site with many hyperlinks, one of which will guide you to a breeder in your general geographic area. The American Kennel Club also provides the telephone number of the CTCA secretary, who can direct you to reputable breeders in your region. Because careful breeders do not have more than a few litters a year, please be prepared to place your name on a waiting list. Waiting several months for a good-quality, healthy Cairn Terrier puppy is well worth the effort.

After contacting a reputable breeder, you may find yourself in an intensive interview. Cairn breeders take the greatest care in placing their puppies with just the right families or individuals, so be prepared to answer many questions regarding your living situation, backyard size, ages and sexes of your children, etc. You, on the other hand, have a right and an obligation to ask what genetic testing has been done on the sire and dam of this litter. How have the puppies been socialized so far? What inoculations and deworming have they received? What sort of health guarantee accompanies the puppy that you are considering?

Every single breed of dog—mixed breeds, too—has certain genetic-related problems. Although basically a hardy, healthy breed, the Cairn does have some inherited genetic anomalies. The CTCA web site includes a list of the genetic diseases found in the Cairn Terrier. Read about these before visiting a breeder so that you can ask specific questions regarding the genetic health of the parents of the litter and the puppies themselves. Observe the litter. Cairn puppies should be active, curious, outgoing, affectionate, and playful, interacting eagerly with other dogs and humans. Although small in size, a Cairn Terrier puppy should feel substantial and sturdy in your hand, not fine boned or delicate. This is a working terrier, not one of the Toy breeds! A healthy puppy will have a clean, sweet odor about him with no signs of diarrhea, coughing, or vomiting. The eyes will be clear, bright,

These irresistible Cairn puppies are a result of quality breeding and excellent care.

Any predictions breeders make about a pup's future as a show prospect are based on their experience with past litters that have produced winning show dogs.

and free of discharge. If possible, take the puppy you are considering into a room away from his dam and littermates to observe his behavior. The puppy should possess enough confidence to remain outgoing and interested in his new environment and in you.

SHOW PROSPECT OR PET?

Breeders will probably not sell a puppy before he is 10 to 12 weeks old. By that time, the breeder will already have a good idea who the show prospects are in the litter. He or she will ask you whether you want just a pet or a show dog and will point out the differences between the two. Feel free to ask what exactly is entailed in showing a dog. Many breeders will co-own a show dog with a first-time exhibitor, contributing their very extensive experience in grooming and handling to the novice as part of the co-ownership arrangement. Most people, however, want a good, healthy pet, and such a puppy is available in nearly every litter—even ones planned with show prospects in mind. The reasons for rating a puppy as pet quality have nothing to do with his health or his suitability as a companion. Faults such as a lower tail carriage, undescended testicles, or missing teeth will make the puppy pet quality. Therefore, pet puppies are sold with a neutering requirement that should be fulfilled by the new owner when the pup is six months old.

Breeders often have adult Cairns that are available to go to carefully selected homes. Bitches that have produced several litters are spayed and placed in "retirement homes" for the duration of their lives. Sometimes young dogs of a year or so prove not to be the show dogs the breeder had hoped for and are sold as neutered pets. For those individuals not able or willing to handle the demands of a young puppy, a young adult Cairn is a marvelous addition to the family. Through careful matching of the dogs to their humans, the Cairn Terrier's adaptability makes adjusting to a new home much easier.

ESSENTIAL PAPERWORK
Every breeder should provide you with the following important documents:
• An official application for registration from the American Kennel Club with the breeder signing over the ownership of the puppy to you.
• A three- to five-generation pedigree.
• A diet sheet that outlines the type and amount of food the puppy should eat, as well as how often he should be fed. Such guidelines should include changes according to the puppy's growth.

Cairn Terriers and children are made for each other and thrive in one another's company.

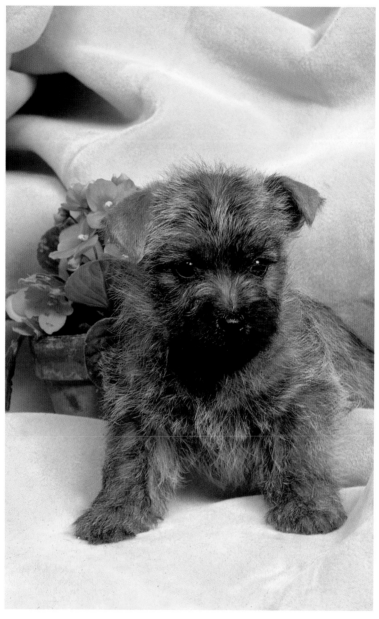

The purchase of any purebred dog entitles you to some important documents: a health record containing a vaccination list, a copy of the dog's pedigree, a registration certificate, a diet sheet, and a health guarantee.

• Documentation from the examining veterinarian as to the physical health and soundness of the puppy, inoculations received with dates, deworming medications administered with dates, or any other pertinent medical data on the puppy.

• A copy of the contract of sale signed by both the seller and the buyer of the puppy, which should include the breeder's health guarantee on the puppy. (Not all breeders use contracts, but many do.)

Temperament and Socialization

A reputable breeder already will have started socializing your new puppy, so be sure to continue. Your youngster must learn to deal gracefully and confidently with all sorts of new and strange environments, some of them quite noisy. Cairns must learn to appreciate humans in all of their various ages, sizes, levels of noise, and ways of moving. Your Cairn must learn to accept visiting dogs—or dogs met out in public places—without being aggressive. The temperament genes that your Cairn inherited will play a major part in his personality, but his human family has a tremendously important role as well. Introduce the Cairn puppy to every new situation you can possibly think of, always ensuring his safety and working to make each experience a happy, pleasant one. Do this by taking the puppy with you to the bank drive-through. (The tellers often give doggy treats!) Take him with you to visit friends, if they approve. With your puppy under

Introducing your puppy to new people, places, and other pets will ensure that he is confident and well-socialized.

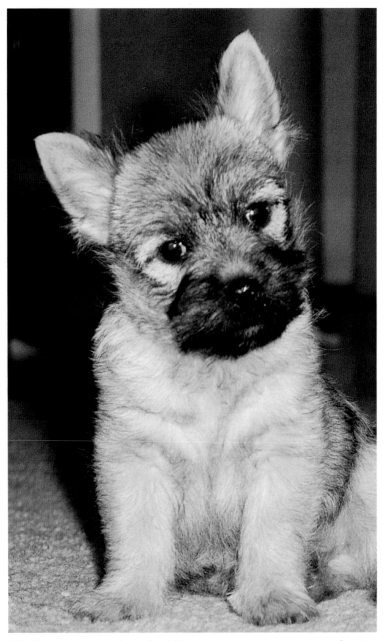

The Cairn puppy you choose should be active, outgoing, responsive, and curious about the world around him.

control on his leash, take him to your child's soccer games, for hikes along nature trails, for strolls on sidewalks next to bustling car and truck traffic, and for walks in the park. Introduce him to strangers, both human and canine—always asking permission first. Some dogs are aggressive toward other dogs, and unbelievably, there are some people who actually don't like dogs!

Cairn Terriers and children are made for each other and thrive in each other's company. Adult supervision should always accompany children and puppy/dog interactions. Older children can often be left on their own with a Cairn, thanks to the sturdy, hardy build of the breed. Together, dog and child can have wonderful adventures and create life-long bonds of companionship. If your home has no children, visit neighbors, friends, or relatives who have children to properly socialize your Cairn puppy to these active, noisy little humans. The window of opportunity in which a puppy can successfully adapt to almost any situation does not last very long. By all means, use these early months of your Cairn's life to mold a confident, resilient dog that can deal calmly with any and all situations.

An integral part of the socialization process involves convincing your puppy that you have the right to handle and examine every single inch of his body, including his mouth. Your Cairn can learn these lessons easily and naturally if you examine his feet, mouth, tail, etc. for just a few moments every day as a part of his quality time with you. Always reward his cooperation with a treat and praise. Whenever it's time for a grooming session or a visit to the veterinarian, you will be forever grateful that you invested the time and effort in teaching your Cairn to stand calmly while being handled or examined.

CARING for Your Cairn Terrier

airn Terriers are noted for being "easy keepers." In other words, they require a small amount of high-quality food to maintain a healthy weight and vitality. Because of this tendency, Cairns are not expensive to maintain. Owners must beware, however, not to overfeed and create a "stuffed sausage" look in a dog that is meant to be lithe and agile. Ribs should not be seen, but be readily felt. No soft layer of fat should be detected between the thumb and forefinger when the skin over the rib cage is pinched gently together. Normal-sized adult hands should be able to span the waist area of a mature Cairn with the opposing thumbs just touching. Keep these guidelines in mind while we discuss feeding your Cairn.

Use only stainless steel feed pans and water dishes. Stainless steel has no harmful chemicals in its composition and can be easily disinfected and run through the dishwasher for cleaning. Water dishes need daily disinfecting before refilling, and feed pans should be run through the dishwasher after every feeding.

A typical 8- to 12-week-old puppy will require 3 meals a day. By 6 months of age, he will be eating just twice a day.

Cairn Terriers are noted for being "easy keepers" because they require only a small amount of food to maintain a healthy weight and vitality.

No discussion of diet is complete without stating that only pure water should be available to your Cairn at all times. After oxygen, water is the most important element required by any mammal's body, both yours and your dog's. We can no longer take for granted that pure water comes out of our faucets. Many municipal water sources are often polluted, which necessitates sanitizing the water with the toxic chemical chlorine. Well water often contains pollutants from a neighbor's septic system or from contamination in the underground aquifer. Distilled bottle water from the grocery store will serve as a short term solution, but the use of a reverse osmosis water purifier will go a long way toward ensuring that both you and your Cairn live long, healthy lives together.

FEEDING PUPPIES

Puppies' stomachs are small; yet the rapidly growing puppy body needs much fuel to grow on, so frequent meals are required. A typical 8- to 12-week-old puppy will eat 3 meals a day: breakfast, lunch, and dinner. Many breeders will vary the content of these meals by giving a milky broth over dry food for breakfast and meat with a bit of hot water over dry food for lunch and dinner. Soon, around three months of age, the lunchtime ration can be eliminated from the puppy's regimen. Allow the pup himself to let you know when it is time to discontinue a meal — he will not be as interested in this meal, because he just isn't that hungry due to increased volume of intake at breakfast and dinner. Small puppies, still needing frequent feedings, will require approximately one-sixth of a cup of dry food three times a day. As the puppy grows, increase the amount of dry food as the number of times fed decreases. By 14 weeks of age, a Cairn puppy will be eating just twice a day, breakfast and dinner, and consuming around one-third of a cup of dry meal plus a large tablespoon of meat at each feeding. Very young pups demand specific nutrients for proper growth and bone density and so should be fed only dry kibble specially formulated for growing puppies. However, at twelve weeks of age, puppies should be transferred to regular adult rations to prevent diet-caused bone and joint problems from a too-rich diet.

To B.A.R.F. or Not to B.A.R.F.?—Feeding Raw and Natural Foods

During the last ten years, dog breeders and owners have witnessed explosive growth in information on how to properly feed dogs.

Always be sure to feed your dog age-appropriate food. For example, very young puppies demand specific nutrients for proper growth and bone density.

Many canine nutritionists and veterinarians have shattered the long-held view that the commercial dog food companies always know what is the best diet for our dogs.

DNA studies have proven that the genetic difference between the domestic dog and the wolf is less than one percent. Therefore, canine nutritionists have looked closely at what wolves and other wild canids eat. Corn (and wheat), which makes up the basis for much of the commercial dry kibble, does not happen to be a foodstuff, which wolves consume. Raw flesh, organs, and bone plus the vegetable contents in the stomachs of the herbivores killed by the wolves constitute a wolf's diet. Some veterinarians and canine nutritionists, therefore, suggest that dogs be fed a diet much more closely resembling that of the wild relatives on the family tree. Hopefully, this section will clarify the essential points of the various raw diets and give options on combining raw food with all-natural kibble.

B.A.R.F. Is Not What You Think!

The name "B.A.R.F." is not what you think! It's an acronym that stands for "bones and raw foods," first coined by Dr. Ian Billinghurst, an Australian veterinarian. He wrote two books, *Give Your Dog a Bone* and *Grow Your Pups with Bones*, which became immensely popular among dog owners who began putting his recommendations

Providing your Cairn with a well-balanced and healthy diet will keep him in excellent condition throughout his life.

into practice. So, what do B.A.R.F. feeders feed? They give their dogs:

1. Raw meaty bones (RMBs)—chicken, lamb, pork, beef, fish, rabbit, venison
2. Ground or chunked meats of the same animals
3. Organ meats
4. Pulverized vegetables and leafy greens
5. Fruits
6. Nuts and seeds
7. Oils: primarily flaxseed oil and fish body oil
8. Dairy products such as yogurt and cottage cheese
9. Probiotics and digestive enzymes

Of course, the phrase "raw bones" was the source of my initial shock when I first heard about the B.A.R.F. diet. I discovered, however, that it is when bones are cooked that they dry out and tend to splinter, making them prime candidates for perforating digestive organs on their way down. Raw, meaty bones, however, are much more soft and pliable. Yes, there have been some documented cases of pieces of bone causing intestinal impactions in dogs fed raw bones. If you have a dog that bolts down his food like the proverbial pig (I have several of those!) and would probably do the same thing with a raw chicken wing, you may feel more comfortable feeding a packaged raw food product. These products contain raw bone ground up in the meat. The absolutely marvelous benefit of feeding raw bone—whether ground or whole—to your dog is

Some experts believe that feeding your dog an all-natural diet ensures better overall health and quality of life.

clean, healthy teeth and gums with sweet breath. That's right! No more "doggy breath" that can curdle your stomach or cement-like plaque to scrape off of Rover's teeth! Something about the raw bone in the diet changes the biochemistry of the dog's saliva to prevent tartar buildup and gingivitis.

Another major objection that most people have to feeding their dogs a raw diet is the fear of poisoning their dogs with bacteria-laden meat. However, the digestive systems of both dogs and cats are especially adapted to handling bacteria ingested with raw food. For extra careful dog owners, food-grade hydrogen peroxide can safely disinfect raw meat as

There are a number of ways you can improve the quality of the diet you offer your Cairn. It's been noted that feeding raw meats, cooked grains, fruits, and vegetables may decrease the chances of your pet developing chronic illnesses.

well as fruits and vegetables. One tablespoon of 3 percent food-grade hydrogen peroxide mixed into a cup of water per pound of meat will kill any harmful bacteria.

To aid neophytes just embarking upon feeding raw diets, there are a number of resources available to provide the needed information. The list below includes the names of the acknowledged experts in feeding raw foods and their books, with a short blurb regarding the contents:

Dr. Ian Billinghurst, *Give Your Dog a Bone* and *Grow Your Pups with Bones.*

This book recommends a diet of 50 percent RMBs with 50 percent vegetables and supplements. It is the easiest diet to follow.

Wendy Volhard, *The Holistic Guide for a Healthy Dog* (with Kerry Brown, DVM).

This diet recommends a diet high in grains and calcium received from bone meal rather than RMBs. It is very restrictive.

Kymythy Schultze, *Ultimate Pet Diet: Natural Nutrition for Dogs and Cats.*

This diet does not allow grains or dairy products. It is good for dogs with cancer or allergies.

Richard H. Pitcairn, DVM, *Dr. Pitcairn's Complete Guide To Natural Health For Cats and Dogs.*

This diet contains a variety of individually balanced receipes. It is high in grains and calcium comes from bone meal instead of RMBs. It also includes quite a bit of yeast.

Pat McKay, *Reigning Cats and Dogs.*

This diet is very similar to that of Schultze's listed above.

Juliette de Baircli Levy, *The Complete Herbal Handbook for the Dog and Cat.*

Good results have been reported over many decades from those using her diet. It can be difficult for beginners to follow.

Maryann Mott, *Nutrition for Dogs.*

This book offers comprehensive information on nutrition know-how and special diets for all canine stages.

Back to Basics

Until recently, zoologists had classified dogs and wolves as separate species. One of the fruits of the canine genome project is the new

Your Cairn should have a well-balanced diet that includes the necessary amounts of fats, proteins, carbohydrates, and vitamins.

Proper nutrition is imperative to your dog's health and promotes longevity.

knowledge that, genetically, not enough difference exists between dogs and wolves to separate them into two different species. In fact, dogs share more genetic material with wolves than they do with coyotes or jackals. Therefore, in many ways, dogs are wolves with a thin veneer of civilization on them from living for so long as companions of humans. What do wolves eat? They eat raw meat, organs, the stomach contents of herbivores they kill, and some of the bone as they seek to consume the marrow inside. It does indeed make sense that the more closely we feed our dogs that same diet, the healthier and more fit they will be.

Feeding Options

Most people have remained unaware that multiple choices exist in how and what they feed their dogs. Actually, a number of options are available to dog owners:

1. Buy commercial grocery store brands of kibble, either fed dry or with a commercial canned food added.

2. Purchase all-natural kibble and add that brand's canned food.

3. Personally cook a customized diet for your dog.

4. Feed all-raw foods with supplements added.

5. Feed raw, ground meat with ground raw bones and an all-natural top-quality kibble.

The purists who feed a strictly raw diet to their dogs would probably say that one should never combine raw food with processed kibble. In ideal situations, it would indeed be best to feed totally raw, unprocessed

As your dog ages, the best way to determine if his diet is sufficient is by checking his weight, muscle mass, and level of activity. An older, overweight Cairn will have a shorter life than one in good, lean condition.

foods to our dogs. However, many of us travel a great deal to dog shows, leaving behind a number of brood bitches, puppies, and stud dogs in the care of long suffering, overworked spouses or dog sitters. The extra work entailed in preparing a raw diet for multiple dogs may be more of a burden than we feel fair to place on our canine caregivers. Also, the time and energy demands on dog owners with careers and/or children may make the option of combining raw food with a more healthy, all-natural kibble most appealing. Fortunately, there do exist companies out there trying to provide such alternative food choices.

So, back to our original question posed by the title of this section: "to B.A.R.F. or not to B.A.R.F.?" Well, that depends on your lifestyle, your dog's age and specific health issues, how many dogs you have to feed, and how dependent you are upon others to care for your dogs while you travel. However, if you have educated yourself in all of the current available information on canine nutrition, you can at least make an informed, intelligent decision on what to feed your dogs.

To further assist you in a continuing educational process, this article concludes with an extensive list of web sites on canine health and nutrition.

Web Sites:
1. **www.barfdiet.com:** ready-made, commercial raw diets.
2. **www.-scf.usc.edu/~animal/canine/raw.html:** articles, including some written by veterinarians, for personal research.
3. **www.naturalholistic.com:** articles written by Dr. Larry Berstein, DVM, on various health and nutrition related topics.
4. **www.whole-dog-journal.com:** web site for the newsletter dealing with canine health and nutrition information. The WDJ accepts no advertising to maintain an unbiased, objective point of view.
5. **www.drianbillinghurst.com:** web site for the Australian vet who developed the B.A.R.F. diet.
6. **www.secondchanceranch.org/rawmeat.html:** an article that condemns raw meat diets.
7. **www.geocities.com/~lyncamp/mybluedog.html:** Dr. Billinghurst's rebuttal to the above article.
8. **www.minden.com/rawlinks.htm:** raw feeding links and mailing lists.
9. **www.petpower.com/pglaicia2.shtml:** canine nutrition advice from a Ph.D., certified nutritional consultant.

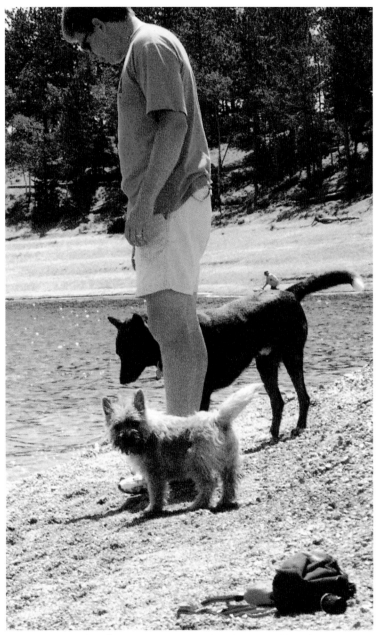

Physical activity benefits your Cairn's mental and emotional health, as well as his body.

A Cairn is often called "the lazy man's terrier," because, compared to other terriers, his coat is not difficult to maintain.

10. **http://home.earthlink.net/~pawsreflect/nutrition.html:** articles and references; this site was organized by Betty Lewis, RVT, Dr. A.N.
11. **www.concentric.net/~Liganje/NatSea/index.html:** a Seattle-based site, but a great compilation of references for easy access.
12. **www.-sci.lib.uci.edu/HSG/Vet.html#JVET:** online veterinary journals.

FEEDING THE OLDER CAIRN

Consult with a canine nutritionist and compare the fat and protein levels of the top all-natural dog foods for the appropriate senior diet for your Cairn. Health issues may dictate how much protein and fat content in the diet will benefit your older dog. Remember to look at the dog, not the amount of food in his dish to determine whether or not he is eating the correct amount of food. An elderly Cairn carrying too much weight will have both a shorter

Design an exercise program that is appropriate for your dog's age and energy level.

and sicker life than one in good lean flesh. Continue adding a wheat germ oil capsule and half a teaspoon of kelp every day for the life of the dog, because these inexpensive supplements will go far toward maintaining the health of your Cairn.

NEUTERED CAIRNS

At about nine months of age, a Cairn has reached his full height, although he will still "body up" or fill out in a maturing process later on—sometimes not until two years of age. However, pets that have been neutered gain weight very easily. They should be placed on "low-fat" kibble if weight gain becomes a problem, and they should be exercised more extensively.

CRATE TRAINING

All dogs, but especially terriers, are den animals. A basic, primal need of every Cairn is to have his very own enclosed, safe place to den. A crate, or kennel, fulfills that need, plus provides a safe mode

The Nylabone® Fold-Away Pet Carrier is easy to set up and makes a great "den" for your Cairn.

of transportation when the dog travels in a car. Therefore, it is essential that your Cairn sleeps and travels in a crate. Just as you do not drive or ride in a car without a seat belt fastened securely for safety, so your Cairn must ride in his crate for safety. Bungee cords can be used to fasten the crate securely into the vehicle. Your dog must also learn to go into his crate on command and remain there quietly with the door shut until such time as you let him out. Houseguests who are allergic to dogs or who fear them will appreciate your thoughtfulness. When forced rest is required due to an illness or injury, your dog will not be upset because he knows his crate to be a familiar, welcome den. An ideal crate is the Nylabone® Fold-Away Pet Carrier. Not only does it make a great home, it sets up easily and folds away quickly for easy storage.

Your Cairn will have already been introduced to a crate by the time you take him home with you. You will simply continue his education in this artificial den you have provided for him. Because a puppy does not want to soil his sleeping area, he will usually be able to go all night without having an accident. An occasional accident is normal until the puppy is around 12 to 14 weeks. A double-sided fleece pad placed in the bottom of the crate with a thick, white towel folded in half and placed on top of the pad will serve as a comfortable bed. Each morning, check the white towel for any signs of blood, vomit, discharge, or fecal material. This provides a wonderful opportunity to perform a quick, daily health check on your Cairn. If the towel hasn't been soiled, turn it to a clean side for that night's use. Both the towel and the pad should then be washed with bleach frequently. Spray disinfectant on all surfaces inside the crate and wipe out. Where dogs are concerned, "cleanliness is next to Godliness"! In hot summer weather, a wire crate will provide more ventilation.

The Cairn's crate can be placed next to your bed so that he bonds well with you, and you can comfort him if he needs reassurance during the night as a new puppy. After a few comforting words from you, if whining or barking continues, give a sharp rap on top of the crate and tell him in a firm, low voice, "No whine!" or "No bark!" When the puppy has quieted, raise the pitch of your voice and soothingly tell him, "G-o-o-d puppy." We generally keep a puppy by our bed until he is about five months old, at which time he goes down to the dog room to sleep in his own crate with the other dogs that each have one as well.

Puppies can be fed in their crates and can be left in them for up to two hours while you run errands, go to the store, etc. They greatly aid in housetraining and in reducing both separation anxiety and its resultant destructive behavior. Leave a favorite toy or chew-stick for the puppy to enjoy while you are gone.

EXERCISE

Cairn Terriers come from a legacy of hard working, no-nonsense terriers. Although not everyone cares to hike five miles a day with their

Cairn and then send him into a badger den, every Cairn Terrier owner must understand the breed's energy level and its need for daily, vigorous exercise. Such physical activity benefits the dog's body as well as his mental health. Cairns boast a keen intelligence that must be stimulated with positive activities or those busy little brains will create activities that you may not approve of at all!

Every Cairn should have a large, safely fenced backyard where he can race around in his daily silly streaks. This yard should have toys, both bought and homemade, so the Cairn can entertain himself. Of course,

Trimming your dog's nails is an important part of his grooming routine. Also check for cracked footpads or swollen areas.

Having the proper tools, such as a soft brush and grooming table, will make grooming easier and more comfortable for your dog.

Regular grooming sessions combined with an all-over body check can help you to stay on top of your Cairn's physical condition.

the yard provides much more fun if a human shares the good times with his dog. In addition to the exercise yard, long walks at an extended trot to develop muscles, plus free runs in a safe area at least three to four times a week will create a calm, happy, and healthy Cairn.

Many of the canine sports that will be discussed in the training section can fulfill exercise needs for both you and your dog. We face a rapid rise in obesity, which seems to extend to our dogs as well. What better way to become leaner and more fit than to have "the best little pal in the world" as your partner in achieving a longer, healthier life.

GROOMING

A Cairn is called "the lazy man's terrier" because compared with other terrier breeds, a Cairn's coat is not at all difficult to maintain. Because you made handling every inch of your Cairn's body (including his mouth) part of the socialization process while he was still a puppy, grooming him will simply be an extension of that socialization. There are some basic grooming tools needed, such as a grooming table with an arm and noose to restrain the dog while he is being groomed. Keep a bag of treats in your grooming box and reward your clever Cairn frequently while he is on the table so that he thinks of the grooming table as a fun place. The following schedule breaks down the required grooming tasks.

Once a Week

File back your Cairn's nails to the correct short length using a cordless nail groomer, which eliminates sharp edges and allows you to maintain much shorter nails without causing bleeding or pain. This tool can be found at major discounts stores or in a wholesale dog supply catalog.

Use a spray bottle to spritz coat conditioner thoroughly throughout the coat and a pin brush to brush against the grain of the hair first, and then with the grain—except on the head furnishings, which should always be brushed forward and full.

Every Two Weeks

Recently, a new grooming tool became available that makes grooming a pet Cairn so much easier! "The Mars Coat King", either in the "fine" or the "extra-fine" blade, will do a marvelous job on the body of a Cairn, from the neck to the elbow, the back, sides, and belly, and the hindquarters down to the stifle (knee). Take care not to rake too hard on the belly, because the tool is sharp enough to cut the skin in that sensitive area. With this tool, then, only the head, tail, and legs need worked with the finishing knife.

For those Cairns sporting a heavy undercoat and "ruff" around their neck, it may be necessary to follow-up with the finishing knife after using the Mars tool on the neck to thin out the hair enough to lie down and allow the neck and slope of shoulder to be seen.

Using a fine stripping knife and your index finger and thumb, "top off" the coat all over the

Keeping your pet well groomed is important to his health and well-being.

Proper oral hygiene keeps your Cairn's teeth clean and his breath fresh.

body, removing any long hairs and thinning out areas on the sides and front of the neck that tend to grow "a ruff."

Strip off extra hair around the feet with a knife. Cut out hair on the inside of the pads of each foot and between the toes. A foot devoid of hair on the underside will not collect weed seeds, mud, snow balls, etc. and will keep a tight foot. Laying the bottom blade of the curved scissors on the grooming table, follow the outline of the foot and trim all the way around it.

Clean the hair off the top third of each ear until only the soft velvet-like fur is left and then cut the outside edges of each ear for a neat, prick ear.

Carefully cut hair around the outline of the anus to keep that area clean. On males, carefully cut hair around the sheath of the penis, while on bitches do the same around the vulva and urethra. Hair left in the genital areas only serves to collect bacteria and cause infections.

Spray every inch of the dog's coat with coat conditioner and brush out with a pin brush. Use this every two-week grooming session to examine every inch of the dog's body, including his eyes and ears for any wound, growth, or foul smell that might indicate a health problem. Clean inside the ears with an antiseptic baby wipe.

Once a Month

With a double-sided dental tool, thoroughly scrape all tartar and plaque from the dog's teeth. The dental tool cannot damage the tooth enamel, no matter how hard you have to push. Run the sharp tip of the dental tool up under the gums all along the gumline to break up any bacterial growth between the teeth and gums. Don't worry if you see a bit of blood oozing from the gums, it is normal. Use an antiseptic wipe to clean the tool as you scrape and end by wiping the gums and teeth with a cloth.

Drain the anal glands—the two anal sacs, one on either side of the anus that gradually fills with a brown, smelly fluid. In prehistoric times, some of this fluid passed out of the dog's body with each bowel movement and contributed to the marking of the dog's territorial boundaries. Modern dog foods do not contain the roughage necessary to naturally drain these anal glands, so humans must literally lend a hand. Lift the dog's tail with one hand and with the other hand, hold a paper towel over the anus. Using your forefinger and thumb on the anal sacs, squeeze firmly in and toward the center of the anus. The anal fluid can exit rather explosively; hence the need for the paper towel. Due to the foul smell of the anal fluid, some baby powder applied to the anal area will make your Cairn sweet smelling again. Contrary to old wives' tales about worms, dogs scooting their bottoms on the ground are really trying to drain their uncomfortably full anal glands. As dogs age, the anal fluid becomes increasingly viscous causing the glands to become impacted, leading to infection. Therefore, older Cairns should have their anal glands drained as frequently as every two weeks.

TRAINING Your Cairn Terrier

HOUSETRAINING

Most Cairn Terriers housetrain quite easily and quickly. Many breeders use newspaper in their puppy pens, so the youngsters already tend to go to newspapers spread out on the floor to eliminate. "Tend to" are key words here, because there are several factors that attribute to housetraining accidents. The muscles responsible for bladder control in a puppy are still quite immature. If the puppy is absorbed in playing, by the time he realizes that he needs to urinate, he may be too far from the papers to make it in time. Then, too, physics is meaningless to a puppy. If his front feet are on the newspapers, he thinks his whole body is also. Many times this mistaken idea results in puddles just off the edge of the papers, squarely on your carpet! Patiently teach your puppy that he must go to the middle of the papers to urinate by placing him there repeatedly. He'll catch on within a week or so.

If the weather permits, begin teaching your puppy the following phrases: "Do you want to go outside?" and "Do you need to go potty?"

Highly intelligent, most Cairn Terriers housetrain quite easily and quickly.

68

Teaching your Cairn Terrier good manners and obedience skills will ensure that he will become a treasured member of the family for years to come.

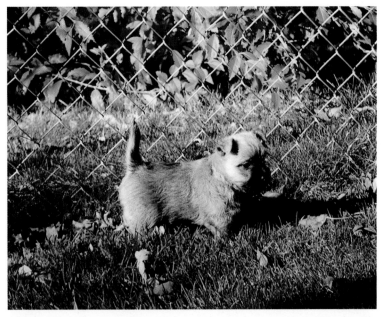

If you take your puppy to the same place to eliminate every time, he'll know what is expected of him. Reinforce what he has learned by praising him when he relieves himself in the correct area.

As soon as he has finished eating or immediately after he wakes from a nap, use these phrases as you encourage him to follow you to the door. Take him outside while continuing to tell him, "Go potty." As soon as he eliminates, raise the pitch of your voice and praise him. In every aspect of dog training, lower your voice to correct and raise it to praise. A lowered voice mimics the growl of a puppy's mother as she would discipline him, and you now take her place as the authority figure in his life.

As early as nine or ten weeks old, puppies can learn that they must go outside to eliminate after meals and naps. Does this mean that they never have accidents anymore? No indeed! Remember those immature muscles that control bladder function? Add that factor to a puppy's very short attention span, and accidents will continue to happen for several months. Patience and consistency will be the keys to success in any training endeavor, including housetraining.

By six months of age, the puppy should be fairly trustworthy with only the rare incidence of eliminating in the house. One final word here: A hiccuping puppy is a puppy that has to urinate. No one seems to have any idea why these two physical symptoms are related, but they are. When you realize that your puppy has the hiccups, take him immediately outside to eliminate.

Crate Training

All dogs are den animals, especially terriers. Your Cairn Terrier's crate will be his den or safe place. Wire crates serve hot weather climates better because of the increased air circulation. When needed, padded covers can be made or purchased to surround the wire crate. Solid, high-impact plastic crates offer more protection from the cold and from injury during travel. Prepare the crate with soft padding and a clean towel. Place a soft, stuffed toy in the crate for the puppy to snuggle up against while sleeping. Position the crate against the bedside of the human responsible for the care and training of the puppy, keeping in mind that a child may not hear or respond to the needs of a puppy during the night. Make sure that the puppy has eliminated just before placing him in his crate for the night (with a puppy-sized dog biscuit treat), around 9:30 or 10:00 pm. Sometimes covering the crate door with a towel to reinforce that this is the end to the day's activities helps to quiet the puppy.

Patience and consistency are the keys to success in any training endeavor, including housetraining.

A 9- to 10-week-old puppy should be able to sleep through the night with no bed-wetting and wake up around 5:30 or 6:00 am. If during the night the puppy wakes and whimpers, simply tell him, "You're all right, no whining." Reinforce if necessary with a quick smack on the top of the crate repeating, "No whining." Usually, the puppy will quiet and return to sleep unless he truly needs to eliminate, in which case a trip to the newspapers or outside will be in order.

If you repeat the command, "In your crate" or "Kennel," and reward him with a treat when he obeys, your puppy will soon eagerly enter his crate whenever told to do so. Puppies can be fed and placed in their crates for morning and afternoon naps. Small children need to be taught that the crate belongs to the puppy, and when the puppy is in his crate, the child may not ever bother him. Crates can also be used for "time out" when a puppy becomes too wild or misbehaves. Just as your child loves his room, even though he sometimes is sent there for disciplinary reasons, your puppy will soon learn to love his crate as his special place in the household. Also, a crate becomes an essential traveling haven for your puppy, ensuring his safety in the car. No dog should ever ride in a car without being properly secured.

To nurture the bond between you and your dog, establish yourself as the pack leader from the beginning of your relationship.

You can begin training your young Cairn puppy as soon as you bring him home.
By starting obedience training early, you can keep him from learning bad habits.

BASIC OBEDIENCE

Many people do not realize just how much a young puppy is capable of learning and wait too long to begin training. As soon as you bring that precious Cairn puppy home, begin educating him. The same is true for dogs as it is for people—learning is for life! The first and most essential lesson a puppy must learn is that humans are "alpha," the top authority over him in the new pack that he has joined. Even the youngest, most vulnerable member of the human family must still be "alpha" to a dog. Your puppy learned at a very early age that his mother not only provided for all of his physical and emotional needs, but she also demanded canine manners from him and disciplined him instantly if he became too "cheeky." However, she quickly forgave and reassured him of his place within the pack.

Once your puppy leaves all that was familiar to him with his mother and siblings, he will now slip easily into his position within the human pack family if he sees that similar rules apply here, too. Your puppy can feel confident if he knows that humans now occupy the alpha position that his canine mother held. He can trust that you will meet all his needs while defining clear limits for his behavior to keep him safe. If he defies your alpha authority—and he probably will—by struggling on the grooming table or growling if you take a toy or food pan from him, simply grasp the scruff of his neck and stare him down. In other words, assert your authority in a similar manner that his mother or other adult member of the dog pack would use to teach him his place in the family hierarchy. Lower your voice to a firm, growling "No!" and stare into his eyes without blinking. The rules of canine etiquette say that the first one to avert the eyes or turn the head slightly to one side while looking away loses this dominance contest. Therefore, you absolutely must win! Continue staring into his eyes until he averts his gaze or looks away. Then you can raise the pitch of your voice and praise him enthusiastically. You've won! You're alpha again! Soon he will gracefully accept your authority in health care and grooming matters. The benefits of a clear alpha position on your part come in the form of a well-mannered happy puppy that looks to you for assurance and guidance.

The socialization process qualifies as some of the first learning that your Cairn puppy experiences with you. Also, as you handle

Training classes are a good way for your Cairn to learn basic obedience and to improve his social skills. These eager students perform a perfect sit/stay.

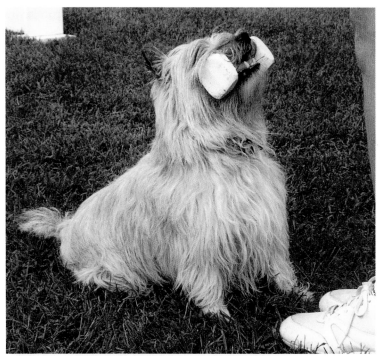

The key to training any Cairn Terrier is to make obeying commands fun for him— turn training sessions into games with various rewards and offer praise for correct responses.

every part of your puppy's body on a daily basis, whether he objects to such handling or not—remember, you are alpha in this relationship—he is learning that he can trust you. He discovers that it is safe to obey you and that you will not harm him. Indeed, he will come to enjoy these sessions if you use a gentle massage technique and speak to him in an affectionate voice as you work.

OBEDIENCE CLASSES

Many wonderful books and videos are available to help make the training process easy and problem free. Your Cairn puppy's breeder can recommend his or her favorites. There is also an equal amount of materials that cover the subject of more structured, disciplined obedience training. This kind of work should take place in the context of an obedience class. Dogs trained exclusively at home will perform there perfectly, but lose all control when away from the home setting.

Therefore, dogs need additional training in new environments among other dogs. Obedience training gives a more reserved or timid dog great self-confidence. For the overly bold or energetic dog, obedience training gives him the self-discipline to manage those traits. Choose your obedience trainer with care. Many instructors do not understand or enjoy terriers. Search for a trainer who appreciates the intelligence and independence of a Cairn Terrier and knows that the breed cannot be trained as one would train a Doberman Pinscher or Golden Retriever.

The key to training any Cairn Terrier is to make obeying your commands fun for him. Cairn Terriers have three basic responses to any command: "No," "Make me," and "Make it worth my while." You want to prevent his outright disobedience and avoid a power struggle, and you certainly want to make it worth his while to obey you. Turning training sessions into games with various rewards waiting for him at the game's successful conclusion can do that. Your enthusiastic participation in the exercise, praise coupled with a food reward, or playtime with a

Versatile and agile, the Cairn Terrier can excel at a variety of activities when properly trained. Stonebridge Trick 'r Treat, CD, tackles the high jump retrieve with ease.

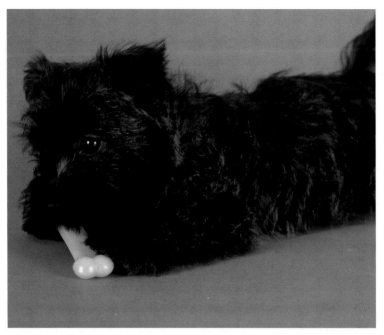

Your Cairn can become easily bored, so remember to keep lessons short, varied, and end them with playtime and a treat, like a Nylabone®.

favorite toy can convince your Cairn that obeying you reaps fun and profit for him.

If you would like more information on obedience clubs and competitions, explore these specific links at the AKC web site: *www.akc.org.*

SPECIAL COMMANDS

Some commands that may not be part of an obedience class instruction or found in a book but are still quite helpful in living with a dog are as follows:

"Back"—This is useful when the dog is crowding in front of you at a doorway.

"Over"—Sometimes one needs to simply have the dog step over to the side, off of a newspaper, or onto a rug.

"Leave it"—This can be used to send the dog away from any object, animal, or situation you deem necessary.

"No stealing"—This prevents the dog from stealing food, socks, slippers, etc.

"Don't even think it"—Use this when the dog has not yet misbehaved, but you see in his eyes that it's coming.

ACTIVITIES AND EVENTS FOR YOU AND YOUR CAIRN TERRIER

Versatile and adaptable describe the Cairn better than any other adjectives. Given these attributes, Cairn Terriers can provide more fun for their owners in more varied ways than perhaps any other breed of dog. The breed standard for the Cairn uses words such as "hardy," "agile," "working terrier," and "lithe." Couple these characteristics with a keen intelligence and a Cairn owner has a dog that is ready for anything!

Earthdog Trials

Allowing your Cairn to pursue the work he has been bred to do for hundreds of years has to be one of the most rewarding activities for both of you. The intensity with which a Cairn Terrier focuses his mind and every muscle of his body on the quarry he hunts is unique to that experience. No other activity you will ever engage in with your Cairn will equal that total, concentrated effort and sheer joy your dog experiences in the

Agility was made for Cairn Terriers! Every skill demanded in the event— climbing, tunneling, lithe twisting, and speed—are second nature to him, making him a top-notch competitor.

Earthdog trials can be very rewarding for your Cairn because they offer him an opportunity to show off his natural hunting and scenting abilities.

hunt. It is no surprise then that a Cairn's favorite thing to do in all the world is to go after vermin!

The American Kennel Club offers earthdog titles that can be earned by small terriers and Dachshunds at sanctioned earthdog trials. Under the *Performance Events* section on the AKC web site *(www.akc.org)*, the earthdog regulations describe in detail how a trial is conducted. In many areas of the country, terrier and Dachshund owners have organized earthdog clubs to hold trials and offer training and mentoring to beginners in this sport—both human and canine. Contact your local all-breed dog club to locate a terrier or Dachshund breeder who can direct you to the nearest earthdog organization.

Earthdog clubs often hold terrier races, both flat races and races over hurdles. Terriers run in pursuit of a fox or coyote tail dragged swiftly across the course and into a nine-inch diameter opening at the opposite end. The first terrier through the "den opening" wins

The time you invest in training your Cairn will benefit both of you for a lifetime.

the race. Dogs are muzzled to prevent squabbles in the heat of the chase. These races provide great fun for dogs and handlers alike and give those terriers that prefer to work above ground an opportunity to shine.

Agility

Agility was absolutely made for Cairn Terriers! Every skill demanded in agility requires exactly the conformational abilities of a Cairn. Agility even meets the mental needs of terriers—it's a game! All of the obstacles designed for agility are second nature for Cairns and highlight their skills in climbing, tunneling, lithe twisting and turning, and speed. Basic obedience training must provide the foundation for any dog to enter agility training. Most obedience clubs have an agility group as part of the organization, but this sport is so popular now that many cities have clubs devoted solely to agility training and competition. The AKC also offers agility titles that are earned at separate agility trials as part of an obedience competition or an AKC all-breed dog show. Again, the AKC web site holds much useful information on this sport, which is the fastest growing dog sport in the country.

For those who find workouts at the gym boring, agility gives us the exercise we need while we're running the course with our dogs. Even better, we're so focused on our dogs that we don't realize how much of a workout we've had in the process—just that we've had a great time!

Obedience and Tracking

Obedience classes and competitions have a long and respected history, so most new Cairn owners know at least a bit about them. Although not all Cairn Terries will enjoy or excel in obedience competition, some truly love this work, probably thanks to how their handlers have presented it to them. If obedience work is shown as an enjoyable game well worth the Cairn's while, then he will excel at it. Because basic obedience is the foundation and springboard for all other canine sports, your Cairn needs to attain a certain proficiency in obedience. Just remember that a Cairn Terrier gets bored quickly and easily, so keep lessons short, varied, and end them with playtime. Unlike other breeds, Cairns do not need daily practice. In fact, too much repetition will make them sour as a lemon about obedience work.

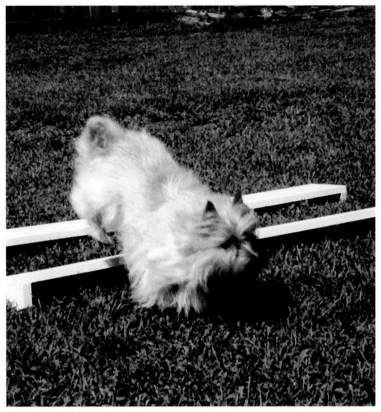

Basic obedience is the foundation for all other canine sports. This Cairn performs the broad jump with ease.

In advanced obedience work, dogs learn scent discrimination—how to choose the right object from a variety of items placed some distance away as the one that holds the handler's scent. Such work blends easily into actual tracking titles, also offered by the AKC. Because of the Cairn Terrier's incredibly keen sense of smell, Cairns excel and have great fun in tracking. The AKC site provides multiple hyperlinks to further information regarding tracking with your dog.

Some search and rescue organizations have discovered the worth of a smaller, well-trained tracking dog that can enter collapsed buildings to search for missing people. Such work in dark, tight spaces comes so naturally to the Cairn Terrier that worked the rocky fox and badger dens on the Isle of Skye in Scotland for centuries.

One activity that grew out of obedience training and provides the fun element needed to break up work sessions is flyball. Usually, four dogs compete, sometimes in relay teams. The dogs race down to the end of their track to hit a lever protruding from a box with their paw. This action causes a tennis ball to fly out of the box and into the air. The dog catches the ball and races back to give it to the handler. As in the terrier races, the flyball course can be flat or can have jumps set up. Many Cairns relish ball playing, so this sport provides great enjoyment for them and their handlers. If you want to know more about flyball, an excellent web site is *http://muskie.fishnet.com/~flyball.*

Canine Freestyle

Sometimes called "musical freestyle," this sport is the newest canine activity available to dog owners. Freestyle has rapidly gained enthusiasts all across the country and may soon challenge agility as the fastest growing canine sport. Again, a foundation of obedience training provides the starting point for freestyle training. Using a musical composition that pleases both the dog and the handler,

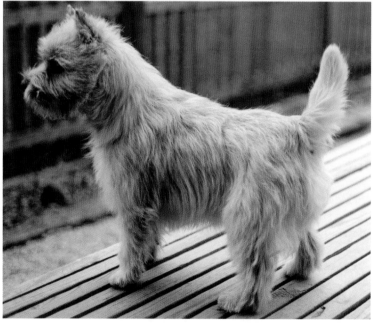

With proper training, there's no limit to what your Cairn Terrier can accomplish.

Showing your dog requires dedication and patience, but most of all, it should be enjoyable for both dog and owner.

choreography is developed to complement the mood and rhythm of the music. Everything from top 40 to jazz to waltzes to salsa have provided delightful musical accompaniment to freestyle routines that allow dog and handler to "dance." Freestyle enthusiasts wax lyrical about the almost mystical bond that develops between handler and dog. Perhaps the intense teamwork played out in the rhythm and melodies that infuse freestyle contribute to such impressions.

Given the Cairn's agile footwork and his natural love of fun and games, he is an ideal candidate for freestyle. Cairn owners involved in this sport have all agreed that their dogs prefer freestyle to any other canine activity. So, if you love dancing and working closely with your dog, then freestyle should delight both you and your Cairn Terrier. Two web sites with more detailed information on canine freestyle are *www.canine-freestyle.org* and *www.woofs.org/wcfo/index.html.*

Therapy Dogs

Perhaps one of the most rewarding efforts for you and your Cairn Terrier to participate in is therapy dog work. Cairns love humans and adapt quickly to various machines and mechanical devices that accompany people in a hospital or nursing home setting, which makes them marvelous therapy dogs. Again, basic obedience training is the starting point for therapy dog work. Therapy dog organizations assist Cairn owners in locating the therapy dog group nearest them and will train and prepare dog and owner for any and all situations they may encounter in hospitals, rehabilitation centers, or nursing homes. Therapy dog organizations exist in every part of the country, but the Southwest Canine Corps of Volunteers (SCCV) based in Albuquerque, New Mexico, is an example of an organized, well-run group that works hand in hand with the medical staff at each facility in which therapy

The Cairn Terrier's love of people makes him an excellent candidate for therapy dog work. Ch. Patter's Mzzz Magnolia could brighten up anyone's day.

dogs visit. The SCCV training program is extensive. Through such canine/handler preparation and thoughtful cooperation with doctors and nurses, real miracles happen on a regular basis as the healing touches of therapy dogs encourage new hope and health in patients. To locate a therapy dog group in your area or research more information about therapy dogs, go to the following web sites: *www.therapydogs.com* and *www.tdi-dog.org.*

Junior Showmanship

Through the AKC program of junior showmanship competition, youngsters from 10 to 18 years of age can learn to handle their dogs in the show ring with poise and accomplishment. By earning points in competition with other children of their own age group, junior handlers can become eligible to compete at the Westminster Kennel Club show held in New York City each February for the title of Best Junior Handler. These talented, skilled junior handlers often go on to successful careers as professional handlers or breeders/exhibitors of dogs from their own kennels.

Junior showmanship is an excellent way to build a young person's confidence in the show ring. Junior handlers are judged solely on their ability and skill in presenting their dogs.

In junior handling, the child's performance, not the dog's, is what is judged. Having said that, however, the overall impression made by the team of handler and dog counts a great deal in the junior handler's success in the ring. Therefore, a champion quality dog that is beautifully groomed is a necessity for the junior handler. Some of the most successful teams in junior showmanship include of a retired champion that now has embarked on a second career as a junior showmanship dog. There are definite rules and guidelines to follow in junior showmanship competition. The AKC web site holds an extensive list of hyperlinks under the "Junior Showmanship" section that will provide you with a great deal of valuable information on this activity.

Because of the Cairn Terrier's irrepressible love for children, he is a perfect candidate for junior showmanship. Cairns are most forgiving of a child's bumbling first attempts at handling and remain patient teachers and companions during the child's years in competition. The wonderful bond that grows between the Cairn and child enables the junior to experience that exhilarating sensation of a human and dog functioning as one. Especially during adolescence when a young person's body grows so quickly and his or her feet seem as large as gunboats, junior showmanship can prove invaluable in helping the child learn how to handle those teenage years gracefully. All the many details and canine facts that need to be memorized help to focus and discipline a child's mind. The child must also remember where to put which part of the dog's body— as well as his own—and when to do it. How should he carry himself? How should he walk? How fast? Meeting all these physical demands and controlling movement helps the child to acquire a physical grace and ease that many of his peers lack. In addition, proper manners must be observed in addressing the judge, and good sportsmanship must be practiced with the others competing in his class. All in all, junior showmanship has proven a marvelous experience for thousands of youngsters in their sometimes difficult transition to young adulthood.

Conformation

Exhibiting in the conformation ring serves the purpose of identifying which dogs possess enough superior qualities that they should be used in breeding. Sometimes, the notion of winning at all costs, expensive publicity, and oversized egos cloud that original

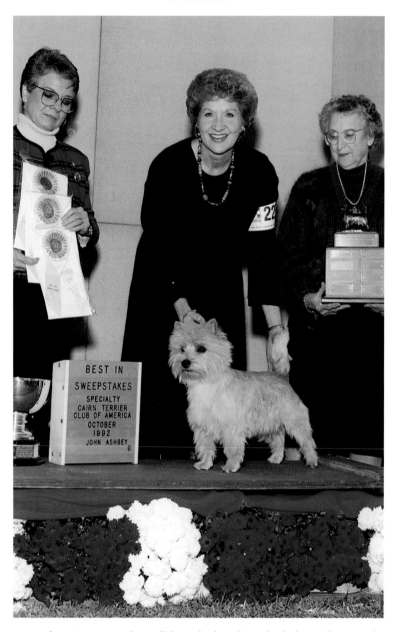

In conformation, your dog will be judged on how closely he conforms to the standard for the breed. The author Sandra Murray and Best in Sweepstakes winner Cairncroft Iron Horse.

purpose, but future breeding stock is truly what the conformation ring is all about. Just as every single breed judged is compared to the standard of perfection, each Cairn Terrier competing is also judged against his breed standard. How each judge interprets that standard becomes a bit subjective. Hence, there are different winners on different days. However, the standard provides a guide for "type," which is the essence of what makes the Cairn Terrier unique to any other breed. The standard should also guide the judge as to the physical condition of each Cairn he examines for the work that the Cairn Terrier was bred to do. If a Cairn's structure or movement would prohibit him from performing a hard day's work in the field, then that dog is neither fit to win nor to reproduce.

If you have arranged with your breeder to own or co-own a show-quality Cairn puppy, then he or she will mentor you through several years of intensive learning. Proper handling, feeding, conditioning, and grooming of your Cairn Terrier for the show ring takes years to learn. Be patient with yourself and settle in for the long haul. Joining a regional Cairn Terrier club as well as the Cairn Terrier Club of America will provide you with a great many educational tools to advance your understanding of the breed and its presentation in the show ring. The CTCA web site *(www.cairnterrier.org)* can direct you to the regional Cairn club nearest you as well as information on how to join the national parent club.

Many people lack the perseverance necessary for a career in dog showing. For the few who do hang in there, the rewards of all those hours of training and preparation are indeed sweet when the judge hands you that purple ribbon, earning your Cairn more points toward his AKC championship.

Your breeder can also recommend excellent books and videotapes that will help you become a better handler of your show-quality Cairn Terrier. An objective breeder will teach you how to see the faults in your beloved, perfect-to-you Cairn, because a perfect dog hasn't been born yet—and won't be. That's one of the ironies of dog showing and breeding. We keep striving for this "impossible dream," or the perfect dog, which is totally unobtainable. But when we come close and see that almost perfect Cairn literally float around the ring with presence, style, and soundness, there is no thrill quite like it!

HEALTH CARE

Veterinary medicine has become far more sophisticated than what was available to our ancestors. This can be attributed to the increase in household pets and, consequently, the demand for better care for them. Also, human medicine has become far more complex. Today, diagnostic testing in veterinary medicine parallels human diagnostics. Because of better technology, we can expect our pets to live healthier lives, thereby increasing their life spans.

THE FIRST CHECKUP

You will want to take your new puppy/dog in for his first checkup within 48 to 72 hours after acquiring him. Many breeders strongly recommend this checkup and so do the humane shelters. A puppy/dog can appear healthy, but he may have a serious problem that is not apparent to the layman. Most pets have some type of a minor flaw that may never cause a real problem.

Unfortunately, if he/she should have a serious problem, you will want to consider the consequences of keeping the pet and the

It's a good idea to take your Cairn puppy to the vet within 48 to 72 hours after acquiring him.

attachments that will be formed, which may be broken prematurely. Keep in mind there are many healthy dogs looking for good homes.

This first checkup is a good time to establish yourself with the veterinarian and to learn the office policy regarding their hours and how they handle emergencies. Usually, the breeder or another con-scientious pet owner is a good reference for locating a capable veterinarian. You should be aware that not all vets give the same quality of service. Please do not make your selection based on the

On the initial visit, your veterinarian should check your pup's overall condition and discuss the proper diet for him.

least expensive clinic, as they may be shortchanging your pet. There is the possibility that it will eventually cost you more due to improper diagnosis, treatment, etc. If you are selecting a new veterinarian, feel free to ask for a tour of the clinic. You should inquire about making an appointment for a tour, because all clinics are working clinics, and therefore, may not be available all day for sightseers. You may worry less if you see where your pet will be spending the day if he ever needs to be hospitalized.

THE PHYSICAL EXAM

Your veterinarian will check your pet's overall condition, which includes listening to the heart; checking the respiration; feeling the abdomen, muscles, and joints; checking the mouth, which includes gum color and signs of gum disease, along with plaque buildup; checking the ears for signs of an infection or ear mites; examining the eyes; and, last but not least, checking the condition of the skin and coat.

He should ask you questions regarding your pet's eating and elimination habits and invite you to relay your questions. It is a good idea to prepare a list so as not to forget anything. He should discuss the proper diet and the quantity to be fed. If this differs from your breeder's recommendation, you should convey to him what the breeder's choice is and see if he approves. If he recommends changing the diet, this should be done over a few days so as not to cause a gastrointestinal upset. It is customary to take in a fresh stool sample (just a small amount) to test for intestinal parasites. It must be fresh, preferably within 12 hours, because the eggs hatch quickly and after hatching will not be observed under the microscope. If your pet isn't obliging, the technician can usually take a sample in the clinic.

IMMUNIZATIONS

It is important that you take your puppy/dog's vaccination record with you on your first visit. In the case of a puppy, presumably the breeder has seen to the vaccinations up to the time you acquired custody. Veterinarians differ in their vaccination protocol. It is not unusual for your puppy to have received vaccinations for distemper, hepatitis, leptospirosis, parvovirus, and parainfluenza every two to three weeks from the age of five or six weeks. Usually, this is a combined injection and is typically called the DHLPP. The DHLPP is given through at least 12 to 14 weeks of age, and it is customary to continue with another parvovirus vaccine at 16 to 18 weeks. You may wonder why so many immunizations are necessary. No one knows for sure when the puppy's maternal antibodies are gone, although it is customarily accepted that distemper antibodies are gone by 12 weeks. Usually, parvovirus antibodies are gone by 16 to 18 weeks of age. However, it is possible for the maternal antibodies to be gone much earlier or even at a later age. Therefore, immunizations are started at an early age. The vaccine will not give immunity as long as there are maternal antibodies.

The rabies vaccination is given at three or six months of age, depending on your local laws. A vaccine for bordetella (kennel cough) is advisable and can be given any time from the age of five weeks. The coronavirus is not commonly given unless there is a problem locally. The Lyme vaccine is necessary in endemic areas. Lyme disease has been reported in 47 states.

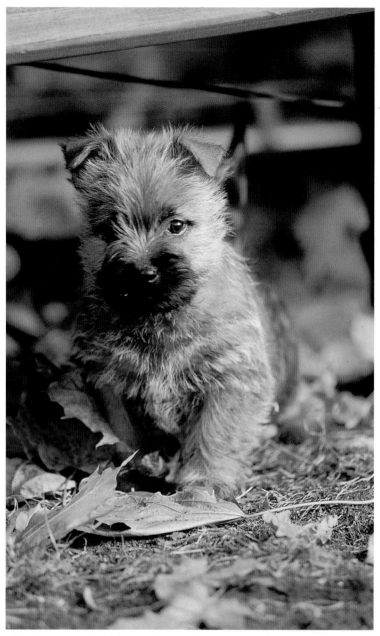

If you begin proper health care right from the start, you will ensure that your puppy will lead a full and active life.

Distemper

Distemper is virtually an incurable disease. If the dog recovers, he is subject to severe nervous disorders. The virus attacks every tissue in the body and resembles a bad cold with a fever. It can cause a runny nose and eyes and cause gastrointestinal disorders, including a poor appetite, vomiting, and diarrhea. The virus is carried by raccoons, foxes, wolves, mink, and other dogs. Unvaccinated youngsters and senior citizens are very susceptible. This is still a common disease.

Hepatitis

Hepatitis is a virus that is most serious in very young dogs. It is spread by contact with an infected animal or its stool or urine. The virus affects the liver and kidneys and is characterized by high fever, depression, and lack of appetite. Recovered animals may be afflicted with chronic illnesses.

Leptospirosis

Leptospirosis is a bacterial disease transmitted by contact with the urine of an infected dog, rat, or other wildlife. It produces severe

Puppies receive maternal antibodies that protect them during the first weeks of life. After this time, they must receive vaccinations to prevent certain canine diseases.

Maintaining your Cairn's immunization schedule and booster shots will increase the longevity of his life.

symptoms of fever, depression, jaundice, and internal bleeding and was fatal before the vaccine was developed. Recovered dogs can be carriers, and the disease can be transmitted from dogs to humans.

Parvovirus

Parvovirus was first noted in the late 1970s and is still a fatal disease. However, with proper vaccinations, early diagnosis, and prompt treatment, it is a manageable disease. It attacks the bone marrow and intestinal tract. The symptoms include depression, loss of appetite, vomiting, diarrhea, and collapse. Immediate medical attention is of the essence.

Rabies

Rabies is shed in the saliva and is carried by raccoons, skunks, foxes, other dogs, and cats. It attacks nerve tissue, resulting in paralysis and death. Rabies can be transmitted to people and is virtually always fatal. This disease is reappearing in the suburbs.

Bordetella (Kennel Cough)

The symptoms of bordetella are coughing, sneezing, hacking, and retching accompanied by nasal discharge usually lasting from a few days to several weeks. There are several disease-producing organisms responsible for this disease. The present vaccines are helpful but do not protect for all the strains. It usually is not life threatening, but in some instances it can progress to a serious bronchopneumonia. The disease is highly contagious. The vaccination should be given routinely for dogs that come into contact with other dogs, such as through boarding, training class, or visits to the groomer.

Coronavirus

Coronavirus is usually self-limiting and not a life-threatening disease. It was first noted in the late '70s about a year before parvovirus. The virus produces a yellow/brown stool, and there may be depression, vomiting, and diarrhea.

Lyme Disease

Lyme disease was first diagnosed in the United States in 1976 in Lyme, CT, in people who lived in close proximity to the deer tick. Symptoms may include acute lameness, fever, swelling of joints,

If your Cairn is not his usual cheery, happy self, he may be sick. If you notice a change in your dog's behavior, consult your vet to have your dog examined.

and loss of appetite. Your veterinarian can advise you if you live in an endemic area.

Booster Shots

After your puppy has completed his puppy vaccinations, you will continue to booster the DHLPP once a year. It is customary to booster the rabies one year after the first vaccine and then, depending on where you live, it should be boostered every year or every three years. This depends on your local laws. The Lyme and corona vaccines are boostered annually, and it is recommended that the bordetella be boostered every six to eight months.

Annual Visit

I would like to stress the importance of the annual checkup, which would include booster vaccinations, a check for intestinal

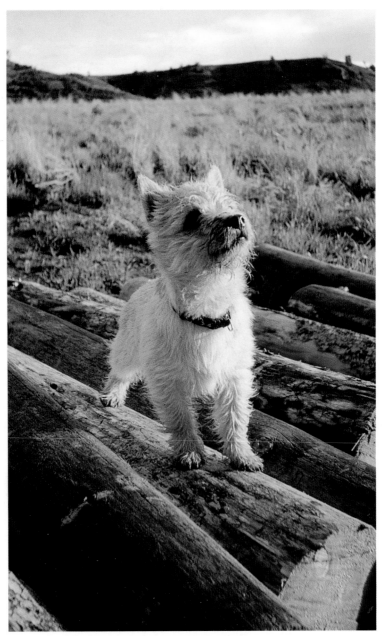

As your dog ages, his health needs will change. Keep veterinary visits regular and all vaccines current.

Whenever you need to take your Cairn to the vet, he should be in his crate. The Nylabone® Fold-Away Pet Carrier makes transporting your dog easier.

parasites, and a test for heartworm. Today, in our very busy world, it is rush, rush, and see "how much you can get for how little." Unbelievably, some nonveterinary establishments have entered into the vaccination business. More harm than good can come to your dog through improper vaccinations, possibly from inferior vaccines and/or the wrong schedule. More than likely, you truly care about your companion dog, and over the years you have devoted much time and expense to his well being. Perhaps you are unaware that a vaccination is not just a vaccination. There is more involved. Please follow through with regular physical examinations. It is so important for your veterinarian to know your dog, and this is especially true during middle age and through the geriatric years. Your older dog may require more than one physical a year. The annual physical is good preventive medicine. Through early diagnosis and subsequent treatment, your dog can maintain a longer and better quality of life.

INTESTINAL PARASITES

Hookworms

Hookworms are almost microscopic intestinal worms that can cause anemia and, therefore, serious problems, including death, in young puppies. Hookworms can be transmitted to humans through penetration of the skin. Puppies may be born with them.

Roundworms

Roundworms are spaghetti-like worms that can cause a potbellied appearance and dull coat, along with more severe symptoms such as vomiting, diarrhea, and coughing. Puppies acquire these while in the mother's uterus and through lactation. Both hookworms and roundworms may be acquired through ingestion.

Whipworms

Whipworms have a three-month life cycle and are not acquired through the dam. They cause intermittent diarrhea, usually with

Dogs can pick up diseases and parasites from each other, so be sure your Cairn has had all of his vaccinations before taking him out to make friends.

The importance of consulting a vet on the diagnosis of internal disorders cannot be overstressed—a relatively common problem, such as listlessness or loss of appetite, could also be a sign of something more serious.

mucus. Whipworms are possibly the most difficult worm to eradicate. Their eggs are very resistant to most environmental factors and can last for years until the proper conditions enable them to mature. Whipworms are seldom seen in the stool.

Intestinal parasites are more prevalent in some areas than others. Climate, soil, and contamination are big factors contributing to the incidence of intestinal parasites. Eggs are passed in the stool, lay on the ground, and then become infective in a certain number of days. Each of the above worms has a different life cycle. Your dog's best chance of becoming and remaining worm-free is to always pooper-scoop your yard. A fenced-in yard keeps stray dogs out, which is certainly helpful.

Having a fecal examination done on your dog twice a year, or more often if there is a problem, is recommended. If your dog has a positive fecal sample, he will be given the appropriate medication and you will be asked to bring back another stool sample in a certain period of time (depending on the type of worm), and then he will be rewormed. This process goes on until he has at least two negative samples. Different types of worm require different medications. You will be wasting your money and doing your dog an injustice by buying over-the-counter medication without first consulting your veterinarian.

If you notice that your dog is scratching excessively, check him for parasite infestation and get appropriate treatment from your vet.

OTHER INTERNAL PARASITES

Coccidiosis and Giardiasis

Coccidiosis and giardiasis, which are protozoal infections, usually affect pups, especially in places where large numbers of puppies are brought together. Older dogs may harbor these infections, but do not show signs unless they are stressed. Symptoms include diarrhea, weight loss, and lack of appetite. These infections are not always apparent in the fecal examination.

Tapeworms

Seldom apparent on fecal floatation, tapeworms are diagnosed frequently as rice-like segments around the dog's anus and the base of the tail. Tapeworms are long, flat, and ribbon-like, sometimes several feet in length, and made up of many segments about five-eighths of an inch long. The two most common causes of tapeworm found in the dog are:

(1)   The larval form of the flea tapeworm parasite matures in an intermediate host, the flea, before it can become infective. Your dog acquires this by ingesting the flea through licking and chewing.

(2)   Rabbits, rodents, and certain large game animals serve as intermediate hosts for other species of tapeworm. If your dog eats one of these infected hosts, he can acquire tapeworms.

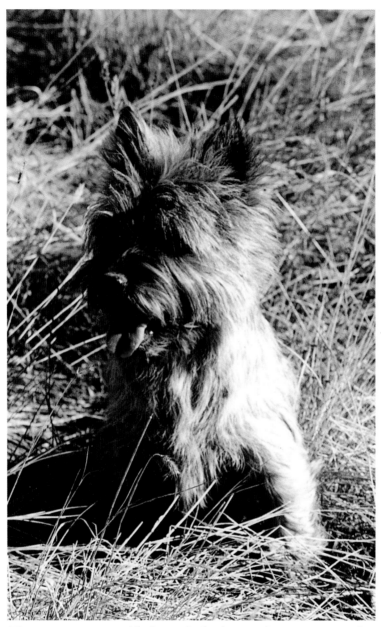

There are many parasites, like fleas and ticks, that your dog may encounter when playing outside. Be sure to check your Cairn's coat thoroughly when he comes in from the outdoors.

Heartworm Disease

Heartworm is a worm that resides in the heart and adjacent blood vessels of the lung that produces microfilaria, which circulate in the bloodstream. It is possible for a dog to be infected with any number of worms from one to a hundred that can be 6 to 14 inches long. It is a life-threatening disease, expensive to treat, and easily prevented. Depending on where you live, your veterinarian may recommend a preventive year-round and either an annual or semiannual blood test. The most common preventive is given once a month.

EXTERNAL PARASITES

Fleas

Fleas are not only the dog's worst enemy, but also enemy to the owner's pocketbook. Preventing is less expensive than treating, but regardless, we'd prefer to spend our money elsewhere. Likely, the majority of our dogs are allergic to the bite of a flea, and in many cases, it only takes one flea bite. The protein in the flea's saliva is the culprit. Allergic dogs have a reaction, which usually results in a "hot spot." More than likely, such a reaction will involve a trip to the veterinarian for treatment. Yes, prevention is less expensive. Fortunately, today there are several good products available.

If there is a flea infestation, no one product is going to correct the problem. Not only will the dog require treatment, so will the environment. In general, flea collars are not very effective, although there is an "egg" collar now available that will kill the eggs on the dog. Dips are the most economical, but they are messy. There are some effective shampoos and treatments available through pet shops and veterinarians. An oral tablet arrived on the American market in 1995 and was popular in Europe the previous year. It sterilizes the female flea, but will not kill adult fleas. Therefore, the tablet, which is given monthly, will decrease the flea population but is not a "cure-all." Dogs that suffer from flea-bite allergy will still be subjected to the bite of the flea. Another popular parasiticide is permethrin, which is applied to the back of the dog in one or two places, depending on the dog's weight. This product works as a repellent, causing the flea to get "hot feet" and jump off. Do not confuse this product with some of the organophosphates that are also applied to the dog's back.

Some products are not usable on young puppies. Treating fleas should be done under your veterinarian's guidance. Frequently, it is necessary to combine products, and the layman does not have knowledge regarding possible toxicities. It is hard to believe, but there are a few dogs that do have a natural resistance to fleas. Nevertheless, it would be wise to treat all pets at the same time. Don't forget your cats. Cats just love to prowl the neighborhood, and, consequently, return with unwanted guests.

Adult fleas live on the dog, but their eggs drop off into the environment. There, they go through four larval stages before reaching adulthood, and thereby are able to jump back on the poor unsuspecting dog. The cycle resumes and takes between 21 to 28 days under ideal conditions. There are environmental products available that will kill both adult fleas and larvae.

Ticks

Ticks can carry Rocky Mountain Spotted Fever, Lyme disease, and can cause tick paralysis. They should be removed with tweezers. Try to pull out the head because the jaws carry disease. There is a tick preventive collar that does an excellent job. Ticks automatically back out on those dogs wearing collars.

Hair loss and itching may indicate a mite infestation. See your vet for proper diagnosis and care.

In an effort to maintain bloodlines, most breeders will ask that you have your puppy spayed or neutered.

Sarcoptic Mange

Sarcoptic mange is a mite that is difficult to find on skin scrapings. The pinnal reflex is a good indicator of this disease. Rub the ends of the pinna (ear) together and the dog will start scratching with his foot. Sarcoptes are highly contagious to other dogs and to humans, although they do not live long on humans. They cause intense itching.

Demodectic Mange

Demodectic mange is a mite that is passed from the dam to her puppies. It commonly affects youngsters aged three to ten months. Diagnosis is confirmed by skin scraping. Small areas of alopecia around the eyes, lips, and/or forelegs become visible. There is little itching, unless there is a secondary bacterial infection. Some breeds are afflicted more than others.

Cheyletiella

Cheyletiella causes intense itching and is diagnosed by skin scraping. It lives in the outer layers of the skin of dogs, cats, rabbits, and humans. Yellow-gray scales may be found on the back and the rump, top of the head, and the nose.

TO BREED OR NOT TO BREED

More than likely, your breeder has requested that you have your puppy neutered or spayed. Your breeder's request is based on what is healthiest for your dog and what is most beneficial for your breed. Experienced and conscientious breeders devote many years to developing a bloodline. In order to do this, they make every effort to plan each breeding in regard to conformation, temperament, and health. This type of breeder does his best to perform the necessary testing (i.e., OFA, CERF, testing for inherited blood disorders, thyroid, etc.). Testing is expensive and sometimes very disheartening when a favorite dog doesn't pass his health tests. The health history pertains not only to the breeding stock, but to the immediate ancestors. Reputable breeders do not want their offspring to be bred indiscriminately. Therefore, you may be asked to neuter or spay your puppy. Of course, there is always the exception, and the breeder may agree to let you breed your dog under his direct supervision. This is an important concept. More and more effort is being made to breed healthier dogs.

Spay/Neuter

There are numerous benefits to spaying or neutering your dog at six months of age. Unspayed females are subject to mammary and ovarian cancer. In order to prevent mammary cancer, she must be spayed prior to her first heat cycle. Later in life, an unspayed female may develop a pyometra (an infected uterus), which is definitely life threatening.

Spaying is performed under a general anesthetic and is easy on the young dog. As you might expect, it is a little harder on the older dog, but that is no reason to deny her the surgery. The surgery removes the ovaries and uterus. It is important to remove all the ovarian tissue. If some is left behind, she could remain attractive to males. In order to view the ovaries, a reasonably long incision is necessary. An ovariohysterectomy is considered major surgery.

Neutering the male at a young age will inhibit some characteristic male behavior that owners frown upon. Some boys will not hike their legs and mark territory if they are neutered at six months of age. Also, neutering at a young age has hormonal benefits, lessening the chance of hormonal aggressiveness.

Surgery involves removing the testicles but leaving the scrotum. If there should be a retained testicle, the male definitely needs to be neutered before the age of two or three years. Retained testicles can develop cancer. Unneutered males are at risk for testicular cancer, perineal fistulas, perianal tumors and fistulas, and prostatic disease.

Intact males and females may be prone to housetraining accidents. Females urinate frequently before, during, and after heat cycles, and males tend to mark territory if there is a female in heat. Males may show the same behavior if there is a visiting dog or guests.

Surgery involves a sterile operating procedure equivalent to human surgery. The incision site is shaved, surgically scrubbed, and draped. The veterinarian wears a sterile surgical gown, cap, mask, and gloves. Anesthesia should be monitored by a registered technician. It is customary for the veterinarian to recommend a pre-anesthetic blood screening, looking for metabolic problems, and an ECG rhythm strip to check for normal heart function. Today, anesthetics are equal to human anesthetics, which enables your dog to walk out of the clinic the same day as surgery.

Some folks worry about their dogs gaining weight after being neutered or spayed. This is usually not the case. It is true that some dogs may be less active so they could develop a problem, but most are just as active as they were before surgery. However, if your dog should begin to gain, you need to decrease his food and see to it that he gets a little more exercise.

MEDICAL PROBLEMS

Anal Sacs

Anal sacs are small sacs on either side of the rectum that can cause the dog discomfort when they are full. They should empty when the dog has a bowel movement. Symptoms of inflammation or impaction are excessive licking under the tail and/or a bloody or sticky discharge from the anal area. Breeders recommend emptying the sacs on a regular schedule when bathing the dog. Many veterinarians prefer this isn't done unless there are symptoms. You can express the sacs by squeezing them (at the five and seven o'clock positions) in and up toward the anus. Take precautions not to get in the way of the foul-smelling fluid that is expressed. Some dogs object to this procedure, so it would be wise to have someone hold the head. Scooting is caused by anal-sac irritation and not worms.

Colitis

The stool may be frank blood or blood tinged and is the result of inflammation of the colon. Colitis, sometimes intermittent, can be the result of stress, undiagnosed whipworms, or perhaps idiopathic (no explainable reason). If intermittent bloody stools are an ongoing problem, you should probably feed a diet higher in fiber. Seek professional help if your dog feels poorly and/or the condition persists.

Conjunctivitis

Many breeds are prone to conjunctivitis. The conjunctiva is the pink tissue that lines the inner surface of the eyeball, except the clear, transparent cornea. Irritating substances such as bacteria, foreign matter, or chemicals can cause it to become reddened and swollen. It is important to keep any hair trimmed from around the eyes. Long hair stays damp and aggravates the problem. Keep the

As a responsible Cairn Terrier owner, you should have a basic understanding of the medical problems that affect the breed.

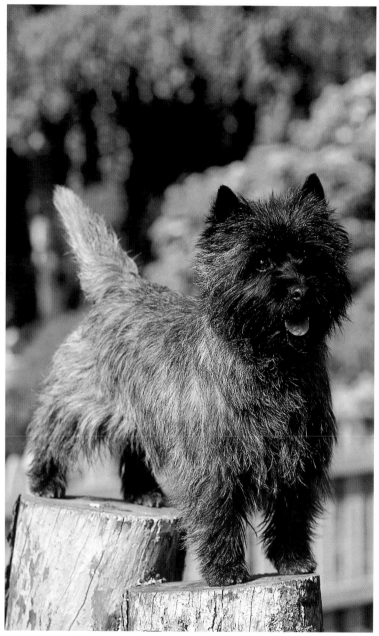

Your Cairn will need annual checkups to maintain his good health and minimize any future problems.

eyes cleaned with warm water and wipe away any matter that has accumulated in the corner of the eyes. If the condition persists, you should see your veterinarian. This problem goes hand in hand with keratoconjunctivitis sicca.

Ear Infection

Otitis externa is an inflammation of the external ear canal that begins at the outside opening of the ear and extends inward to the eardrum. Dogs with pendulous ears are prone to this disease, but breeds with upright ears also have a high incidence of problems. Allergies, food, and inhalents, along with hormonal problems, such as hypothyroidism, are major contributors to the disease. For those dogs that have recurring problems, you need to investigate the underlying causes if you hope to cure them.

Be careful never to get water in the ears. Water provides a great medium for bacteria to grow. If your dog swims or you inadvertently get water in his ears, use a drying agent. You can use an at-home preparation of equal parts of three-percent hydrogen peroxide and 70-percent rubbing alcohol. Another preparation is equal parts of white vinegar and water. Your veterinarian, alternatively, can provide a suitable product. When cleaning the ears, be careful using cotton tip applicators, because they make it easy to pack debris down into the canal. Only clean what you can see.

If your dog has an ongoing infection, don't be surprised if your veterinarian recommends sedating him and flushing his ears with a bulb syringe. Sometimes this needs to be done a few times to get the ear clean. The ear must be clean so that medication can come into contact with the canal. Be prepared to return for rechecks until the infection is gone. This may involve more flushings if the ears are very bad.

For chronic or recurring cases, your veterinarian may recommend thyroid testing, etc., and a hypoallergenic diet for a trial period of 10 to 12 weeks. Depending on your dog, it may be a good idea to see a dermatologist. Ears shouldn't be taken lightly. If the condition gets out of hand, surgery may be necessary. Please ask your veterinarian to explain proper ear maintenance for your dog.

Flea Bite Allergy

Flea bite allergy is the result of a hypersensitivity to the bite of a flea and its saliva. It only takes one bite to cause the dog to chew or

Chemicals, allergies to food and drugs, stress, and even sunburn can cause damage to your Cairn's skin and coat. Consult your vet if conditions persist.

scratch himself raw. Your dog may need medical attention to ease his discomfort. You need to clip the hair around the "hot spot" and wash it with a mild soap and water, and you may need to do this daily if the area weeps. Apply an antibiotic anti-inflammatory product. Hot spots can occur from other trauma, such as grooming.

Interdigital Cysts

Check for interdigital cysts on your dog's feet if he shows signs of lameness. They are frequently associated with staph infections and can be quite painful. A home remedy is to soak the infected foot in a solution of a half teaspoon of bleach in a couple of quarts of water. Do this two to three times a day for a couple of days. Check with your veterinarian for an alternative remedy; antibiotics usually work well. If there is a recurring problem, surgery may be required.

Lameness

Lameness may only be an interdigital cyst or it could be a mat between the toes, especially if your dog licks his feet. Sometimes it is hard to determine which leg is affected. If your dog is holding up his leg, you need to see your veterinarian.

Skin

Frequently, poor skin is the result of an allergy to fleas, inhalants, or food. These types of problems usually result in a staph dermatitis. Dogs with food allergies usually show signs of severe itching and scratching. Some dogs with food allergies never once itch. Their only symptom is swelling of the ears with no ear infection. Food allergy may result in recurrent bacterial skin and ear infections. Your veterinarian or dermatologist will recommend a good restricted diet. It is not wise for you to hit and miss with different dog foods. Many of the diets offered over the counter are not the hypoallergenic diet you are led to believe. Dogs acquire allergies through exposure.

Inhalant allergies result in atopy, which causes licking of the feet, scratching the body, and rubbing the muzzle. They may be seasonable. Your veterinarian or dermatologist can perform intradermal testing for inhalant allergies. If your dog should test positive, then a vaccine may be prepared. The results are very satisfying.

Tonsillitis

Usually, young dogs have a higher incidence of tonsillitis than the older ones. Older dogs have built up resistance. It is very contagious. Sometimes it is difficult to determine if the condition is tonsillitis or kennel cough because the symptoms are similar. Symptoms include fever, poor eating, swallowing with difficulty, and retching up a white, frothy mucus.

DENTAL CARE for Your Dog's Life

So, you have a new puppy! Anyone who has ever raised a puppy is abundantly aware of how this new arrival affects the household. Your puppy will chew anything he can reach, chase your shoelaces, and play "tear the rag" with any piece of clothing he can find. When puppies are newly born, they have no teeth. At about four weeks of age, puppies of most breeds begin to develop their deciduous or baby teeth. They begin eating semi-solid food, biting and fighting with their littermates, and learning discipline from their mother. As their new teeth come in, they inflict pain on their mother's breasts, so feeding sessions become less frequent and shorter. By six or eight weeks, the mother will start growling to warn her pups when they are fighting too roughly or hurting her as they nurse too much with their new teeth.

Puppies need to chew. It is a necessary part of their physical and mental development. They develop muscles and necessary life skills as they drag objects around, fight over possession, and vocalize alerts and warnings. Puppies chew on things to explore their world. They are using their sense of taste to determine what is food and what is not. How else can they tell an electrical cord from a lizard? At about four months of age, most puppies begin shedding their baby teeth. Often, these teeth need some help to come out to make way for the permanent teeth. The incisors (front teeth) will be replaced first. Then, the adult canine or fang teeth erupt. When a baby tooth is not shed before the permanent tooth comes in, veterinarians call it a retained deciduous tooth. This condition will often cause gum infections by trapping hair and debris between the permanent tooth and the retained baby tooth. Puppies that are given adequate chew toys will exhibit less destructive behavior, develop more physically, and have less chance of retained deciduous teeth.

During the first year, your dog should be seen by your veterinarian at regular intervals. He will let you know when to bring your puppy in for vaccinations and parasite examinations. At each visit, your vet should inspect the lips, teeth, and mouth as part of a complete physical examination. You should take some part in the maintenance of your dog's oral health. Examine your dog's mouth weekly

Maintaining healthy teeth and gums are an important part of your dog's general care. Check and brush his teeth regularly.

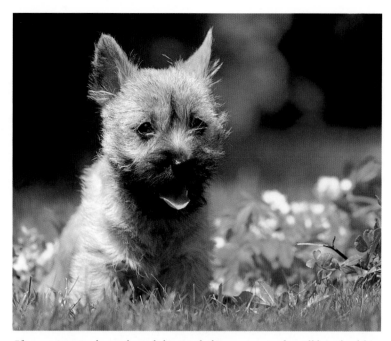

If you train your dog with good chewing habits as a puppy, he will have healthier teeth throughout his life.

throughout his first year to make sure there are no sores, foreign objects, tooth problems, etc. If your dog drools excessively, shakes his head, or has bad breath, consult your veterinarian. By the time your dog is six months old, his permanent teeth are all in and plaque can start to accumulate on the tooth surfaces. This is when your dog needs good dental-care habits to prevent calculus buildup on his teeth. Brushing is best—that is a fact that cannot be denied. However, some dogs do not like their teeth brushed regularly, or you may not be able to accomplish the task. In this case, you should consider a product that will help prevent plaque and calculus buildup, like any of the dental devices available from Nylabone®.

By the time dogs are four years old, 75 percent of them have periodontal disease. It is the most common infection in dogs. Yearly examinations by your vet are essential to maintaining your dog's good health. If he detects periodontal disease, he or she may recommend a prophylactic cleaning. To do a thorough cleaning, it will be necessary to put your dog under anesthesia. With modern gas anesthetics and monitoring equipment, the procedure is pretty

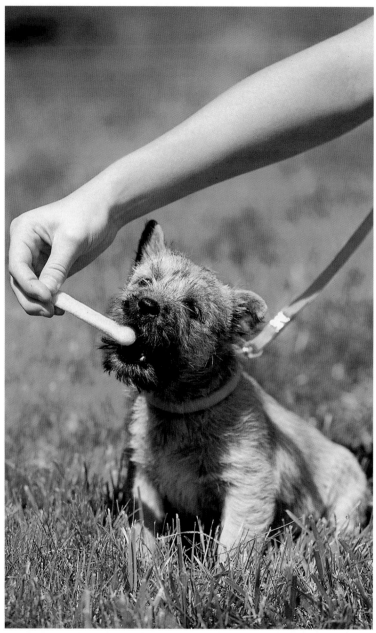

Providing your Cairn puppy with safe chew toys, like Nylabones®, promotes good oral health and keeps him occupied.

safe. Your veterinarian will scale the teeth with an ultrasound scaler or hand instrument. This removes the calculus from the teeth. If there are calculus deposits below the gum line, the veterinarian will plane the roots to make them smooth. After all of the calculus has been removed, the teeth are polished with pumice in a polishing cup. If any medical or surgical treatment is needed, it is done at this time. The final step would be fluoride treatment and your follow-up treatment at home. If the periodontal disease is advanced, the veterinarian may prescribe a medicated mouth rinse or antibiotics for use at home. Make sure your dog has safe, clean, and attractive chew toys, like Nylabones®, and healthy treats.

As your dog ages, professional examination and cleaning should become more frequent. The mouth should be inspected at least once a year. Your vet may recommend visits every six months. In the geriatric patient, organs such as the heart, liver, and kidneys do not function as well as when your dog was young. Your vet will probably want to test these organs' functions prior to using general anesthesia for dental cleaning. If your dog is a good chewer and you work closely with your vet, he can keep all of his teeth all of his life. However, as your dog ages, his sense of smell, sight, and taste will diminish. He may not have the desire to chase, trap, or chew his toys. He will also not have the energy to chew for long periods, as arthritis and periodontal disease could make chewing painful. This will leave you with more responsibility for keeping his teeth clean and healthy. The dog that would not let you brush his teeth at one year of age, may let you brush his teeth now that he is ten years old.

If you train your dog with good chewing habits as a puppy, he will have healthier teeth throughout his life.

TRAVELING with Your Dog

The earlier you start traveling with your new puppy or dog, the better. He needs to become accustomed to traveling. However, some dogs are nervous riders and become carsick easily. It is helpful if he starts any trip with an empty stomach. Do not despair, as it will go better if you continue taking him with you on short, fun rides. How would you feel if every time you rode in the car you stopped at the doctor's office for an injection? You would soon dread that nasty car. Older dogs that tend to get carsick may have more of a problem adjusting to traveling. Those dogs that are having serious problems may benefit from medication prescribed by the veterinarian.

Do give your dog a chance to relieve himself before getting into the car. It is a good idea to be prepared for a clean up with a leash, paper towels, bag, and terry cloth towel.

When in the car, the safest place for your dog is in a fiberglass or wire crate, although close confinement can promote carsickness in some dogs.

An alternative to the crate would be to use a car harness made for dogs and/or a safety strap attached to the harness or collar. Whatever you do, do not let your dog ride in the back of a pickup truck unless he is securely tied on a very short lead. I've seen trucks stop quickly, and, even though the dog was tied, he fell out and was dragged.

Another advantage of the crate is that it is a safe place to leave your dog if you need to run into the store. Otherwise, you wouldn't be able to leave the windows down. Keep in mind that while many dogs are overly protective in their crates, this may not be enough to deter dognappers. In some states, it is against the law to leave a dog in the car unattended.

Never leave a dog loose in the car wearing a collar and leash. More than one dog has killed himself by hanging. Do not let him put his head out an open window. Foreign debris can be blown into his eyes. When leaving your dog unattended in a car, consider the temperature. It can take less than five minutes to reach temperatures over 100 degrees Fahrenheit.

TRIPS

Perhaps you are taking a trip. Give consideration to what is best

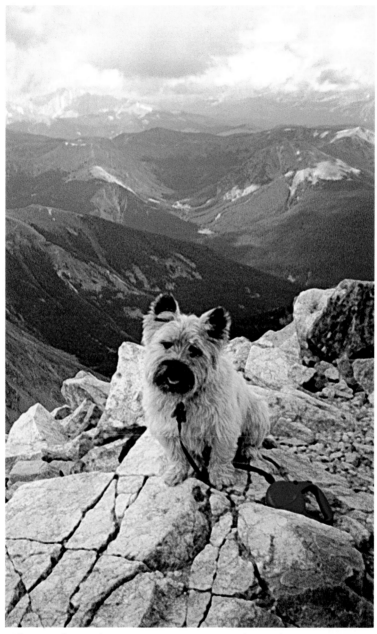

When traveling with your canine companion, make sure he is wearing proper identification that includes your name and phone number.

for your dog—traveling with you or boarding. When traveling by car, van, or motor home, you need to think ahead about locking your vehicle. In all probability you have many valuables in the car and do not wish to leave it unlocked. Perhaps most valuable and not replaceable is your dog. Give thought to securing your vehicle and providing adequate ventilation for him. Another consideration for you when traveling with your dog is medical problems that may arise and little inconveniences, such as exposure to external parasites. Some areas of the country are quite flea infested. You may want to carry flea spray with you. This is even a good idea when staying in motels. Quite possibly you are not the only occupants of the room.

Unbelievably, many motels and even hotels do allow canine guests, even some very first-class ones. Gaines Pet Foods Corporation publishes *Touring With Towser*, a directory of domestic hotels and motels that accommodate guests with dogs. Their address is Gaines TWT, PO Box 5700, Kankakee, IL, 60902. Call ahead to any motel that you may be considering and see if they accept pets. Sometimes it is necessary to pay a deposit against room damage.

Before planning a trip, give serious consideration to what would be best for your dog—traveling with you or boarding. Make sure he is up to it physically and mentally.

The management may feel reassured if you mention that your dog will be crated. If you do travel with your dog, take along plenty of baggies so that you can clean up after him. When we all do our share in cleaning up, we make it possible for motels to continue accepting our pets. As a matter of fact, you should practice cleaning up everywhere you take your dog.

Depending on where your are traveling, you may need an up-to-date health certificate issued by your veterinarian. It is good policy to take along your dog's medical information, which would include the name, address, and phone number of your veterinarian, vaccination record, rabies certificate, and any medication he is taking.

AIR TRAVEL

When traveling by air, you need to contact the airlines to check their policy. Usually, you have to make arrangements up to a couple of weeks in advance when traveling with your dog. The airlines require your dog to travel in an airline-approved fiberglass crate. These can be purchased through the airlines, but they are also readily available in most pet-supply stores. If your dog is not accustomed to a crate, it is a good idea to get him acclimated to it before your trip. The day of the actual trip you should withhold water about 1 hour ahead of departure and food for about 12 hours. The airlines generally have temperature restrictions that do not allow pets to travel if it is either too cold or too hot. Frequently, these restrictions are based on the temperatures at the departure and arrival airports. It's best to inquire about a health certificate. These usually need to be issued within ten days of departure. You should arrange for nonstop, direct flights, and if a commuter plane is involved, check to see if it will carry dogs. Some don't. The Humane Society of the United States has put together a tip sheet for airline traveling. You can receive a copy by sending a self-addressed, stamped envelope to:

The Humane Society of the United States
Tip Sheet
2100 L Street NW
Washington, DC 20037.

Regulations differ for traveling outside of the country and are sometimes changed without notice. Well in advance of your trip you need to write or call the appropriate consulate or agricultural

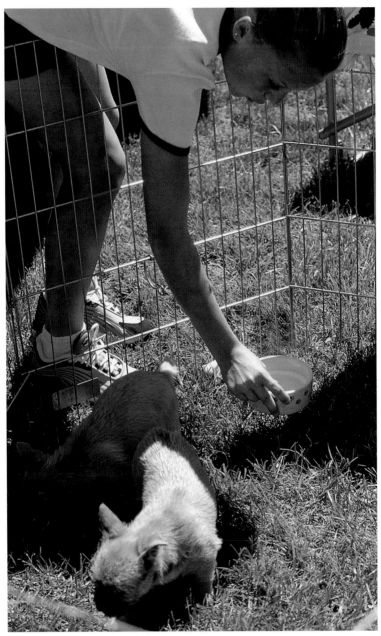

If you must leave your dog behind, there are two options for care: a kennel or a qualified pet sitter. Ask other pet owners or your vet for recommendations.

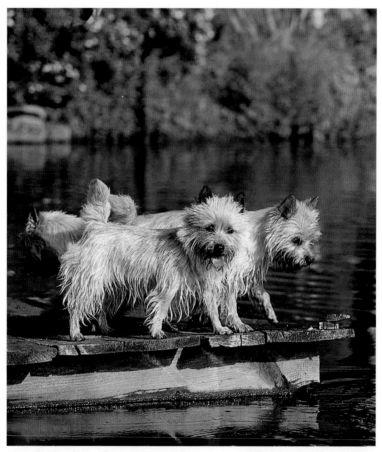

Traveling with your dog requires a lot of preparation. When making arrangements, confirm that your hotel and places at your destination, like parks and beaches, welcome dogs.

department for instructions. Some countries have lengthy quarantines (six months), and many differ in their rabies vaccination requirements. For instance, it may have to be given at least 30 days ahead of your departure.

Do make sure your dog is wearing proper identification including your name, phone number, and city. You never know when you might be in an accident and separated from your dog, or your dog could be frightened and somehow manage to escape and run away.

Another suggestion would be to carry in-case-of-emergency instructions. These would include the address and phone number of a relative or friend, your veterinarian's name, address, and phone number, and your dog's medical information.

BOARDING KENNELS

Perhaps you have decided that you need to board your dog. Your veterinarian can recommend a good boarding facility or possibly a pet sitter that will come to your house. It is customary for the boarding kennel to ask for proof of vaccination for the DHLPP, rabies, and bordetella vaccines. The bordetella should have been given within six months of boarding. This is for your protection. If they do not ask for this proof, I would not board at their kennel. Ask about flea control. Those dogs that suffer flea-bite allergy can get in trouble at a boarding kennel. Unfortunately, boarding kennels are limited as to how much they are able to do.

For more information on pet sitting, contact NAPPS:
National Association of Professional Pet Sitters
1200 G Street, NW
Suite 760
Washington, DC 20005.

Some pet clinics have technicians that pet sit and that board clinic patients in their homes. This may be an alternative for you. Ask your veterinarian if they have an employee that can help you. There is a definite advantage to having a technician care for your dog, especially if he is on medication or is a senior citizen.

You can write to the ASPCA for a copy of *Traveling With Your Pet:* ASPCA, Education Department, 441 E. 92nd Street, New York, NY 10128.

IDENTIFICATION and Finding the Lost Dog

There are several ways of identifying your dog. The old standby is a collar with dog license, rabies, and ID tags. Unfortunately, collars have a way of being separated from dogs and tags fall off. We're not suggesting you shouldn't use a collar and tags. If they stay intact and on the dog, they are the quickest form of identification.

For several years, owners have been tattooing their dogs. Some tattoos use a number with a registry. Herein lies the problem, because there are several registries to check. If you wish to tattoo your dog, use your social security number. Humane shelters have the means to trace it. It is usually done on the inside of the rear thigh. The area is first shaved and numbed. There is no pain, although some dogs do not like the buzzing sound. Occasionally, tattooing is not legible and needs to be redone.

The newest method of identification is microchipping. The microchip is a computer chip that is no larger than a grain of rice. The veterinarian implants it by injection between the shoulder blades. The dog feels no discomfort. If your dog is lost and picked up by the humane society, they can trace you by scanning the microchip, which has its own code. Most microchip scanners are

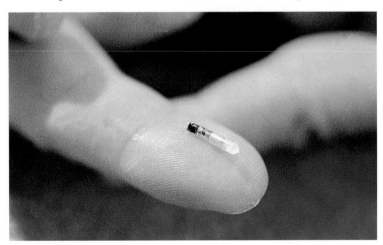

The newest method of identification is microchipping; a chip no bigger than a grain of rice is implanted under your dog's skin.

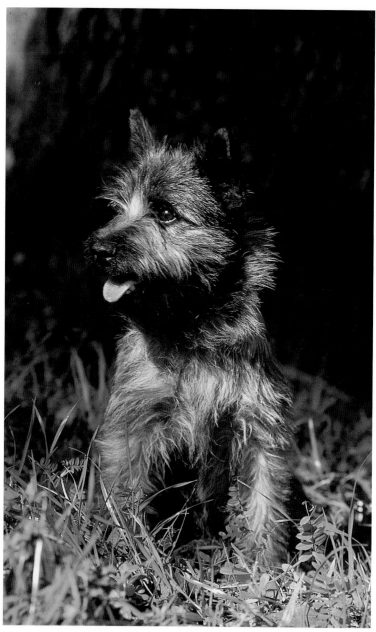

It is a good idea to have a clear, recent photo of your dog to distribute in the event that he becomes lost.

Responsible pet owners do everything they can to ensure the safety of their canine companions, especially when they are left unsupervised.

friendly to other brands of microchips and their registries. The microchip comes with a dog tag saying that the dog is microchipped. It is the safest way of identifying your dog.

FINDING THE LOST DOG

Most people would agree that there would be little worse than losing your dog. Responsible pet owners rarely lose their dogs. They do not let their dogs run free because they don't want harm to come to them. Not only that, but in most, if not all, states there is a leash law.

Beware of fenced-in yards. They can be a hazard. Dogs find ways to escape either over or under fences. Another fast exit may be through the gate that perhaps someone left unlocked.

Below is a list that will hopefully be of help to you if you lose your pet. Remember, don't give up, keep looking. Your dog is worth your efforts.

1. Contact your neighbors and put flyers with a photo on it in their mailboxes. Information you should include would be the dog's name, breed, sex, color, age, source of identification, when your dog was last seen and where, and your name and phone numbers. It may be helpful to say that the dog needs medical care. Offer a *reward*.

2. Check all local shelters daily. It is also possible for your dog to be picked up away from home and end up in an out-of-the-way shelter. Check these, too. Go in person. It is not

enough to call. Most shelters are limited on the time they can hold dogs before they are put up for adoption or euthanized. There is the possibility that your dog will not make it to the shelter for several days. He could have been wandering or someone may have tried to keep him.

3. Notify all local veterinarians. Call and send flyers.

4. Call your breeder. Frequently, breeders are contacted when one of their breed is found.

5. Contact the rescue group for your breed.

6. Contact local schools—children may have seen your dog.

7. Post flyers at the schools, groceries, gas stations, convenience stores, veterinary clinics, groomers, and any other places that will allow them.

8. Advertise in the newspaper.

9. Advertise on the radio.

BEHAVIOR and Canine Communication

tudies of the human/animal bond point out the importance of the unique relationships that exist between people and their pets. Those of us who share our lives with pets understand the special part they play through companionship, service, and protection. For many, the pet/owner bond goes beyond simple companionship; pets are often considered members of the family. A leading pet food manufacturer recently conducted a nationwide survey of pet owners to gauge just how important pets were in their lives. Here's what they found:

- 76 percent allow their pets to sleep on their beds
- 78 percent think of their pets as their children
- 84 percent display photos of their pets, mostly in their homes
- 84 percent think that their pets react to their own emotions
- 100 percent talk to their pets
- 97 percent think that their pets understand what they're saying

Are you surprised?

Senior citizens show more concern for their own eating habits when they have the responsibility of feeding a dog. Seeing that their

For many, the pet/owner bond goes beyond companionship; pets are considered members of the family.

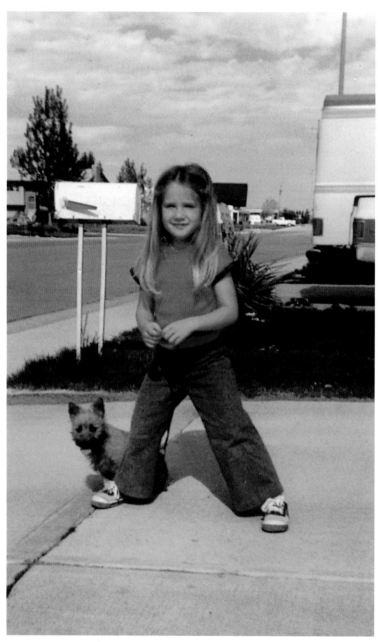

Having your child take part in caring for a family pet is a good lesson in responsibility. It also helps a child to feel comfortable and secure around animals.

dogs are routinely exercised encourages the owners to think of schedules that otherwise may seem unimportant to a senior citizen. The older owner may be arthritic and feeling poorly, but with respon-sibility for his dog he has a reason to get up and get moving. It is a big plus if his dog is an attention seeker that will demand such from his owner.

Over the last couple of decades, it has been shown that pets relieve the stress of those who lead busy lives. Owning a pet has been known to lessen the occurrence of heart attack and stroke.

Many single folks thrive on the companionship of their dogs. Lifestyles are very different from a long time ago, and today more individuals seek the single life. However, they receive fulfillment from owning dogs.

Most likely, the majority of dogs live in family environments. The companionship they provide is well worth the effort involved. In my opinion, every child should have the opportunity to have a family dog. Dogs teach responsibility through the understanding of their care, feelings, and even respect for their life cycles. Frequently, those children who have not been exposed to dogs grow up afraid of them, which isn't good. Dogs sense timidity, and some will take advantage of the situation.

Providing a loving and stimulating environment for your Cairn is important for his physical and emotional well-being. Be sure to spend quality time with your pet, like playtime with his favorite Nylabone® toys.

Socialization with his littermates will help your Cairn pup to get along with other dogs when he is older.

Today, more dogs are working as service dogs. Since the origination of the Seeing Eye dogs years ago, we now have dogs trained to aid the deaf. Also, dogs are trained to provide service for the handicapped and are able to perform many different tasks for their owners. Search and rescue dogs, with their handlers, are sent throughout the world to assist in the recovery of disaster victims. They are lifesavers.

Therapy dogs are very popular with nursing homes, and some hospitals even allow them to visit. The inhabitants truly look forward to their visits. They wanted and were allowed to have visiting dogs to hold and love.

Nationally, there is a Pet Awareness Week to educate students and others about the value and basic care of our pets. Many countries take an even greater interest in their pets than Americans do. In those countries, pets are allowed to accompany their owners into restaurants and shops, etc. In the US, this freedom is only available to our service dogs. Even so, we think very highly of the human/animal bond.

CANINE BEHAVIOR

Canine behavior problems are the number-one reason that pet owners dispose of their dogs, either through new homes, humane shelters, or euthanasia. Unfortunately, there are too many owners who are unwilling to devote the necessary time to properly train their dogs. On the other hand, there are those who are not only concerned about inherited health problems but are also aware of the dog's mental stability.

You may realize that a breed and his group relatives (i.e., sporting, hounds, etc.) show tendencies toward behavioral characteristics. An experienced breeder can acquaint you with his breed's personality. Unfortunately, many breeds are labeled with poor temperaments, when actually the breed as a whole is not affected but rather only a small percentage of individuals within the breed.

Inheritance and environment contribute to the dog's behavior. Some naïve people suggest inbreeding as the cause of bad temperaments. Inbreeding only results in poor behavior if the ancestors carry the trait. If there are excellent temperaments behind the dogs, then good breeding practices will promote good temperaments in the offspring. Did you ever consider that inbreeding is what sets the characteristics of a breed? A purebred dog is the end result of inbreeding. This does not spare the mixed-breed dog from the same problems. Mixed-breed dogs are frequently the offspring of purebred dogs.

Not too many decades ago most dogs led a different lifestyle than what is prevalent today. Usually, mom stayed home, so the dog had human companionship and someone to discipline him if needed. Not much was expected from the family pet. Today's mom works, and everyone's life is at a much faster pace.

The dog may have to adjust to being a "weekend" dog. The family is gone all day during the week, and he is left to his own devices for entertainment. Some dogs sleep all day waiting for their families to come home, and others become wigwam wreckers if given the opportunity. Crates do ensure the safety of the dog and the house. However, he could become physically and emotionally crippled if he doesn't get enough exercise and attention. We still appreciate and want the companionship of our dogs, although we expect more from them. In many cases, we tend to forget dogs are just that—*dogs* not human beings.

SOCIALIZING AND TRAINING

Many prospective puppy buyers lack experience regarding the proper socialization and training needed to develop the type of pets

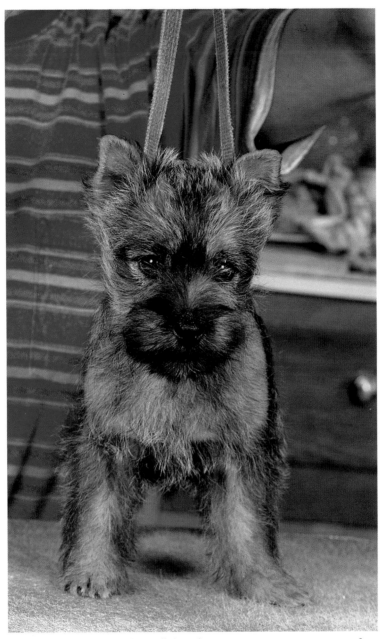

Every experience a puppy has will shape his temperament. Proper training from an early age will help your Cairn become a well-adjusted, well-mannered adult.

we all desire. In the first 18 months, training does take some work. It is easier to start proper training before there is a problem that needs to be corrected.

The initial work begins with the breeder. The breeder should start socializing the puppy at five to six weeks of age and cannot let up. Human socializing is critical up through 12 weeks of age and is likewise important during the following months. The litter should be left together during the first few weeks, but it is necessary to separate the pups by ten weeks of age. Leaving them together after that time will increase competition for litter dominance. If puppies are not socialized with people by 12 weeks of age, they will be timid in later life.

The eight- to ten-week age period can be a fearful time for puppies. They need to be handled very gently by children and adults. There should be no harsh discipline during this time. Starting at 14 weeks of age, the puppy begins the juvenile period, which ends when he reaches sexual maturity around 6 to 14 months of age. During the juvenile period, he needs to be introduced to

Breeders usually begin socializing their puppies at five to six weeks of age. It's vital to your pup's development that you continue this socialization process.

Life will be easier for your dog if you expose him at a young age to the necessities of life—proper behavior and restraint.

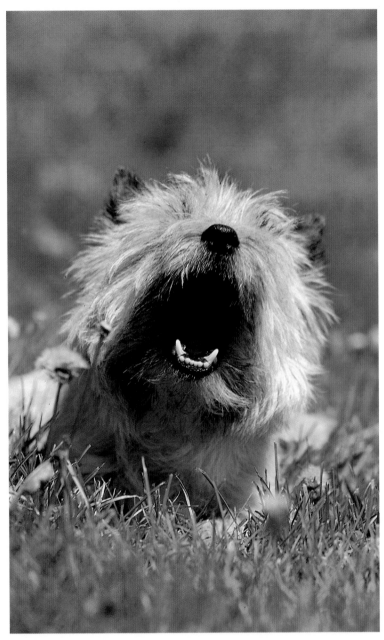

Learning how a dog communicates will help you to better understand particular behaviors. For example, your dog may be barking excessively to get attention.

strangers (adults, children, and other dogs) on the home property. At sexual maturity, he will begin to bark at strangers and become more protective. Males start to lift their legs to urinate, but you can inhibit this behavior by walking your boy on leash away from trees, shrubs, fences, etc.

Perhaps you are thinking about getting an older puppy. You need to inquire about the puppy's social experience. If he has lived in a kennel, he may have a hard time adjusting to people and environmental stimuli. Assuming he has had a good social upbringing, there are advantages to an older puppy.

Training includes puppy kindergarten and a minimum of one to two basic training classes. During these classes, you will learn how to train your youngster. This is especially important if you own a large breed of dog. It is somewhat harder, if not nearly impossible, for some owners to be the alpha figure when their dog reaches adult size. You will be taught how to properly restrain your dog. This concept is important. Again, it puts you in the alpha position. All dogs need to be restrained many times during their lives. Believe it or not, some of the worst offenders are the eight-week-old puppies that are brought to our clinic. They need to be gently restrained for a nail trim, but the way they carry on you would think we were killing them. In comparison, their vaccination is a "piece of cake." When we ask dogs to do something that is not agreeable to them, their worst comes out. Life will be easier for your dog if you expose him at a young age to the necessities of life—proper behavior and restraint.

UNDERSTANDING THE DOG'S LANGUAGE

Most authorities agree that the dog is a descendent of the wolf. The dog and the wolf have similar traits. For instance, both are pack oriented and prefer not to be isolated for long periods of time. Another characteristic is that the dog, like the wolf, looks to the leader—alpha—for direction. Both the wolf and the dog communicate through body language, not only within their packs but with outsiders.

Every pack has an alpha figure. The dog looks to you, or should look to you, to be that leader. If your dog doesn't receive the proper training and guidance, he very well may replace you as alpha. This would be a serious problem and is certainly a disservice to your dog.

Your dog's body language can often tell you how he is feeling. For instance, he may show dominance by not parting with toys in his mouth or may be possessive with his food bowl.

Eye contact is one way the alpha wolf keeps order within his pack. You are alpha so you must establish eye contact with your puppy. Obviously, your puppy will have to look at you. Practice eye contact, even if you need to hold his head for five to ten seconds at a time. You can give him a treat as a reward. Make sure your eye contact is gentle and not threatening. Later, if he has been naughty, it is permissible to give him a long, penetrating look. There are some older dogs that never learned eye contact as puppies and cannot accept eye contact. You should avoid eye contact with these dogs since they feel threatened and will retaliate as such.

BODY LANGUAGE

The play bow, when the forequarters are down and the hindquarters are elevated, is an invitation to play. Puppies play fight, which helps them learn the acceptable limits of biting. This is necessary later in their lives. Nevertheless, an owner may be falsely reassured by the playful nature of his dog's aggression. Playful aggression toward another dog or human may be an indication of serious aggression in the future. Owners should never play fight or play tug-of-war with any dog that is inclined to be dominant.

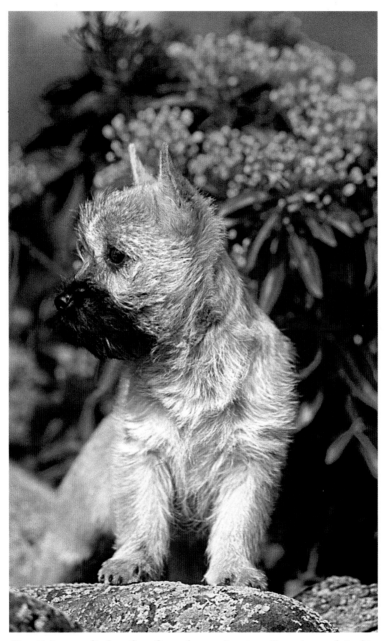

Your Cairn may display a fear of new places or situations. Be patient and give him time to get used to what is unfamiliar to him.

Signs of submission are:

1. Avoids eye contact.

2. Active submission—the dog crouches down, ears back and tail lowered.

3. Passive submission—the dog rolls on his side, with his hindlegs in the air, and frequently urinates.

Signs of dominance are:

1. Makes eye contact.

2. Stands with ears up, tail up, and the hair raised on his neck.

3. Shows dominance over another dog by standing at right angles over him.

Dominant dogs tend to behave in characteristic ways such as:

1. The dog may be unwilling to move from his place (i.e., reluctant to give up the sofa if the owner wants to sit there).

2. He may not part with toys or objects in his mouth and may show possessiveness with his food bowl.

3. He may not respond quickly to commands.

4. He may be disagreeable for grooming and dislikes being petted.

Dogs are popular because of their sociable nature. Those that have contact with humans during the first 12 weeks of life regard them as a member of their own species—their pack. All dogs have the potential for both dominant and submissive behavior. Only through experience and training do they learn to whom it is appropriate to show which behavior. Not all dogs are concerned with dominance, but owners need to be aware of that potential. It is wise for the owner to establish his dominance early on.

A human can express dominance or submission toward a dog in the following ways:

1. Meeting the dog's gaze signals dominance. Averting the gaze signals submission. If the dog growls or threatens, averting the gaze is the first avoiding action to take—it may prevent attack. It is important to establish eye contact in the puppy. The older dog that has not been exposed to eye contact may see it as a threat and will not be willing to submit.

2. Being above the dog signals dominance; being lower signals submission. This is why, when attempting to make friends with a strange dog or catch the runaway, one should kneel down to his level. Some owners see their dogs become dominant when allowed on the furniture or on the bed. Then the dog is at the owner's level.

3. An owner can gain dominance by ignoring all the dog's social initiatives. The owner pays attention to the dog only when he obeys a command.

No dog should be allowed to achieve dominant status over any adult or child. Ways of preventing this are as follows:

1. Handle the puppy gently, especially during the three- to four-month period.

2. Let the children and adults handfeed him and teach him to take food without lunging or grabbing.

3. Do not allow him to chase children or joggers.

4. Do not allow him

When a dog is showing signs of aggression, you should speak calmly and firmly give a command he understands, such as sit.

to jump on people or mount their legs. Even females may be inclined to mount. It is not only a male habit.

5. Do not allow him to growl for any reason.

6. Don't participate in wrestling or tug-of-war games.

7. Don't physically punish a puppy for aggressive behavior. Restrain him from repeating the infraction and teach an alternative behavior. Dogs should earn everything they receive from their owners. This would include sitting to receive petting or treats, sitting before going out the door, and sitting to receive the collar and leash. These types of exercises reinforce the owner's dominance.

Young children should never be left alone with a dog. It is important that children learn some basic obedience commands so they have some control over the dog. They will gain his respect.

If you have attempted to correct a behavior and still have problems, contact your local dog trainer or behaviorist for some advice.

FEAR

One of the most common problems dogs can experience is being fearful. Some dogs are more afraid than others. On the lesser side, which is sometimes humorous to watch, dogs can be afraid of a strange object. They act silly when something is out of place in the house. We call this trait perceptive intel-ligence. He realizes the abnormal within his known environment. He does not react the same way in strange environ-ments since he does not know what is normal.

On the more serious side is a fear of people. This can result in backing off, seeking his own space and saying "leave me alone," or it can result in an aggressive behavior that may lead to challenging the person. Respect that the dog wants to be left alone and give him time to come forward. If you approach the cornered dog, he may resort to snapping. If you leave him alone, he may decide to come forward, which should be rewarded with a treat.

Some dogs may initially be too fearful to take treats. In these cases it is helpful to make sure the dog hasn't eaten for about 24 hours. Being a little hungry encourages him to accept the treats, especially if they are of the "gourmet" variety.

Dogs can be afraid of numerous things, including loud noises and thunderstorms. Invariably, the owner rewards (by comforting) the dog when he shows signs of fearfulness. When your dog is frightened, direct his attention to something else. Don't dwell on his fright.

AGGRESSION

Some different types of aggression are: predatory, defensive, dominance, possessive, protective, fear induced, noise provoked, "rage" syndrome (unpro-voked aggression), maternal, and aggression directed toward other dogs. Aggression is the most common behavioral problem encountered. Protective breeds are expected to be more aggressive than others, but with the proper upbringing they can make very dependable companions. You need to be able to read your dog.

Many factors contri-bute to aggression, including genetics and environment. An improper environment, which may include living conditions, lack of social life, excessive punishment, being attacked or frightened by an aggressive dog, etc., can all influence a dog's behavior. Even spoiling him and giving too much praise may be detrimental. Isolation and the lack of human contact or exposure to frequent teasing by children or adults also can ruin a good dog.

Lack of direction, fear, or confusion lead to aggression in those dogs that are so inclined. Any obedience exercise, even the sit and down, can direct the dog and overcome his fear and/or confusion. Every dog should learn these commands as a youngster, and there should be periodic reinforcement.

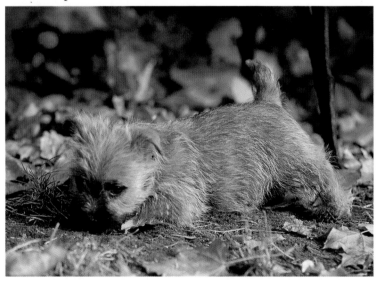

Puppies may sometimes tend to show improper behavior, like barking or digging. Correct these behaviors with firm, positive reinforcement.

When a dog is showing signs of aggression, you should speak calmly (no screaming or hysterics) and firmly give a command that he understands, such as the sit. As soon as your dog obeys, you have assumed your dominant position. Aggression presents a problem because there may be danger to others. Sometimes it is an emotional issue. Owners may consciously or unconsciously encourage their dogs' aggression. Other owners show responsibility by accepting the problem and taking measures to keep it under control. The owner is responsible for his dog's actions, and it is not wise to take a chance on someone being bitten, especially a child. Euthanasia is the solution for some owners, and in severe cases this may be the best choice. However, few dogs are that dangerous and very few are that much of a threat to their owners. If caution is exercised and professional help is gained early on, most cases can be controlled.

Some authorities recommend feeding a lower protein (less than 20 percent) diet. They believe this can aid in reducing aggression. If the dog loses weight, vegetable oil can be added. Veterinarians and behaviorists are having some success with pharmacology. In many cases, treatment is possible and can improve the situation.

If you have done everything according to "the book" regarding training and socializing and are still having a behavior problem, don't procrastinate. It is important that the problem gets attention before it is out of hand. It is estimated that 20 percent of a veterinarian's time may be devoted to dealing with problems before they become so intolerable that the dog is separated from his home and owner. If your veterinarian isn't able to help, he can refer you to a behaviorist.

PROBLEMS

Barking

Barking is a habit that shouldn't be encouraged. Some owners desire their dogs to bark so as to be watchdogs. Most dogs will bark when a stranger comes to the door.

The new puppy frequently barks or whines in the crate in his strange, unfamiliar environment, and the owner reinforces the puppy's bad behavior by going to him during the night. This is a no-no. Smack the top of the crate and say, "Quiet," in a loud, firm voice. Puppies don't like to hear the loud noise of a crate being banged. If the barking is sleep-interrupting, the owner should take

Teach your Cairn Terrier how you want him to behave. Obedience training can encourage good behavior and correct undesirable behavior.

crate and pup to the bedroom for a few days until the puppy becomes adjusted to his new environment. Otherwise, ignore the barking during the night.

Barking can be a breed trait or a bad habit learned through the environment. It takes dedication to stop the barking. Attention should be paid to the cause of it. Does the dog seek attention, does he need to go out, is it feeding time, is it occurring when he is left alone, is it a protective bark, etc.? Overzealous barking can be a breed tendency. When barking presents a problem for you, try to stop it as soon as it begins.

There are electronic collars available that are supposed to curb barking. There are some disadvantages to the collar. If the dog is barking out of excitement, punishment is not the appropriate treatment. Presumably, there is the chance the collar could be activated by other stimuli and thereby punish the dog when he is not barking. If you decide to use one, you should seek help from a person with experience with that type of collar. Nevertheless, the root of the problem needs to be investigated and corrected.

In extreme circumstances (usually when there is a problem with the neighbors), some people have resorted to having their dogs

Although what you may consider to be problem behaviors—like chewing, biting, or digging—are natural behaviors to your dog, most can be controlled or prevented.

Bored dogs relieve their frustrations through mischievous behavior. Be sure to provide your Cairn with enough physical activity and attention to keep him out of trouble.

debarked. Be cautioned that the dog continues to bark, but usually only a squeaking sound is heard. Frequently, the vocal cords grow back. Probably the biggest concern is that the dog can be left with scar tissue, which can narrow the opening to the trachea.

Jumping Up

A dog that jumps up is a happy dog. Nevertheless, few guests appreciate dogs jumping on them. Clothes get footprinted and/or snagged.

Some trainers believe in allowing the puppy to jump up during his first few weeks. If you correct him too soon and at the wrong age, you may intimidate him. Consequently, he could be timid around humans later in his life. However, there will come a time, probably around four months of age, that he needs to know when it is okay to jump and when he is to show off good manners by sitting instead.

Some authorities never allow jumping. If you are irritated by your dog jumping up on you, then you should discourage it from the beginning. A larger breed of dog can cause harm to a senior citizen. Some are quite fragile. It may not take much to cause a topple that could break a hip.

How do you correct the problem? All family members need to participate in teaching the puppy to sit as soon as he starts to jump up. The sit must be practiced every time he does it. Don't forget to praise him for his good behavior. If an older dog has acquired the habit, grasp his paws and squeeze tightly. Give a firm, "No." He'll soon catch on. Remember, the entire family must take part. Each time you allow your dog to jump up you go back a step in training.

Providing your Cairn with a large, fenced-in area outdoors will offer him the exercise and stimulation he needs, as well as keep him from running off when unsupervised.

Biting

All puppies bite and try to chew on your fingers, toes, arms, etc. This is the time to teach them to be gentle and not to bite hard. Put your fingers in your puppy's mouth, and if he bites too hard then say "easy" and let him know he's hurting you. Squeal and act like you have been seriously hurt. If the puppy plays too rough and doesn't respond to your corrections, then he needs "time out" in his crate. You should be particularly careful with young children and puppies that still have their deciduous (baby) teeth. Those teeth are like needles and can leave little scars on youngsters.

Biting in the more mature dog is something that should be prevented at all costs. If it occurs, quickly let him know in no uncertain terms that biting will not be tolerated. When biting is directed toward another dog (dog fight), don't get in the middle of it. Some authorities recommend breaking up a fight by elevating the hind legs. This would only be possible if there was a person to handle each dog. Obviously, it would be hard to fight with the hind legs off the ground. A dog bite is serious and should be given attention. Wash the bite with soap and water and contact your doctor. It is important to know the status of the offender's rabies vaccination.

Your dog must know who is boss. When biting occurs, you should seek professional help at once. On the other hand, you must not let your dog intimidate you and be so afraid of a bite that you can't discipline him. Professional help through your veterinarian, dog trainer, and/or behaviorist can give you guidance.

Digging

Bored dogs release their frustrations through mischievous behavior such as digging. Dogs shouldn't be left unattended outside, even if they are in a fenced-in yard. Usually, the dog is sent to "jail" (the backyard) because the owner can't tolerate him in the house. The culprit feels socially deprived and needs to be included in the owner's life. The owner has neglected the dog's training. The dog has not developed into the companion we desire. If you are one of these owners, then perhaps it is possible for you to change. Give him another chance. Some owners object to their dogs' unkempt coat and doggy odor. See that he is groomed on a regular schedule and look into some training classes.

Submissive Urination

Submissive urination is not a housetraining problem. It can occur in all breeds and may be more prevalent in some. Usually, it occurs in puppies, but occasionally it occurs in older dogs and may be in response to physical praise. Try verbal praise or ignoring your dog until after he has had a chance to relieve himself. Scolding will only make the problem worse. Many dogs outgrow this problem.

Coprophagia

Also know as stool eating, coprophagia sometimes occurs without a cause. It may begin with boredom and then becomes a habit that is hard to break. Your best remedy is to keep the puppy on a leash and keep the yard picked up, so he won't have an opportunity to get into trouble. Your veterinarian can dispense a medication that is put on the dog's food that makes the stool taste bitter. Of course, this will do little good if your dog cleans up after other dogs.

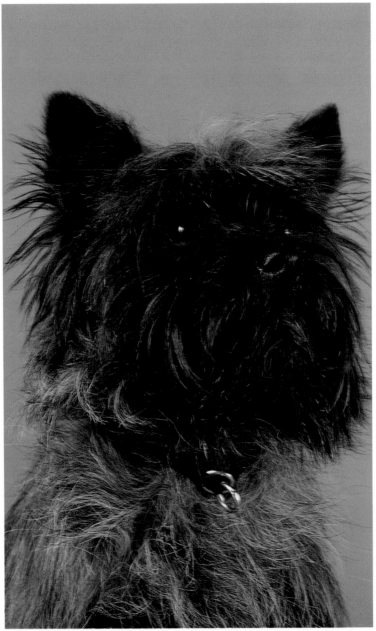

Your Cairn Terrier will look to you, his owner, for the discipline and guidance he needs to become a well-behaved pet and treasured companion.

The Runaway

There is little excuse for a dog to run away, because dogs should never be off leash except when supervised in a fenced-in yard.

Many prospective owners want to purchase a female because they believe a male is inclined to roam. It is true that an intact male is inclined to roam, which is one of the reasons a male should be neutered. However, females will roam also, especially if they are in heat. Regardless, these dogs should never be given this opportunity. A few years ago one of our clients elected euthanasia for her elderly dog because he radiographically appeared to have an intestinal blockage. The veterinarian suggested it might be a corncob. She assured him that was not possible because they hadn't had any. Apparently, he roamed and raided the neighbor's garbage, and you guessed it—he had a corncob blocking his intestines. Another dog

At times, your Cairn may challenge you by breaking some rules, but he must always know that you are the boss in the relationship.

Because Cairn Terriers bond so strongly to their owners, your love and companionship is necessary to their overall happiness and emotional stability.

raided the neighbor's garbage and died from toxins from the garbage.

To give the benefit of the doubt, perhaps your dog escapes or perhaps you are playing with your dog in the yard and he refuses to come when called. You now have a runaway. Help! The first thing to remember is when you finally do catch your naughty dog, you must not discipline him. The reasoning behind this is that it is quite possible there could be a repeat performance, and it would be nice if he would respond to your sweet command the next time you used the recall.

Always kneel down when trying to catch the runaway. Dogs are afraid of people standing over them. Also, it would be helpful to have a treat or a favorite toy to help entice him to your side. After that initial runaway experience, start practicing the recall with your dog. You can let him drag a long line (clothesline), and then randomly call him and reel him in. Let him touch you first. Reaching for the dog can frighten him. Each time he comes reward him with a treat, and, eventually, he should get the idea that this is a nice experience. The long line prevents him from really getting out of hand. At least with the long line you can step on it and stop him.

Food Guarding

If you see signs of your puppy guarding his food, you should take immediate steps to correct the problem. It is not fair to your puppy to feed him in a busy environment where children or other pets may interfere with his eating. This can be the cause of food guarding. Puppies should be fed in their crates where they do not feel threatened. Another advantage of this is that the puppy gets down to the business of eating and doesn't fool around. Perhaps you have seen possessiveness over the food bowl or his toys. Start by feeding him out of your hand, and teach him that it is okay for you to remove his food bowl or toys and that you most assuredly will return them to him. If your dog is truly a bad actor and intimidates you, try keeping him on leash and perhaps sit next to him making happy talk. At feeding time, make him work for his reward (his dinner) by doing some obedience command such as sit or down. Before your problem gets out of control, you should get professional help. If he is out of control over toys, perhaps you should dispose of them or at least put them away when young children are around.

Mischief and Misbehavior

All puppies and even some adult dogs will get into mischief at some time in their lives. You should start by "puppy proofing" your house. Even so, it is impossible to have a sterile environment. For instance, if you would be down to four walls and a floor, your dog could still chew a hole in the wall. What do you do? Remember puppies should never be left unsupervised, so let us go on to the trusted adult dog that has misbehaved. His behavior may be an attention getter. Dogs, and even children, are known to do mischief even though they know they will be punished. Your puppy/dog will benefit from more attention and new direction. He may benefit from a training class or by reinforcement of the obedience he has already learned. How about a daily walk? That could be a good outlet for your dog, time together, and exercise for both of you.

Separation Anxiety

Separation anxiety occurs when dogs feel distress or apprehension about being separated from their owners. One of the mistakes owners make is to set their dogs up for their departure. Some authorities recommend paying little attention to the pet for at least ten minutes before leaving, and for the first ten minutes after you arrive home. The dog isn't cued to the fact you are leaving, and if you keep it low key, he learns to accept it as a normal everyday occurrence. Those dogs that are used to being crated usually accept your departure. Dogs that are anxious may have a serious problem and wreak havoc on the house within a few minutes after your departure. You can try to acclimate your dog to the separation by leaving for just a few minutes at a time, and returning and rewarding him with a treat. Don't get too carried away. Plan on this process taking a long time. A behaviorist can set down a schedule for you. Those dogs that are insecure, such as ones obtained from a humane shelter or those that have changed homes, may present more of a problem.

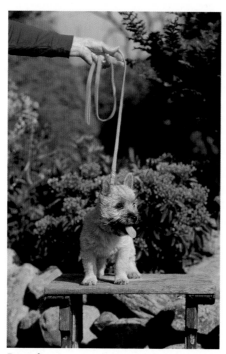

Discipline is necessary at any age. Your Cairn will pay more attention and try harder if he is praised for his efforts and rewarded for good behavior.

Punishment

A puppy should learn that correction is sometimes necessary and should not question your authority. An older dog that has never received correction may retaliate. There may be a time for physical punishment, but this does not mean hitting the dog. Do not use newspapers, fly swatters, etc. One type of correction that is used by the mother dog when she corrects her puppies is to

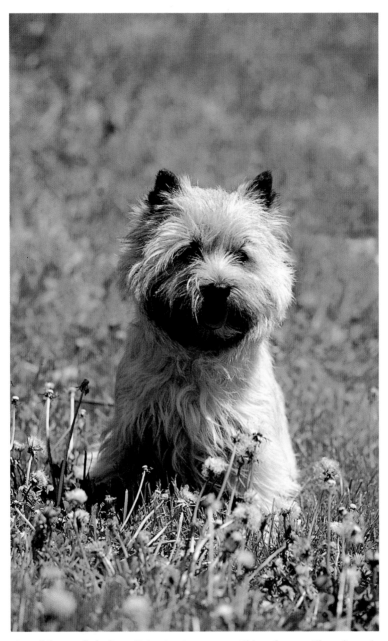

A confident and obedient Cairn is a joy to own. Although you will need to take the time to train him properly, it will be well worth the effort.

take the puppy by the scruff and shake him *gently*. For the older, larger dog, you can grab the scruff, one hand on each side of his neck, and lift his legs off the ground. This is effective because dogs feel intimidated when their feet are off the ground. Timing is of the utmost importance when punishment is necessary. Depending on the degree of fault, you might want to reinforce punishment by ignoring your dog for 15 to 20 minutes. Whatever you do, do not overdo corrections or they will lose value.

The most important advice to you is to be aware of your dog's actions. Even so, remember dogs are dogs and will behave as such, even though we might like them to be perfect little people. You and your dog will become neurotic if you worry about every little indiscretion. When there is reason for concern—don't waste time. Seek guidance. Dogs are meant to be loved and enjoyed.

REFERENCES

Valerie O'Farrell. *Manual of Canine Behavior*. British Small Animal Veterinary Association.

Brian Kilcommons. *Good Owners, Great Dogs*. Warner Books.

RESOURCES

Cairn Terrier Club of America
Corresponding Secretary: Sandra Murray
PO Box 279
Woodland Park, CO 80866-0279
www.cairnterrier.org

American Kennel Club
Headquarters:
260 Madison Avenue
New York, NY 10016

Operations Center:
5580 Centerview Drive
Raleigh, NC 27606-3390

Customer Services:
Phone: (919) 233-9767
Fax: (919) 816-3627
www.akc.org

The Kennel Club
1 Clarges Street
London
W1J 8AB
Phone: 087 0606 6750
Fax: 020 7518 1058
www.the-kennel-club.org.uk

The Canadian Kennel Club
89 Skyway Avenue
Suite 100
Etobicoke, Ontario, Canada
M9W 6R4
Order Desk & Membership: 1-800-250-8040
Fax: (416) 675-6506
www.ckc.ca

The United Kennel Club, Inc.
100 E. Kilgore Road
Kalamazoo, MI 49002-5584
(616) 343-9020
www.ukcdogs.com

INDEX

12.99   892-06

LEWIS
            Lewis, Beverly,
                  The sacrifice

DATE DUE

NO 03 04	617		

Winchester Public Library
2117 Lake Street
Winchester, WI 54557

DEMCO

The Sacrifice

BEVERLY LEWIS

·

The Sacrifice

BETHANYHOUSE
PUBLISHERS
MINNEAPOLIS, MINNESOTA

The Sacrifice
Copyright © 2004
Beverly Lewis

Cover design by Dan Thornberg

The portion of a poem cited in chapter thirty-four is as quoted in *A Joyous Heart* by Corrie Bender, published by Herald Press of Scottdale, Pennsylvania, in 1994. The author of the poem is unknown.

All rights reserved. No part of this publication may be reproduced, stored in a retrieval system, or transmitted in any form or by any means—electronic, mechanical, photocopying, recording, or otherwise—without the prior written permission of the publisher and copyright owners.

Published by Bethany House Publishers
11400 Hampshire Avenue South
Bloomington, Minnesota 55438
www.bethanyhouse.com

Bethany House Publishers is a division of
Baker Publishing Group, Grand Rapids, Michigan.

Printed in the United States of America

ISBN 0-7642-2872-2 (Paperback)
ISBN 0-7642-2875-7 (Hardcover)
ISBN 0-7642-2876-5 (Large Print)
ISBN 0-7642-2877-3 (Audio Book)

Library of Congress Cataloging-in-Publication Data

Lewis, Beverly, date-
    The sacrifice / by Beverly Lewis.
        p.   cm. — (Abram's daughters ; 3)
    ISBN 0-7642-2875-7 (hardcover : alk. paper) —ISBN 0-7642-2872-2 (pbk.) —ISBN 0-7642-2876-5 (large-print pbk.)
    1. Lancaster County (Pa.)—Fiction. 2. Amish women—Fiction. 3. Young women—Fiction. 4. Sisters—Fiction. 5. Amish—Fiction. I. Title II. Series: Lewis, Beverly, date. Abram's daughters ; 3.
    PS3562.E9383S23   2004
    813'.54—dc22

2003028149

Dedication

For

Jeannette Green,

wonderful friend and "sister."

Beautiful in every way.

By Beverly Lewis

ABRAM'S DAUGHTERS

The Covenant

The Betrayal

The Sacrifice

The Prodigal

❖ ❖ ❖

THE HERITAGE OF LANCASTER COUNTY

The Shunning

The Confession

The Reckoning

❖ ❖ ❖

The Postcard

The Crossroad

❖ ❖ ❖

The Redemption of Sarah Cain

October Song

*Sanctuary**

The Sunroom

❖ ❖ ❖

The Beverly Lewis Amish Heritage Cookbook

www.beverlylewis.com

*with David Lewis

BEVERLY LEWIS, born in the heart of Pennsylvania Dutch country, fondly recalls her growing-up years. A keen interest in her mother's Plain family heritage has led Beverly to set many of her popular stories in Lancaster County.

A former schoolteacher and accomplished pianist, Beverly is a member of the National League of American Pen Women (the Pikes Peak branch) and the Society of Children's Book Writers and Illustrators. She is the 2003 recipient of the Distinguished Alumnus Award at Evangel University, Springfield, Missouri, and her blockbuster novel, *The Shunning*, recently won the Gold Book Award. Her bestselling novel *October Song* won the Silver Seal in the Benjamin Franklin Awards, and *The Postcard* and *Sanctuary* (a collaboration with her husband, David) received Silver Angel Awards, as did her delightful picture book for all ages, *Annika's Secret Wish*. Beverly and her husband have three grown children and one grandchild and make their home in the Colorado foothills.

Prologue

Come June, the first song of the whippoorwill reminds me of berry picking . . . and bygone days. Although it has been over two years since Jonas Mast left for Ohio, I still wonder about him, along with my older sister, Sadie, and am able to pray for their happiness more readily than at first.

Especially now, at summer's onset, when strawberries are ripe and ready for pies and preserves, I think of Jonas. He loved strawberry-rhubarb pie like nobody's business, and both his mamma and mine made it for him with sugar *and* raw honey, so it was nothing short of wonderful-good. "Desserts are s'posed to be plenty sweet," Mamma has said for as long as I can remember. This, with her irresistible wide-eyed smile. These days Sadie is the one baking such delicious fruit pies for Jonas.

Now and again I feel almost numb for the way things turned out between Jonas, Sadie, and me. Close as I was to each of them, it seems they should have cared enough to send some word early on—prior to Bishop Bontrager's strict decree—offering an explanation. Anything would've been

9

better than this dreadful silence. It's the not knowing how things got so *verkehrt*—topsy-turvy—that causes the most frustration in me. The lack of word from Ohio confirms my worst fears. I expect even now Sadie probably wonders if I have any idea she is married to Jonas, or that I feel strongly she stole him away from me. How on earth does she live with herself?

I'm slowly accepting the split between my beau and me, since it would be wrong to pine for a man who belongs to another. Most folk just assume I've passed the worst of it and am moving on with life. They will never know truly, because I tend to go about things rather cheerfully . . . and, too, so much time has passed since that devastating autumn. It does still puzzle me, if I think on it, how one minute we were so happily planning our wedding, and then, clear out of the blue, a most peculiar letter arrived saying Jonas suspected Gideon Peachey of carrying a torch for me. Even though I promptly wrote to reassure him of my devotion and love, I never again heard from him. Downright baffling it is.

Of course, if Jonas were privy to my *present* friendship with Smithy Gid, he might have a little something to go on. But, back then, nothing was further from the truth. Fact was, my heart belonged wholly to Jonas, and nothing and no one could make me think otherwise. Not Smithy Gid, nor his sister Adah, my closest friend. Not even dear *Dat* and Mamma, though my father has long hoped Gid might one day win my affections.

With the revelation of Aunt Lizzie's secret to me—to Mary Ruth and Hannah, too—my father's and grandfather's health seems much improved and both Mamma and Aunt

Lizzie have a new spring in their step, in spite of the vacant spot at the supper table. Sadie's absence is a constant source of worry, especially since she's been shunned from the Gobbler's Knob church. And Dat was right; the bishop—after a reasonable time—insisted Sadie's letters be returned unopened. It's no wonder she stopped writing along about Christmastime after leaving for Ohio. I wish to heavens I might've been allowed to read those things she wrote to us.

Some days it seems as if my sister has been away for years on end. But if that were true, I'd be thought of as a *maidel* by now, which I'm surely not. I am still only nineteen—a few years under the limit of the expected marrying age—though if Smithy Gid had his way, he and I would be hitched up already.

The berry patch calls to me even now as I help Dat with morning milking. Seems there's something nearly sacred about creeping along the mounded rows, the blissful buzz of nature in my ears, long runners tripping at my bare feet as the blistering sun stands high and haughty in the sky and the tin bucket steadily fills with plump red fruit. Being out there alone with the birds and the strawberry plants, beneath the wide and blue heavenly canopy, soothes my soul and sets my world aright. At least for a time . . .

Part One

❖ ❖ ❖ ❖

What doth the Lord require of thee,

but to do justly, and to love mercy,

and to walk humbly with thy God?

—Micah 6:8

Chapter One

The morning Mamma quietly announced her baby news, Leah hung back a bit, standing near the kitchen door, while her twin sisters, especially Mary Ruth, were overjoyed at Mamma's being in the family way again. Many of the Old Order viewed it as shameful to share such things with unmarried children, but both Mamma and Dat felt otherwise and didn't hesitate to include their four eldest daughters, though discreetly.

"Since Lydiann's a toddler and not so little anymore, it'll be fun to have a baby around again," declared Mary Ruth.

"And wonderful-*gut* for Lydiann to have a close-in-age brother or sister." Hannah's smile stretched from ear to ear as she seemingly took the news in her stride, much as Dat must surely have, too, when Mamma told him in private earlier.

Leah had suspected nothing of this from Dat, although he'd had plenty of opportunity to say something during early-morning chores. Her father had never been one to speak of personal things; she knew this firsthand, because, for some time now, she had been asking for information relating to her

15

own birth, to no avail. "For goodness' sake, Leah," he would say each time she brought it up, "be grateful the Good Lord made you healthy and strong, that you were born headfirst. What else wouldja care to know?"

But there were certain things she *did* ponder, such as who her first father might be. Lizzie, however, seemed unable to discuss the subject. *Is it too hard to dredge up the past?* Leah wondered. Or was Lizzie simply unwilling to bring it up for fear of implicating a member of the Hickory Hollow Amish church, miles away? There were also nagging questions concerning the day Leah was born in the Ebersol Cottage, but she couldn't bear to ask them of Lizzie.

Mary Ruth broke the stillness, glancing furtively at Leah as she said, "Maybe Dat will finally get a *real* son."

"Aw, pity's sake," Mamma said, shaking her head at Mary Ruth. She went to sit on the wooden bench next to the kitchen table, fanning herself with the hem of her long black apron. Her round face was flushed from the heat of the wood stove, where she had two strawberry pies baking.

"But . . . if the baby is a girl," Hannah spoke up, "there'll be less sewing to do."

Leah spoke at last. "Only if we get busy and make plenty of little afghans 'tween now and December. Lydiann was a spring baby, don't forget."

At this Leah caught Mamma's sweet and gentle smile. "That's my Leah, always leaning toward the practical."

Mary Ruth continued to chatter, asking where Lydiann would sleep once the wee one came.

Quickly Hannah suggested, "Why, she can sleep with us. Ain't so, Mary Ruth?"

Mamma laughed at that. "I daresay there wouldn't be much sleeping goin' on. Not as wiggly as that one is!"

Leah turned and slipped outdoors, going to the hen house, where she scattered feed to the chickens. Inside, she leaned against the rickety wall, watching them peck the ground near her bare feet. "Honestly," she said right out, "I don't know whether to be happy or sad about a new baby."

The hens paid her no mind, but the lone rooster cocked his head and eyed her curiously. In all truth, she had forced a smile about Mamma expecting a little one come next Christmas. Here, with only the chickens for company, she recalled the months before two-year-old Lydiann came into the world. Mamma had been ever so tired . . . nauseated, too. At close to forty-five, she was not nearly as energetic and strong as in years past, but there *were* a good many women that age or older in the family who had no trouble birthing babies. Leah was glad her mother came from a long line of such women. Indeed, she was happy at the prospect of Dat's having his first son should the baby turn out to be a boy.

Heading out of the hen house toward the barnyard, Leah was suddenly aware of Smithy Gid calling to her from the brink of the cornfield. *"Wie geht's,* Leah. Do ya have a minute?"

Out of habit, she glanced toward the back door, curious if Mamma or one of the twins was observing her with Gid, who was not only breathless from running, but his eyes were strangely aglow. "What is it?" she asked.

He grinned down at her. "I've got a whole new litter of German shepherd pups, and I think there's another dog Abram—your pop—might just take a shinin' to."

It was common knowledge Dat wanted a third dog, after having purchased from Gid his second German shepherd, Blackie, well over a year ago. "With a houseful of women folk, another male dog might be worth thinkin' about. 'Least I won't be so outnumbered anymore," he'd said that very morning, chuckling heartily.

She walked alongside Gid to the barn, listening as he described the various puppies' coloring.

"Does Dat know about the recent pups?" she asked.

"He oughta, 'cause I ain't been talkin' to myself all these weeks." They both laughed at that; then Gid added, "I believe Abram's just waitin' for the gut word."

She felt her cheeks warm. "Then you best be tellin' *him*."

His eyes lit up. "Well, now, I wanted to tell you, Leah."

She held her breath, scared he might take this opportunity to say more, them alone this way.

And he did, too . . . at least started to. "I've been wantin' to ask ya something."

She took a small step back. In fact, she had been inching away from him, romantically at least, her whole life long, and for all good reason. She had always loved her second cousin Jonas, though she had made a conscious effort to bury her bitter sadness, hiding it from her family and especially from Smithy Gid, who remained a right good friend as he'd always been—even more so lately. Yet Leah shuddered at the thought of Gid showing kindness to her out of mere pity. Surely their friendship was more special than that. But she had no intention of leading him on just because he was clearly fond of her.

Ach, she groaned inwardly, wishing someone—*anyone*—

might come flying into the barn. But no one did, and not even the barn doves, high in the rafters, made a sound as the smithy's son reached for her hand. "Uh, Gid . . ." What she really wanted to tell him was *please don't say another word*, but the words got trapped in her throat. She knew all too well the ache of rejection, and the way his eyes were intent on hers just now, it would be downright unkind to hurt him.

He was still holding her hand as the slow creaking of the windmill behind the barn broke the stillness. "Adah and her beau are going for supper in Strasburg next Saturday night. I thought it might be fun if you and I rode along."

No two ways about it, *riding along* simply meant double courting and Gid knew it. Sighing, she gently pulled her hand away, staring down at her toes. *What should I say?*

"If you want to talk it over with Adah, I don't mind." His words were like thin reeds in a swamp compared to his usual self-assured manner. Inside, Smithy Gid was most likely standing on tiptoes. Furthermore, she suspected he had been ever so eager to spend an evening with her for quite some time, hoping to double up with her first cousin Sam Ebersol, Uncle Jesse's youngest son, along with Gid's sister Adah. But Leah also knew Gid wouldn't be asking her twice. If she didn't give her answer now, she'd have to seek him out in the next day or so. Because at twenty-two—three years her elder—Smithy Gid was to be treated with the respect he deserved.

"I'll think on it." She trembled, afraid he might take her reply as a *maybe*.

Truth be told, she figured he was working his way to ask her to go "for steady," and right soon. To be true to herself, she knew she ought to refuse. Yet looking on the bright side, allowing Gid to court her would convince the People, especially Mamma and Aunt Lizzie, that she'd regained her balance, so to speak, that her shattered heart was on the mend. Wasn't it about time for that, anyway? Jonas was happy with someone else; why shouldn't *she* marry, as well? And, too, it had been ingrained in her all her days that to follow the Lord God's will for her life, she must marry and bear many children, as many as the Good Lord saw fit to give her and her future husband.

One thing was sure, Leah enjoyed her barn chats with Gid while pitching hay to the field mules or redding up the haymow for summertime Preaching services. It was downright pleasant to have a young man of Gid's reputation thinking of her as a good friend. Other times, she almost wished he might fix his gaze on a girl whose heart was truly available, like, for instance, any number of her cousins—dozens of Ebersols to choose from in Gobbler's Knob alone.

Naturally Gid wanted to marry well before his sister Adah. Even his youngest sister, Dorcas, was seeing someone seriously, or so Adah had confided in Leah recently. A knotty problem for Gid, being the eldest of the family and the only son and still unmarried, though it was clear thus far he'd set his cap for no one other than Leah.

Daily this weighed heavily on her mind, especially because Smithy Gid was such a fine young man. Why should she forfeit having a family of her own just because things between her and Jonas had fizzled? She could simply marry the farm boy who'd waited for her all these years, couldn't she?

She watched Smithy Gid walk back through the cornfield, holding her breath and not knowing for sure the right answer to his invitation. *I'll ask Mamma what to do,* she thought and headed out the barn door.

Leah found Mamma in the potting shed, fanning herself. "Another hot day, ain't?"

To this her mother nodded, and Leah began to share her uncertainty. "Smithy Gid invited me to go ridin' with him, Mamma. What do you think 'bout that—if you were me, I mean?"

Mamma moved the potting soil around in the earthen jar before speaking. She stopped her work and looked at Leah with a fond expression. "Seems to me if you care the least at all for him, why not see where it leads? He's a right nice young man."

" 'Tis easy to see Dat thinks so," Leah offered. She wouldn't ask for a comparison between Gid and Jonas; Mamma had made it known years ago how fond she was of Jonas.

"Far as I can tell, Gid's been sweet on you for a long time."

She thought on that. "Honestly there are times I think it *would* be fun to go somewhere with Gid, at least with another couple along."

Mamma's blue eyes grew more serious, and she set about cleaning the potting soil off the wooden work counter with a hand brush and dustpan. "Sometimes I wonder if you care for Gid simply because his sister is your dearest friend. Have you ever considered that?"

"Adah has little to do with Gid's and my friendship," Leah said quickly. The smithy's son had happily befriended her during her darkest days. They had even gone walking at dusk several times, but mostly their conversations took place in the cow pasture. She worried if allowing herself to warm to his winning smile might in some way betray the depth of love she'd had for Jonas.

"Just so Gid understands where your heart is," Mamma said.

Light streamed in through the windows, casting sunny beams onto the linoleum floor.

Where your heart is . . .

Leah sighed. "Whatever do you mean?"

Mamma sat tall and still, her gaze intent on Leah. "I think you know, dear. Deep within you, a voice is whispering what you should or should not do."

"I can't come right out and tell Smithy Gid that I don't love him as a beau, can I? How cruel that would be."

"You might say instead you think of him as a close brother."

Knowing Gid as she did, if she revealed this truth, he might take it as a challenge to try harder still to win her. "Oh, Mamma, I don't know what to say, honest I don't."

"Then say nothing . . . until you're sure. The Lord will give you the right words when the time comes. God holds the future in His hands . . . always remember this."

Mamma was as wise as any woman she knew—Mamma and Aunt Lizzie both. She thanked the Lord above for allowing her to grow up close to such women, though if she'd had her druthers, she would have preferred to know early on that

Lizzie Brenneman was the woman who'd birthed her. But to dwell on this was futile.

Mamma's words nudged her back to the present. "Why not ask Adah how *she* thinks her brother might react."

"I've thought of that, but I can't bring myself to open my mouth and say what I oughta."

Mamma frowned momentarily. "That's not the Leah *I* know."

Leah forced a smile. Maybe what Mamma was trying to say was *Don't settle for a Gideon Peachey if your heart longs for a Jonas Mast.*

Still, she refused to let Mamma or anyone see the depth of bewilderment that plagued her. It was as if her feet had sprouted long tendrils, like the runners that sometimes tripped her in the berry patch, making it impossible to move forward, tangling her way, keeping her from progressing on the path of her life.

"Are you afraid I'll never marry . . . if I pass up Gid's affection?" she asked suddenly.

"Not afraid, really," Mamma replied. "Just awful sorry if you're not happy in your choice of a husband. 'Tis better to be a contented maidel—like your aunt Lizzie—than a miserable wife, ya know."

Leah had heard similar remarks at the quilting frolics she and her twin sisters attended with Mamma; seemed there was an overabundance of spontaneous advice from the women folk nowadays. But the overall bent of Amish life, at least for a woman, was to marry and have a large family. Anything less was a departure from what the People expected.

All of a sudden she felt overcome with fatigue. The

potting shed had trapped the hot air, and she longed for the cool mossy green of the shaded front yard.

Politely she offered to help Mamma with the rest of her planting, but her mother shook her head.

"Go and have yourself some time alone," she said. "Goodness knows, you must need a rest."

Leah kissed Mamma's cheek and walked around the southeast side of the house, admiring the clear pink hydrangea bushes flourishing there. She sat on the ground and rested in the shadow of an ancient maple, daydreaming that Jonas had never, ever left Gobbler's Knob for his carpentry apprenticeship in Ohio.

Everything would be so different now. . . .

Yet she refused to give in to her emotions. Something as innocent as a daydream was wrong, she knew. Jonas belonged to Sadie now, and she to him.

"God holds the future in His hands." Mamma's confident words echoed in her mind.

Mosquitoes began to bite her ankles, and the sound of the noontime dinner bell prompted her to rouse herself and paste on yet another pleasant face. Leah rose and trudged toward the house.

Chapter Two

Sunday evening the air was so fresh and sweet it was hard for Mary Ruth to imagine a better place to be on such a fine night. She rode next to Hannah down Georgetown Road in the family buggy, chattering on the way to the singing. Once again, Aunt Lizzie had offered to drive, drop them off, and return home with the carriage, since there were no brothers to do the favor. Ever since February, when they turned sixteen and became eligible to attend Sunday singings, Lizzie had been kind—even eager—to drive them.

It had crossed Mary Ruth's mind to ask Leah to take them to the singing, but with Leah past her *rumschpringe* and a baptized church member, she was no longer expected to go to the barn singings, though she was welcome if she desired to, since she *was* still single. Mary Ruth couldn't help but wonder if Leah might have an awful slim chance of marrying now, unless, of course, she succumbed to Smithy Gid.

Mary Ruth felt sure Leah was still in mourning for Jonas, despite that everlasting smile of hers; her sister's cheerful mood didn't fool Mary Ruth one bit.

All in all, Aunt Lizzie was a much better choice for taking them to singings. One thing annoyed Mary Ruth, though—their aunt seemed a little too interested in who rode home with whom. Especially here lately, since the Stoltzfus boys had been bringing the twins home long past midnight every other Saturday. The grown-ups in the house were supposed to play dumb; the age-old custom of turning a deaf ear and a blind eye.

"Do you think Ezra and Elias will bring only one courting buggy to singin' again?" Mary Ruth whispered to her twin, eyes wide with anticipation. "It's such fun double courting, ain't so?"

To this Hannah smiled, shrugging her shoulder and looking nervously at Aunt Lizzie.

Hundreds of lightning bugs blinked over the cornfield like stars fallen glittery white from the heavens as the carriage headed downhill toward Grasshopper Level. A lone doe crept out at dusk and stood on the edge of the woods and watched them pass, as though hesitant to cross a road just claimed by a spirited steed.

"Elias has eyes only for you," Hannah whispered back. "If ya didn't know already."

Mary Ruth reached for her sister's hand and squeezed it. "I should say the same for you 'bout Ezra."

Aunt Lizzie turned her head just then and smiled. "What're you two twittering about?"

"*Ach*, best not to say, *Aendi*," Mary Ruth said quickly.

"Well, s'posin' I try 'n' guess," Aunt Lizzie taunted jovially, wispy strands of her dark hair loose at the brow.

Mary Ruth frowned. "Let's talk 'bout something else."

Their aunt caught on and clammed up, and that was that. Truth was, neither Mary Ruth nor Hannah felt comfortable telling Lizzie that the Stoltzfus boys were ever so fond of them. Since Ezra and Elias were less than a year and a half apart, it was fascinating they should be double-courting. "It's almost like we're going 'for steady' with twin boys, they're so close in age," Mary Ruth had declared to Hannah in the privacy of their bedroom last week.

"Not only that, but if we end up married . . . our children will be double cousins." Shy Hannah's pretty brown eyes had danced at that.

Yesterday afternoon, while stemming strawberries and, later, picking peas, Mamma had hinted she'd heard only a single buggy bringing her dear girls home here lately. Which, of course, could mean just one thing: the boys were either the best of friends and using the same open buggy . . . or they were brothers.

Naturally, with the secrecy surrounding the courting years, their mother knew better than to mention much else. Yet she'd said it with a most mischievous smile and out of earshot of Dat. At the time Mary Ruth had noticed how pretty Mamma looked, her face beaming with joy. Was it because she was with child once again? The women folk often whispered at canning bees and such that a woman in the family way had "a certain glow."

Or . . . maybe it had more to do with Mary Ruth showing an interest in a nice Amish boy; maybe that's what made Mamma smile these days. If so, then surely their mother wasn't nearly as worried as she had been at the end of the twins' eighth grade, a full year ago. The evening of graduation from the Georgetown School, Mary Ruth had out-and-out declared, "I want to attend high school next year!"

However, the very next day Dat had surprised her by taking her aside and talking mighty straight. "Hold your horses now, Mary Ruth." He'd asked her to wait until her rumschpringe to decide such a thing, so this past year she had continued to work three days a week for their Mennonite neighbor, Dottie Nolt, doing light housekeeping and occasional baby-sitting for the Nolts' adopted son, Carl. Along with that, she helped Mamma, as did Hannah and Leah, tending to the family and charity gardens, cleaning house, keeping track of busy Lydiann, and attending quilting frolics. Now that she was courting age, she was also going to Sunday singings with Hannah, who was taking baptismal instruction without her—a terrible sore spot between them.

Since she was "running around" now, Mary Ruth was able to openly read for pleasure, as well as study books at home, but the novelty of getting together with other Plain young people, especially fine-looking boys, had tempered her intense craving for escape into the world of English characters and settings. If she wanted to experience the modern world, she didn't have to rely on fiction any longer. Besides, it was great fun spending time with Elias Stoltzfus, who was as much a free spirit as she, within the confines of the Plain community, of course. She loved riding in his open courting buggy through Strasburg and the outskirts of Lancaster, soaring fast as they could through the dark night—though always in the company of Hannah and Ezra.

"How's Dottie Nolt these days . . . and her little one?" Aunt Lizzie asked unexpectedly.

"Carl moves right quick round the house. Dottie has to watch him awful close," Mary Ruth readily replied.

"I 'spect so. He's what—two now?"

She nodded. "A delightful child, but he's definitely on the go."

The horse turned off the road and headed down a long dirt lane, coming up on the old clapboard farmhouse. Aunt Lizzie pulled on the reins, and the carriage came to a stop. "Well, it certainly looks like a nice gathering of young folks."

Mary Ruth was happy to see the big turnout. What a wonderful-good night for a barn singing, not to mention the ride afterward under the stars with Elias. "Come along, Hannah." She hopped down out of the carriage. "*Denki*, Aunt Lizzie!" she called over her shoulder.

"Don't worry a smidgen 'bout us," Hannah said more softly to Lizzie.

Mary Ruth waited for Hannah to catch up, and then they walked together toward the two-story bank barn in their for-good blue dresses and long black aprons. "Why'd you say that?" asked Mary Ruth. "Do you really think Lizzie worries?"

"Well, I 'spect Mamma does, so I wouldn't be surprised if Aunt Lizzie does, too."

"They ought to know how nice the Stoltzfus family is," Mary Ruth spoke up in defense of Ezra and Elias. "Everybody does."

"*Jah* . . . but our eldest sister's wild rumschpringe days must surely haunt Mamma."

"Our sister was ever so foolish," Mary Ruth said, being careful not to mention Sadie's name outright. They had been forbidden to do so by Dat and the bishop following the *Bann*.

"Foolish, jah. And downright dreadful . . . stealing Leah's beau."

Mary Ruth didn't want to worry herself over things that couldn't be changed. She was caught up in the excitement of the moment and tried hard not to gawk at the many courting buggies lined up in the side yard. *Which one belongs to Elias?* she wondered, a thrill of delight rushing up her spine.

Abram sat next to Ida on the front porch swing, watching the stars come out. He also noticed the lightning bugs were more plentiful than in recent summers, maybe due to frequent afternoon showers. " 'Twas right kind of Leah to settle Lydiann in for the night," he said.

Ida nodded, sighing audibly. "Jah . . . even though she's as tuckered out as I am, prob'ly. She's such a dear . . . our Leah."

"That, she is."

Ida leaned her head gently on his shoulder. At last she said, "We did the right thing treatin' her as our very own all these years."

Hearing his wife speak of their great fondness for Leah made him realize anew that his own affection for Lizzie's birth daughter was as strong as if Ida had given birth to her. For a moment he was overcome with a rare sadness and remained silent.

Their flesh-and-blood Sadie was a different story altogether. Her defiance in not returning home after all this time had stirred up more alarm in him than he cared to voice to beloved Ida.

"The Good Lord's hand rests tenderly on us all," Ida said softly, as if somehow tuned in to his thoughts. "I daresay we'd be in an awful pickle otherwise."

He had to smile at that and reached over to cup her face in his callused hand. Sweet Ida ... always thinking of the Lord God heavenly Father as if He were her own very close friend.

"Where do you think our twins are tonight?" He stared at the seemingly endless cornfield to the east of the house, over toward smithy Peachey's place.

"Don'tcha mean *whom* the girls are with?"

He let out a kindly grunt; Ida could read him like a book. She continued. "Deacon's wife told me in so many words that two of her sons are spending quite a lot of time with Hannah and Mary Ruth."

"Which boys ... surely not the older ones?"

"I'm thinkin' it must be Ezra and Elias." Ida snuggled closer.

"A right fine match, if I say so myself. I best be givin' my approval to Deacon here 'fore long."

He heard the small laugh escape Ida's lips. "Best not get in the way, Abram. Let nature take its course."

"I s'pose you're thinkin' I shouldn't have interfered with Jonas and Leah back when."

Ida sat up quickly and looked at him, her plump hands knit into a clasp in her wide lap. "Leah would be happily married by now if you hadn't held out for Smithy Gid."

"Are ya blamin' *me* for what went wrong?" he said.

Ida pushed her feet hard against the porch floor, making the swing move too fast for his liking. When she spoke at last, her voice trembled. "None of us truly knows what caused their breakup."

He inhaled and held his breath. Ida didn't know what had caused the rift between Jonas and Leah, but *he* knew and all too well. Abram himself had gotten things stirred up but good by raising the troublesome issue of Leah's parentage with Jonas. He had never told her that, at Peter Mast's urging, he'd put Jonas to a fiery test of truth, revealing Lizzie's carefully guarded secret. When all was said and done, Jonas had failed it miserably. "Best leave well enough alone. Jonas is married to our eldest now."

"Jah, and worse things have happened," Ida whispered, tears in her eyes. "But I miss her something awful."

Abram didn't own up to the same. "What's done is done," he said. "Thing is we've got us a son-in-law we may never lay eyes on again. Could be a grandchild by now, too."

"All because our daughter was bent on her own way. . . ."

He leaned back in the swing and said no more. At times an uncanny feeling gnawed at him, made him wonder if Ida— who seemed to know more about Sadie than he did— might've disregarded the bishop and read a few of their eldest's early letters, after the law was laid down about returning them unopened.

But no, now was not the appropriate time to speculate on that. Clearly Ida needed his wholehearted companionship and understanding this night.

Chapter Three

Hannah was surprised how warm the night was, with little or no breeze. Her eyes kept straying toward the moon, and she was grateful for the hush of the evening hour, especially after having sung so robustly. Now she sat eating ice cream in the front seat of the open carriage with Ezra Stoltzfus, who wore a constant if not contagious smile.

She hoped Elias was not able to wrestle the reins away from Ezra tonight. It seemed both boys liked to trade off sitting in the driver's seat of the shiny new carriage. In fact, she was fairly sure they were actually sharing ownership of the courting buggy, though she'd never heard of this done in other families with many sons. As keenly interested as the deacon's boys had been in Mary Ruth and herself for the past several years, it was no wonder Ezra and Elias might share a single buggy now that the foursome were courting age.

Hannah's heart leaped with excitement. She was truly fond of auburn-haired Ezra, but more than that, she was most happy to see Mary Ruth putting aside her dream of becoming a schoolteacher. At least it appeared to be so in the presence of her dashing young beau. If Elias was the reason for Mary Ruth to set aside her perilous goal, then all was well and good and Hannah could simply use the money she'd saved from selling handiwork for something else altogether. If Mary Ruth didn't end up needing the money for future college expenses, maybe several pretty wedding quilts would do.

Thinking about this, Hannah felt she could accept Ezra's affections if for this one reason alone—to keep the double courting going full speed ahead, for the sake of a peaceful household and for Mary Ruth's future as a baptized church member. The latter she knew their parents wished for above all else.

"Let's find another courtin' couple to race," Elias said nearly the minute they were finished eating ice cream.

"Not tonight," Ezra replied firmly.

Hannah bit her tongue. She hoped her beau got his way, being older and all.

"Aw, lookee there. It's Sam Ebersol and Adah Peachey." Elias pointed to an open buggy some distance behind them, then waved his arms, trying to get the couple's attention.

"*I'm* driving," Ezra said at once.

But Elias persisted. "C'mon, it'll be fun. What do you say, Mary Ruth?"

"Sure, why not?" her twin was quick to say.

Hannah grew tense. The last time Elias persuaded his brother to let him race, they'd nearly locked wheels with another courting carriage on the way to a railroad crossing down on Route 372. In the end, Hannah had let out a squeal . . . and Elias had stopped. He'd apologized promptly, saying he hadn't meant any harm by it. He had also said,

"There's plenty other things to do to have fun after singing."

Plenty other things is right, thought Hannah. She figured at the rate he was going, Elias wouldn't be ready to settle down and farm, probably, or marry, for another couple of years. But she'd seen the love-light in her twin's eyes for the redheaded and handsome young man, and in his for pretty Mary Ruth. Sooner or later, the both of them would start thinking about joining church.

Just then Sam and Adah pulled up beside them. "What's goin' on?" asked Sam.

"Thought you might wanna race," Elias called to them from the backseat.

Sam looked at Adah, then answered, "Oh, that's all right. We've got some talking to do, Adah and I."

"Okay, then," Elias said, sitting down.

Hannah was relieved and felt herself relax against the seat. Sam hurried his horse, passing them, and she was glad to see Ezra let Sam gain on him. Ezra, after all, was most steady and dependable. At nearly eighteen, he was taking baptismal instruction classes and might be looking to settle down and marry within a year or so. Hannah wondered if she was truly mature enough, though, to accept if he should ask her to be his wife. Was *she* ready for the duties of home and mother-hood? Mamma's sisters had married young. All except Aunt Lizzie, of course. And Mamma, who, though she'd been but seventeen when first she'd met Dat, had waited until her early twenties to tie the knot.

Behind her, she heard Elias whispering to Mary Ruth, probably with his arm draped around her shoulder; they'd done their share of snuggling, for sure.

Beverly Lewis

As for herself, the rest of the night would be most pleas-ant—watching for shooting stars with Ezra, playing Twenty Questions, and letting him reach for her hand as they slowly made their way back home before dawn.

Once Leah had safely nestled Lydiann into her crib for the night, she crept toward the stairs. Having just kissed the little girl's tiny face, she realized sadly that Sadie might never know about Mamma's coming baby—their new sibling-to-be.

Downstairs, she spotted the tops of her parents' heads through the front room window. She wouldn't think of dis-turbing them. Much of their energy, too, went into thinking of Sadie; Leah was sure it had been so since her sister's shun-ning.

Turning from the room, she decided it was best to leave Dat and Mamma be. They deserved some quiet time together.

She went to the kitchen and poured a glass of water, thinking now of Smithy Gid. More than likely, he could be found in his father's big barn playing with the new brood of pups. "Tonight's the night," she said to herself, "ready or not."

Slipping out the back door, she headed past the barnyard and through the cornfield. She'd kept Gid waiting long enough—too long, really, as he'd made his thoughtful invita-tion to her two days ago. She mustn't be rude and keep him guessing by the hour. She'd had several opportunities to speak privately with him yesterday, but she had still been uncertain, though she knew Gid was as stalwart in his soul as he was in his frame. He wasn't just "as good as gold," as Dat liked to say; Gid was superior to Dat's proverbial gold, and the girl who consented to be his wife would be truly blessed.

Is it to be me? she wondered. *Can I trust the Lord God to guide my faltering steps?*

In vain, she tried to imagine being held in his strong arms. Would she be gladdened by his tender affection . . . ready for their courting days to begin? All these things and more Leah contemplated as her bare feet padded the ground on her way to find the blacksmith's son before Dat and Mamma wondered where on earth she'd taken herself off to on a night set apart for singings.

She found Smithy Gid in the haymow, amusing himself with a new pup. "Hullo," Leah called up to him.

Quickly he rose and made his way down the long ladder to her, carrying the tiny dog. "I wasn't expecting to see you tonight, Leah." He looked at her with gentle eyes. "But it's awful nice," he added with a warm smile.

They stood there looking at each other by lantern light, Leah feeling ever so awkward. She glanced down for a moment, breathed a sigh, and then lifted her face to his. "I'm ready to give you my answer," she said softly.

"Jah?"

"I'll go along to Strasburg with you . . . with Adah and Sam, come Saturday night."

Gid's face lit up like a forbidden electric light bulb. "Wonderful-gut! Denki for comin' here to say so."

She realized at that moment the power her decision had over him. If she'd said otherwise, she could just imagine the look of disappointment that would have transformed his ruddy face. "I best be headin' home," she said.

"Aw, must ya?" His eyes implored her to stay.

"Dat and Mamma don't know I'm gone. I wouldn't want them to fret." She didn't go on to say they were worried enough over Sadie. No doubt he was aware of that; it was to be expected with Gid's mother and Mamma close neighbors and bosom friends. Miriam Peachey had surely heard tell of Mamma's sleepless nights.

"Well, then, I 'spect it's best you return *schnell*—quickly."

At that she moved toward the barn door. "*Gut Nacht*," she said as Gid strolled alongside her.

"Good night, Leah."

She nodded self-consciously and turned to go, walking briskly toward her father's cornfield. Hundreds of stars beckoned her, and she found herself wondering if anyone had ever tried to count them, at least those twinkling over the Ebersol Cottage.

Staring up at the sky, she pondered her decision to go with Gid this one time . . . and his near-gleeful response. *Did I do the right thing?*

The last place Gid wanted to be, now that Leah had told him her good news, was back up in the lonely haymow. He returned the puppy in hand to the whelping box and hurried out behind the barn, toward Blackbird Pond. He had to keep looking at the ground, now murky in the early evening hour, to see if his feet were really touching the grassy path that led through the pastureland and beyond to the lake.

With great joy, he began to count the hours till he would see Leah again, not in Abram's barn or out in the field . . . no, what he most anticipated was their first *real* date. The long ride to Strasburg was nothing to sneeze at as far as time on the road; he must make sure he took along a light lap robe, in case the evening had a chill to it. They would enjoy a fine meal in town with Adah and Sam, then leisurely return to Gobbler's Knob, a round trip of nearly ten miles. All in all, the night would not be so young when he returned Leah to the covering of her father's house.

Gid's heart sang as he picked up his pace and began to run around the wide lake. *Will Leah accept my love at last?*

Chapter Four

Dr. Schwartz plodded upstairs to the second-floor bedroom, where, in the corner of the large room, he found his wife reclining on the leather chaise, sipping a cup of chamomile tea. *Lorraine's nerves must be ragged again tonight,* he thought. He'd learned not to address her when she was in such a state. In the past, when he had attempted to engage her in conversation, she withdrew further still.

As for Henry, he was much more practiced at concealing his misery; he prided himself in his ability to do so. Even Lorraine had no knowledge of his ongoing despair, he was quite certain. On the exterior, his life was as fulfilled now as he had ever hoped it to be—faithful wife, grown sons, and a flourishing medical clinic. With their boys gone from home, he and Lorraine had sufficient time to do as they pleased, which most evenings meant sitting in easy chairs and reading silently, enjoying baroque music, or discussing eldest son Robert's zealous letters and spiritual ambition. Lorraine was increasingly anxious, though, and he had begun to recognize the fact around the time the boys spread their proverbial wings. Continually she invited him to attend church with her and their neighbors, Dottie and Dan Nolt and their toddler-age son. Without exception, he refused, adding to his wife's dejection. Having attended church only sporadically during their adult years, he was by no means interested in jumping on Lorraine's recent religious bandwagon. To her credit, his wife was a woman who knew how to blend persuasion with loving consideration. This fact, over the years, had helped keep their marriage intact.

His misery had not so much to do with Robert's search for God, nor Derek's enlistment in the army and detachment from the family, as his bleak memory of a dark April night when his own frail grandson had experienced both life and death in the space of a few hours. That fateful night had altered Henry's very existence.

Accordingly, each Sunday before Lorraine awakened and the sun rose, he crept downstairs and got into the car, driving down Georgetown Road, past the Ebersol and Peachey farms, turning onto a dirt lane east of the smithy's spread of land. That narrow byway led to the ten acres he'd inherited from his father, Reverend Schwartz. Having decided against ever building a house there, Henry had held on to the grazing land, letting it appreciate in value over the years. More recently, he had thought of offering to sell it to the local blacksmith, if the Amishman was so inclined. Lorraine, however, had suggested the parcel of land remain in the family, perhaps to be given at the appropriate time to Robert as a wedding gift.

Getting out of the car, Henry would go and tend to a small grave unmarked by a headstone, trimming the tall grass away with hand clippers. When finished, he stood in deep contemplation, the little mound of earth his altar and the clipped grass his pew, surrounded by a choir of insects and birds.

Just this morning he had visited the site and stared down at the memorial of his own making, recalling the momentous night he had hauled to the spot a shovel in the trunk of his car. Having paced the ground, he had made a frantic determination for the location of a proper burial. The hollowness in his soul had been undeniable as he pushed hard and deep into the ground—the ball of his foot on the shovel, his arms lifting out the soil one heaping pile at a time. Grave digging was harder work than he had anticipated, both physically and otherwise, but the burial itself had been excruciating. And when the task was complete, the lifeless body of an infant boy lay in the broken earth.

There it was that Henry presented himself to the Creator-God on Sunday mornings, each and every one since that very first, refusing Lorraine's invitation to a church with walls of stone and mortar. Nowhere else drew him like the open-air cathedral where he was the one and only parishioner, the lone visitor to a child's tiny grave.

Startled out of his musing by Lorraine's gentle voice, Henry jerked his head, a piece of mail slipping out of his hands and onto the floor.

"Dear," she said, "be sure to read Robert's letter."

Lorraine had left a pile of their personal mail from Saturday afternoon lying on the dresser for him. He had been much too busy at the clinic to bother thumbing through the bills and such. He stooped now to reach for his eldest's latest letter. "How are things going for him?" he inquired for Lorraine's sake. Hard as it was for him to admit, son Robert was looking for absolute truth—strangely finding it in a group of Bible-believing Mennonites.

"He's planning to come home for Thanksgiving," Lorraine offered, still seated with cup poised in midair.

"Oh?" He nodded absentmindedly. Late November was the perfect time for a visit with his strapping son. Perhaps Robert would consider arriving a few days early so that they might join the enthusiastic turkey shooters over on the wooded hillock across the road. *We'll surprise Lorraine with a plump turkey for our Thanksgiving feast,* he thought, wishing that Derek, too, might be inclined to desire connection with family. Regrettably there had been no word from Derek in the past year, a fact that continued to grieve them. *Yes,* thought Henry. *Our younger son is long gone in more ways than one.*

He settled down with Robert's letter, adjusting his eyeglasses and leaning his head close to the linen stationery in order to follow every line and curve of his firstborn's penmanship.

Thursday, June 16
Dear Mom and Dad,

Thanks for writing, Dad. I received your last letter in the Wednesday mail. And thanks, Mom, for the care packages. Several of my campus friends have gratefully helped me devour your chocolate-chip cookies and banana-nut breads. Because of your delectable gifts, I'm one of the best-fed—and most popular—fellows I know!

I hope to make a trip home for Thanksgiving weekend. Any chance Derry might show up? He continues to snub my letters, but I'd like to see him again . . . it's been too long.

Well, I must head to class. I'll look forward to hearing from you soon.

> *With love to you both,*
> *Robert*

Sighing, Henry blurted out, "What do you make of that, Lorraine?"

"Sounds to me Derry has no intention of keeping in touch with *any* of us." Her voice wavered.

Henry felt sure he knew why; no doubt Derek was suffering a severe bout of old-fashioned guilt, and no wonder. He'd gotten an Amish girl pregnant, only to promptly leave Gobbler's Knob for the army. His son's misbehavior and indifference were an embarrassment. How could Derek ruin the girl's life and simply abandon her?

Henry folded the letter, returning it to the envelope. When it came to guilt, he could relate to having made a few serious mistakes in life—some more earthshaking than others.

"We must celebrate the prospect of seeing Robert again," he said suddenly as he prepared to retire for the night. "We can't go on mourning Derek's appalling attitude."

"Sometimes that's far easier said than done," Lorraine replied, dabbing at her eyes.

He acknowledged the grim fact with a nod of his head. *What else is there to do?*

◆

Soon after Leah started working part-time at the village clinic, she began to recognize her interest in children, especially the youngest ones with obvious injuries. She loved to console or distract them in the waiting room by using the sock puppets Hannah had knitted. She often did the same at home while caring for Lydiann, who, at times, seemed rather accident prone—scraped knees, brush-burned elbows, and all.

Leah had surprised herself with her immediate like for the doctor and his wife; she felt sure she'd met good solid folk, although worlds apart from her in culture and upbringing. There was not one iota of plainness about Henry and Lorraine, but that didn't stop Leah from enjoying their company. The doctor's infectious laughter, though seemingly forced at times, and Lorraine's delicious specialty cakes and breads she set out for the clinic staff during short breaks in the flow of patient traffic made Leah feel most welcome.

This Monday morning she hurried into the clinic and made coffee for the receptionist, as well as the coming patients. That done, she did a bit of dusting, which, before today, had not been one of the things expected of her. Till now she had swept and washed the floors and windows, making doubly sure the examination rooms and miniscule restroom were sanitary, along with sweeping the steps and sidewalk. In many ways she was considered the clinic's sole housekeeper.

Lorraine had recently hinted *she* might need a bit of help, especially with the large kitchen floor and the many knick-knacks that accumulated dust in both the living and sitting rooms of the Schwartz residence. So far Leah hadn't jumped at the opportunity to assist Lorraine with additional tasks, mainly because Mamma's strawberries were coming on awful fast now and there would be plenty to sell at the Ebersols' roadside stand. In fact, at this moment, Mamma and Miriam Peachey were out in the hot sun picking berries while Hannah and Mary Ruth completed the washing. And Lydiann, more than likely, was babbling to Dawdi John next door in the Dawdi Haus. Only occasionally did Mamma ask her father to watch her youngest, but since Leah was expected home in time for the noon meal, Lydiann would be in Dawdi's charge only a short time. After that Leah herself would help tend to her baby sister, along with her afternoon chores outside. By taking Lydiann along with her to the barn and whatnot, she hoped to develop a strong love of the land and the farm animals in the wee toddler. And, too, it wouldn't be long and Lydiann would be someone to talk to while working outdoors—someone besides Gid, that was, and Sam Ebersol's older brother, twenty-year-old Thomas, recently hired by Dat to help with fieldwork part-time.

During a lull between patient appointments, Leah got up the nerve to mention the doctor's grazing land, "not so far from the Peacheys' place," interested to see what Dr. Schwartz might say about it.

When there was little or no direct response to her comment, she forged ahead. "Have you ever thought of putting cattle out there? Such nice grazing it would be."

The good doctor scratched his head and looked nearly disoriented for a few seconds. Then he said, "I've thought of different things over the years. Everything from building a house and barn on it . . . to putting up a stable for horseback riding. In the end, I always come back to its being too great an effort to bother with putting cattle or anything else on it, though."

She paused to study him. Tall and lean, he was a man with plenty of options flitting in his head. But he fell silent, and in a short time another patient came up the walk and in the door.

Leah was surprised to see her mother's cousin Fannie Mast, with young Jake and Mandie in tow. She at first felt sheepish standing there, then pained, remembering Fannie was to have been her mother-in-law. Without meaning to, she found herself gawking at the twins; she hadn't seen them in two years and they'd grown so much.

This woman, equally as plump as Mamma now, if not more so, had always been a bubbly hostess when the Ebersols visited the Mast orchard house on Grasshopper Level, not but a thirty-minute buggy's ride from Gobbler's Knob. Today, though, when Fannie caught Leah's eye, her mouth drooped and she turned away, taking the twins' hands and guiding them to the far corner of the waiting room.

Undaunted, Leah slipped into the short hall, hoping to watch her little cousins toddle with their mamma to one of the examination rooms. She stood behind the doorjamb and peered out as the threesome made their way.

Jake was tall and skinny, much like his big brother Jonas, though his hair was a deep brown and he limped slightly as he tottered along. Leah couldn't tell if he'd hurt himself or if he was still discovering his own stride as a two-year-old. She recalled the first time she'd held him, how she had sensed his helplessness as an infant—a frail one at that.

But it appeared his mother's nurturing touch had made all the difference, just as it had for the sickly lambs and struggling houseplants Fannie was known to nurse back to health.

Dr. Schwartz appeared in the hallway and called Jake's name, then scooped him up in his arms. He touched the top of Mandie's head, speaking quietly to Fannie.

Observing Mandie now, Leah was taken with her dainty features, though altogether different from Jake's—her blue eyes and blond hair showing hints of highlights the color of honey, much lighter than Jonas's.

Attempting to redirect her thoughts from her former beau, she wondered how Fannie must feel seeing her here after all this time, knowing—surely she did—how devoted her first-born son had been to Leah from his earliest teen years. Until he'd turned his attention to Sadie, of course. Did Fannie have any knowledge of Jonas and Sadie, perhaps where they were living in Ohio? Would she even care to say if Leah got up the nerve to ask?

Having been in attendance at the required membership meeting where Bishop Bontrager called for a vote for or against shunning Jonas—most excruciating for her—she understood fully that he had been cut off from his family as entirely as the rest of the People. Unless he returned and repented for breaking the strict covenant, Jonas would be estranged from both the communities of Gobbler's Knob and Grasshopper Level all the days of his life. Leah felt strongly that the bishop had found fault with him because of his keen interest in carpentry. For Jonas to abandon the idea of farming was near heresy!

Sighing now, she was tormented with the image of the smiling Mast children, as well as the solemn face of Fannie, Mamma's once bright and happy relative. *Why is she sour toward me?* she wondered. *Does she blame me for the shun on her son?*

It was Lizzie, not Ida, who spent a good part of the morning picking strawberries with Miriam Peachey when she came to lend a hand. Ida remained indoors, trying to keep herself cool, and all for the best since she had complained of nausea today. Lizzie was more than a little concerned about her sister.

She was glad for the white-pleated candlesnuffer-style sunbonnet Hannah had presented to her just this morning after the twins had hung out the clothes to dry.

"It'll keep the sun off your face," Hannah had said sweetly, entering the kitchen wearing a green choring dress.

"So your nose won't peel something awful ... like last summer's sunburn," Mary Ruth had added, glancing approvingly at her twin.

Since Ida had already taken herself upstairs, Lizzie felt she ought to see who was doing what chores, both indoors and out. Mary Ruth spoke up, declaring she would be the one to look after Lydiann while the clothes dried, and then she'd single-handedly fold everything neatly after the noon meal, once Lydiann was down for a nap. Hannah, on the other hand, volunteered to hoe the large family vegetable garden after the dishes were washed and dried.

With Leah gone for the morning at the clinic, it seemed they might've been a bit shorthanded with Ida resting, but thanks to Miriam, the morning duties would be accomplished in a timely manner.

"Awful kind of you to come over," Lizzie said as she and Miriam moved through the strawberry patch. "Did you suspect Ida might be suffering another bout of mornin' sickness?"

Miriam nodded. "Jah, and she has no business bein' out here in the hot sun."

"Aside from that, I'd have to say she's feeling perty well. She's a strong one, Ida."

They worked together without saying much more for a time. Then Miriam asked softly, looking over her shoulder, "Ida bears most of her pain in silence . . . what with her eldest gone, ain't so?"

"Oh my, ever so much. The girl's shunning has taken its toll. None of us understands why she refused to repent here in Gobbler's Knob. The silence and separation is almost a punishment for all of *us*, too."

Miriam stretched a moment, then resumed picking. "On top of that, Ida tells me she gets ever so blue not hearin' a speck from Fannie." She shook her head sadly. "Why she keeps on writing letters, I just can't figure. If it were me, I'd plain quit."

Lizzie knew well why her sister continued to send letters over to Grasshopper Level. "Bless her heart, she hopes Fannie might write back with some word of our wayward girl . . . though the Masts must be in the dark as much as we are."

"How awful sad for Abram and Ida, having no contact with either their eldest or their only son-in-law," Miriam replied. "And the Masts have kept mighty tight-lipped. Surely something will give sooner or later."

"I can only imagine what it might take to get the two families talking again." Lizzie's pail was nearly full now, and a glance at Miriam's let her know now was as good a time as any for them to hurry inside and cool off a bit with a nice tall glass of iced tea.

Chapter Five

Hannah stole away to the bedroom during the hottest hour of the day and took from the bureau drawer her makeshift writing journal, a simple notebook with yellow lined paper. She wanted to catch up on her diary before it was time to dress around for a double date with Ezra, and Mary Ruth and Elias.

Saturday afternoon, June 25
Dear Diary,

I haven't put my thoughts down on paper every other day like I'd set out to. Now, more than ever, I ought to be recording the events as they happen to my dear twin and me. If Ezra Stoltzfus and his younger brother Elias are to become my and Mary Ruth's husbands someday, it would be an awful shame not to have faithfully written about our double courtship. Goodness knows, my children and grandchildren might one day wish I had.

So . . . I am making an attempt to be more thorough, beginning with what happened today. Mary Ruth confided she has been seriously considering extending her rumschpringe for several more years. This is such a disappointment; I'd hoped she would join church with me. We've done everything else together. Why not this?

Life is ever so unpredictable—makes me wonder if Elias, too, is thinking along the same lines. Obviously he isn't headed toward making his kneeling vow before the membership this fall, since he's not taking baptism classes with Ezra.

Naturally I pleaded with Mary Ruth not to tell another soul, "not till you think gut and hard." Such news would hurt Mamma and Dat even worse than they already are. And Leah . . . oh my, I hate to think what it would do to her if Mary Ruth stalled too long and ended up going her own way. Leah has had more than her share of heartache.

Come tonight, I'm hoping Elias and Mary Ruth sit in the front seat of the courting buggy. They might not be so inclined to smooch that way . . . though it's more awkward for Ezra and me, sitting behind them and having to see what's going on.

When all's said and done, liking a boy so much that you turn your back on the Lord God and the People isn't worth a hill of beans all summer. Knowing Mary Ruth, I expect she'll come round sooner or later.

Respectfully,
Hannah

She closed the notebook and placed it back in the drawer, concealing it with several woolen scarves. Then she went to fill the washbasin with water to freshen up for supper and her evening with Ezra, who had suggested going to Strasburg for some store-bought ice cream. The thought of seeing him again made her feel light inside, and a peace settled over her.

Leah was content with the quietude of the house. Lydiann was napping while Mamma read the Good Book in the big bedroom. Aunt Lizzie worked downstairs in the kitchen, cooking as silently as she could, and Mary Ruth and Hannah were down the hall in their room, most likely preparing to go riding in someone's courting buggy.

Standing at the window, Leah looked down, appreciating the bright green of the enormous trees and the meadow. Dashes of color from the wild flowers scattered here and there caught her eye, and she wondered, *What's Gid thinking? Is he counting the minutes till we sit side by side in his open buggy?*

Slowly she turned from her window, wandered to the corner of the room, and sat in the single cane chair, leaning her elbows hard on her legs, palms cupping her chin. With a great sigh, she began to remove her head covering and the pins in her bun. She shook out her hair, untangling it with her fingers and going over and over the length.

As she began to brush her hair vigorously, she recalled the many times she had brushed or combed Sadie's beautiful blond locks. Often the two of them had taken turns doing so at day's end.

When she was satisfied all the snarls were out, she rose and walked to the bed—the one she and Sadie had shared from the time they were but tiny girls, once Leah was able to sleep in a bed and not roll out.

Do you miss me, sister, as sorrowfully as I miss you?

She felt the strength drain from her legs, and she was compelled to lie down. A short rest might rejuvenate her for the long night ahead. Almost immediately her muscles relaxed as she stretched out on the bed. Sadie's plump pillow was a constant reminder of their many late-night talks, sharing dreams of the future as schoolgirls and on into the early teen years ... and finally rumschpringe. They had always talked of living neighbors to each other as married women. "Our babies will grow up together just like brothers and sisters," Sadie had promised in the fading light.

Leah couldn't bear to think of the children Sadie would give birth to. Such things were too painful still. Reaching over, she slid her hand beneath her sister's pillow, aware of its utter coolness to the touch. *Will I ever see you again?* she wondered. The thought left her torn, and tears came all too fast ... missing Sadie yet not wanting to truly know about her life as Jonas's wife. *No, 'tis best you stay wherever you are....*

◆

When it came time to go out and hitch his horse to the courting buggy, Gid simply told his mother he had "some business in town." It was a common phrase used among the young men in the community on a Saturday night before the no-church Sunday. This, to explain the reason for having cleaned up, put unruly hair to order with a comb, and dressed around in clean black trousers and colorful shirts, though Plain parents all over Lancaster County were mindful it was courting night.

"Oh?" his mamma said, her face shining her delight. "Well, have yourself a good time, hear?"

Pop nodded slowly, smiling faintly before recovering his solemn look. Gid was downright certain his father had at least an inkling Leah would also be going along "to tend to business."

"We won't be waitin' up for you, son," Mamma said, a twinkle in her eyes.

Pop agreed they'd be "goin' to bed with the chickens," so Gid felt assured of their trust, just as all young Amishmen did on such a night. Though he knew they would not interfere with his choice of a girlfriend, he would attempt to guard his relationship with Leah, whatever it was to be, from the eyes and ears of the People as a whole for as long as possible. In fact, he must remind Adah once again to keep quiet about Leah going along with them tonight, just as he wouldn't think of breathing a word that Leah's cousin Sam was seriously courting Adah and, more than likely, soon to marry her. The age-old custom of secrecy was so ingrained into the ritual of courtship, Gid felt sure no one would guess whom he was engaged to when the time finally did come. No, he must woo and win Leah's heart and require his sister to vow absolute secrecy.

Nothing must go wrong, he thought. *I must do things the respectable and right way. Beginning tonight.*

Locusts sang a percussive song as Smithy Gid's best horse pulled the open buggy west from Gobbler's Knob, past the dense woods on the north, heading toward the town of Strasburg. Gid's sister pointed out how pretty the sky was, and Sam Ebersol said he wouldn't be surprised if there was a downright beautiful sunset tonight.

To Gid's left, Leah sat straight and stiff in the seat, as if she wasn't wholly committed to being there. Or, more than likely, she was uneasy with double courting, what with Adah and Sam nearly engaged already. How awkward for her—for them, really. *Yet I'm determined for her to have a right nice time,* thought Gid, holding the reins. *Leah must feel comfortable not only with me, but with my sister and her beau.*

Surely the sweet fragrance of honeysuckle, the shimmer of the first evening star shortly after sunset, and the fact Leah's best girlfriend was along for the ride would enhance her first outing in his black courting buggy. Gid dared not to go so far as to think his mere presence might make the evening altogether pleasant for her.

Behind them in the second seat, Sam began to tell a joke to Adah. Both Adah and Sam laughed out loud when the tall story was over. Gid felt like letting loose with hearty laughter himself, but Leah was only smiling, not laughing at all, so he remained silent. He was, in general, much too self-conscious. He wanted to be himself, to relax and enjoy the ride, the night air so warm and agreeable for such a trip. Frankly he felt nearly helpless to wind down, and it was obvious Leah felt the same.

He was indeed thankful for Sam's wholehearted chortle, which continued for several more jokes, at least until well past Rohrer Mill Road. Soon the horse turned north at Paradise Lane, taking them closer to the Strasburg Pike and then west, past the railroad depot and into the town of Strasburg.

"Did ya hear of the boy who attended his first singing, hooked up with a wild bunch, drank himself full of moonshine, and passed out on the front seat of his own carriage?" Sam asked.

"Ach, what happened?" Adah asked innocently.

"From what I heard—and this is true—his horse simply trotted on home, the drunk youth sleepin' all the while in the buggy."

Gid had heard such stories, too, and he said so but added quickly that there were "some fatal accidents happening under those kinds of circumstances, too." He didn't especially want to be a wet blanket, but, truth was, several young men had been killed that way when their horses galloped right through a red light at a dangerous intersection, the carriage hit broadside by an unsuspecting automobile.

His comment stirred up some talk from Leah, and a few minutes later Sam jumped in with more jokes. With an inward sigh, Gid realized the evening was going to turn out just fine. He felt the tension drain from his jaw, and when he could do so discreetly, he saw that Leah, too, seemed much more tranquil now, her hands not so tightly clasped in her lap.

◆

It was on the ride home from Strasburg, as they made the bend onto Georgetown Road, that Gid spotted two open buggies riding side by side at a fast pace. "Look at that!" he said.

Both Leah and Adah gasped.

"Pity's sake, what're they doin'?" Adah hollered.

Leah held on to the seat with both hands. "Somebody's a *Dummkopp!*"

"Worse than a blockhead," Gid added.

"I should say!" Adah said.

"Let's not get too close, in case. . . ." Leah's voice trailed off.

"Don'tcha worry none," Gid reassured her, wanting to touch her hand but refusing to take advantage of the harrowing situation. Instead, he steered the horse onto the right shoulder and slowed down, allowing some distance between his buggy and the two speeding carriages ahead.

Suddenly he heard a girl's voice from one of the buggies. "Elias, stop!"

"Ach no," Leah whispered.

"What?" Gid leaned near. "Do you recognize someone?"

"My sister . . . Hannah." She turned in her seat now that they had rolled to a halt. "She may be dating one of the deacon's sons."

"Then he oughta know better!" Adah was standing up behind them now for a better look.

The deafening sound of a car horn pierced the stillness. Quick as a wink, one of the buggies fell behind the other, and Gid breathed a sigh of relief. "Too close for comfort."

"You can say that again." Leah put her hands on her throat.

Gid waited a few more minutes, then clicked his cheek and his horse pulled forward. "We could follow the buggy your sister's in," he suggested.

"Gut idea," Adah said.

"Jah, let's follow 'em!" Sam said.

Leah said no more, and Gid wondered if she was worried the Stoltzfus boy might feel threatened somehow, that trailing them might cause a rift between herself and her younger sisters. He certainly understood if she was thinking that way. Leah might've told him, if the two of them had gone riding alone, that Abram's other daughters—she and Sadie, at least—had surely endured enough strain between them to last a lifetime.

Chapter Six

Hannah said not a word to Mary Ruth as they slipped into the house through the kitchen door. She was so upset with Elias—and Mary Ruth for egging him on—all she wanted to do was hurry and undress for bed. *At least in my dreams I won't be ridin' with the likes of Elias Stoltzfus!* she thought, heading for the stairs.

Once the two of them were situated in bed, scarcely needing even a sheet, with the room so stuffy and warm, she was careful to sigh ever so lightly, hoping Mary Ruth wouldn't mention anything. She felt done in from having clung to her seat for dear life, and literally, too! Goodness, she was fairly sure the driver of the car coming straight at them tonight scarcely had enough time to sound the horn, let alone pray that the wild buggy driver could get out of his way.

"I know what you're thinkin'," Mary Ruth whispered on the pillow next to her.

Hannah inhaled and held her breath for a moment, then let it out gradually. "Honestly, I felt I saw my whole life flash in front of my eyes tonight."

"I don't think we were ever in any real danger, Hannah. For pity's sake!"

"Oh, but we *were!* Didn't you see how close that car came to hitting us?"

Mary Ruth was quiet, stirring only enough to turn her back to Hannah.

"Weren't you frightened, Mary Ruth?"

"I *did* feel the hairs on my neck stand straight up, but that was only from excitement, nothin' more. Frankly it was lots of fun." Mary Ruth pulled on the sheet, leaving little for her twin. "Besides, Elias is a right gut driver, really he is."

Hannah thought her sister was sadly mistaken. "Well, if that's what you call fun, then maybe we'd best not go double courting anymore."

"If that's what you want" came the empty reply.

She has no sense of good judgment, Hannah thought. Maybe Mary Ruth preferred to court alone, after all. If so, Hannah didn't quite know how she felt about that, though it *would* give her and Ezra more time to get to know each other. That might be a good thing; however, she wasn't so sure it would be wise to encourage Mary Ruth and Elias to court alone. She hated to think of her twin ending up the way Sadie had . . . and like Aunt Lizzie evidently, too, according to Mamma's account of things most private.

Leah was becoming more and more eager to get home, back to the comfort of her soft bed. The carriage seat felt awful hard now, and Gid seemed too eager to keep driving around in circles. Adah and Sam were silent in the second seat behind them, and she wondered if Adah had dozed off on Sam's shoulder. Surely they weren't smooching, knowing Adah.

Looking to her left, away from Gid, Leah recalled her first-ever kiss. Jonas had shown no hesitancy whatsoever, and as much as she had delighted in the feel of his lips on hers that afternoon in the meadow, she'd also heard clearly Mamma's admonition: *Save lip-kissin' for your husband.* . . .

Well, obviously she and Jonas had been only betrothed, not married, so according to Mamma, she had no business yielding to his embrace. And every day that passed, she pushed away the warm thoughts of her former beau, wishing to high heavens she'd waited to let her husband be the first to kiss her, whoever that was to be.

She had been meaning to ask Aunt Lizzie about all this, or Mamma. If they knew, would they say her disobedience had caused her to lose Jonas in the end? Might Mamma admit such a thing? Was the lip-kissing rule passed down from all the People's mothers to their daughters as keenly important as that? She knew of a good many young married couples that never kissed till their wedding day; some stricter groups even forbid holding hands before marriage.

Wishing the road was better lit than by an occasional yard light whenever they passed the English farmhouses, Leah wondered what time it was and how much longer she'd have to wait to return home.

Out of the blue, Smithy Gid got a talk on, and as tired as she was, she thought it best to lend her ear . . . show respect. "What would you think of going to Strasburg again some-time?" he said.

She wasn't sure if he meant to ask if she enjoyed the visit

62

to the neighboring village or if he was asking her for another date. So, not to confuse him, she mentioned the nice supper they'd had, how awful kind it was of him to include her.

"Didja like the food?" he asked.

"Right tasty, it was. Denki."

"'Twas my first time eating there. Sam has been tellin' me off and on for several weeks that we oughta go."

"So Sam knew of it, then?"

He nodded cheerfully. "That's how I heard of the place."

She was feeling sorry for Gid, truly; he was trying to draw her out of her shell, wanting to make good conversation. "I liked it just fine," she said, putting on a smile. "As gut as home cooking, really."

She saw him glance down to see where her hands were just then, and she was glad she'd folded them on her lap. No sense making things more complicated than they already were, him wanting more than mere friendship and her content with things as they were. For now.

"How would you feel 'bout going to the next singing?" he asked.

"I haven't been for the longest time. Might seem peculiar."

"Maybe you and Adah could ride together, and then . . . I'd be happy to bring you home."

She didn't know what made her say it, but without thinking twice, she simply said, "Sure, Gid. That'd be fine." She hoped they might not end up with Adah and Sam again, though. It was awful complicated riding around the countryside with them when all they talked about was renting or building a house, what they needed in the way of furnishings, and whatnot—typical talk for a serious couple. Surely Gid must either know or strongly suspect this about his sister and Sam.

She looked off toward the horizon line to the west, her thoughts straying hard to Ohio . . . wondering if Sadie and Jonas were still living there. Were they happy as larks? Was it even possible for Sadie to find joy with Leah's first and only love? Quickly she felt ashamed, because it was wrong to begrudge her sister and Jonas anything.

"Sometimes you seem almost lost without your older sister," Gid said unexpectedly.

"Is it that noticeable?"

They rode along in silence for a ways. He surprised her when he slipped his arm around her shoulder, barely touching her as he did. "It pains me so . . . you must know this, Leah."

Then and there, she felt the oddest twinge. She turned and looked at him—really looked. Such compassion in his face, his eyes much too serious now. Usually he was easy to talk to, but this minute she felt awkward, unable to speak. She wanted to please him, to let him know how grateful she was for his caring about her, yet what should she say? What *could* she say?

Slowly he drew her near, letting go the reins and reaching for her ever so gently. "Oh, Leah. I'm awful sorry for what you've been through. . . ."

She couldn't help herself as she began to cry, at once glad Adah and Sam were asleep sitting up in each other's arms. "You're so nice to me, Gid. You've always been so."

He held her fast, and she was surprised at how good it felt to rest in the strength of his arms. Like he was truly a dear and trusted friend, not an anxious young man wanting to get on with courting, hoping she might fall in love with him so he could marry before his younger sisters. No, there was a genuine consideration in his warm embrace, and she laid her head against his burly shoulder.

Two long, sad years had come and gone, and she'd behaved nearly like a widow, never attending singings or corn huskings where young men and women paired up, so distraught she was. She had made up her mind all she wanted was the love of the Lord God and whatever He had in store for her life. She'd even turned her back on the idea of marrying, thinking that if Aunt Lizzie could be happy as a maidel, then why couldn't she?

But now, with these familiar feelings stirring within, what was she to do? Yet, when all was said and done, Leah *was* free to love again. *If I choose to*, she thought, surprising herself.

Sitting this close to Gid, she felt genuinely cared for, looked after . . . even cherished. She was wary of the feeling— she'd missed it so desperately after she and Jonas split up. Now she was afraid it might overcome her, because as they rode along, she suddenly knew she wanted more, wanted to drown her resentment toward Sadie in Gid's loving arms.

When they neared the turnoff to the Peachey farm, he asked, "Do you mind if I walk you home? We could cut through the field, if that's all right with you."

She said she didn't mind, and right then she realized how glad she was. This happy night had completely changed her outlook. Gone was her impatience to get home. Something tender that had died in her was beginning to revive, and at this moment, she felt she might at last be able to cast aside the stranglehold of sadness and animosity hindering her path. *Just look at the smithy and Miriam Peachey . . . how happy they are*, she told herself. If Gid's father was as loving to his mother as Leah had always observed him to be, then Gid would also be a compassionate husband, wouldn't he? How foolish of her to pass up the chance to be loved so dearly, to be so completely adored.

She found herself thinking ahead to what it might be like to accept Gid's hand, to live with him and cherish him, to care for their little ones . . . to be his devoted helpmeet. As thoughtful and kind as he was, how hard would it be to follow her heart—if truly her heart *was* coming round, as it seemed to be?

Lest Leah was getting ahead of herself, she chased such thoughts away, but she was altogether pleased she and Gid had yet another few minutes to spend together this night.

◆

They were enveloped in the green scent of jagged grass and the dank smell of cow pies as they strolled through the wide field between the Ebersol and Peachey farms.

The roof of her father's barn caught Leah's eye, the brilliant reflection of the moon dousing the silvery tin with its whiteness. She heard what she thought was one of their mules braying. Mules weren't nearly as stubborn as some folks seemed to think. They could be coaxed, not easily, but persuaded nevertheless to work the narrowest sections of the field. And mules required less feed and had greater fortitude than horses.

Gid glanced over at the barn. "What's the racket over there?"

"Must be a bat tormenting the livestock." She looked up at Gid. "Ever see one lunge at a mule?"

To this they both laughed, and she welcomed his hand finding hers. His companionably firm clasp made her own hand seem small and almost fragile, and once again she was startled at the long-dormant stirring within. She moved along at his side, keeping pace with his stride.

"Speaking of mules," Gid said halfway across the field, "didja ever hear of certain long-ago ministers sayin' it was offensive to mix God's creatures because our heavenly Father didn't create such an animal in the first place? Like breeding a horse and a donkey to produce a mule."

"Jah, Dat's said as much . . . but we all have mules these days, ain't? So what do you make of that?"

"Sure beats trying to get the field horses to go into steep places or some of the more narrow spots in the field," Gid replied.

They talked slowly as they walked, both seemingly hesitant to call it a night now that they were getting on so well. Now that they were alone with only the moon, the stars, and the blackness of the sky.

Leah's impression of the last full hour with Gid had grown as a little garden in her heart. Never in the most secret landscape of her soul could she have foreseen the joy she felt as she walked with Gid Peachey, picking her way through the thick grazing land, her hand snugly in his.

"What would you say if I told you this is the happiest night of my life?" he came right out and said.

A lump crept into her throat, and she was afraid she might cry again. She dared not try to answer.

He must have understood and squeezed her hand, turning to face her. His wavy light brown hair seemed almost colorless in the glow of the moon. "I hope it's not too forward of me. . . ."

She wondered what he might say and, composing herself, she asked, "What is it, Gid?"

He paused but for a moment. "I'd like to court you, if you . . . well, if you might agree."

She didn't once glance sheepishly at the Ebersol Cottage as she often did when talking with Gid here lately. No, she kept her gaze on him, studying the rugged lines of his face, the unabashed attraction he displayed for her as he leaned slightly forward.

She knew she'd traversed the gamut of feelings, from reluctance at the outset of the evening to this strange yet wonderful sincerity, the way she felt at this moment—surely it wasn't the moonlight and gentle sweet breeze of the wee hours, was it?

Smithy Gid's invitation was hard to resist. "Jah, I'll go for steady with you," she replied.

Then and there, he picked her up and swung her around and around. Her joy knew no bounds, because she had been so sure—in that most secret room of her heart—she would never, ever feel this way again. Yet here she was . . . and she did.

Chapter Seven

June's fair weather swept into the soaring temperatures of midsummer, and Mamma's lilies flourished, amassed in a solid bed of eye-catching pink.

On her way to the outhouse, Mary Ruth happened to brush past them, deep in thought, not paying any mind that her for-good purple dress had gotten some of the golden red pollen smeared on it. When she did notice it, she tried to brush it off with her hand, setting the stain but good. Realizing what she'd done, she hurried back to the house and told Mamma.

"Ach, you must always use adhesive tape to get lily pollen off," Mamma said.

"That or wipe it off with an old rag . . . anything but your hands," Aunt Lizzie said, explaining the natural oils from the skin set the stain.

Mamma continued. "If the stain stays put after using the rag, let the sun bleach it out."

Mary Ruth sighed and looked down at the smudged mess. "Well, now I have nothing to wear to the singing. My other good dress is too snug through the middle."

Aunt Lizzie shook her head. "Then you may just have to stay home and sew a new one tomorrow."

"What?" Mary Ruth didn't catch on to Aunt Lizzie's kidding at first.

Lizzie's face broke into a smile. "Come, let me see what I can do."

Mamma left the kitchen to tend to Lydiann, who was wailing upstairs, and while Aunt Lizzie scrubbed with an old rag, Mary Ruth bemoaned the fact that Hannah was refusing to double court with her. "My twin's not herself," she confided.

Lizzie seemed to perk up her ears. "Why would that be?"

Mary Ruth wouldn't go so far as to say more than "Hannah's persnickety these days . . . been so all summer, really."

"Well, in some cases, that's not such a bad thing," Lizzie said, still scrubbing. "All depends on what a person's bein' particular about, ain't so?"

Good point, thought Mary Ruth. "Still . . . ever since Hannah started taking baptismal classes, she seems aloof."

"For gut reason, I 'spect." Aunt Lizzie stepped back to look over the pollen stain and Mary Ruth herself.

"Why do you think that?"

"I daresay if you consider it carefully, you prob'ly already know."

She knew, all right. She just hated to admit it to anyone, especially Aunt Lizzie. For the longest time it seemed Hannah had been too quiet, almost downhearted. Was it the absence of Sadie . . . the unending silence from Ohio? Or was Hannah peeved at her for not following the Lord in holy baptism as

Hannah herself hoped to do come fall? No one but her twin knew that Mary Ruth had refused, of course. It wasn't something you went around telling, not amongst the People. The women folk would frown and carry on something awful if they knew the Ebersol twins—close in looks, and upbringing— might be heading in different directions, one certainly not in the Old Ways of their forefathers.

Aunt Lizzie was still scrubbing the spot awful hard, and Mary Ruth wondered if she might be attending the singing with a hole in her best dress—or, just as bad, a smeared stain.

"Have you asked Hannah to loan you one of *her* dresses?" Aunt Lizzie's question cut through the stillness.

She hadn't thought of that. "I best not be askin' her for anything."

Lizzie's hands rested hard on her slender hips. "Pity's sake, the two of you have shared nearly everything since you were both just little ones." She frowned and cocked her head, looking awful curious.

"If you promise not to tell, I'll say why," she whispered back.

But Aunt Lizzie surprised her—startled her, really—by backing away and waving her hands in front of her. "No . . . I'm not interested in hearin' or keepin' any more secrets. I've learned a mighty hard lesson."

Aunt Lizzie's response made Mary Ruth feel even more alone and made her want to tell her aunt all the more. But it was no use to plead. Truth was, contrary to what Hannah might say or think, Mary Ruth hadn't fully decided whether or not to join the Amish church. What was the rush, anyway? Hannah could make her covenant this September if she chose, without Mary Ruth tagging along just because they were twins and all. Then, when Mary Ruth was good and ready, she'd decide, and not one moment before. Meanwhile, she wanted to take her time with rumschpringe, just as Dat had said to do back last year. Joining church, after all, was for a lifetime, so it could wait . . . for now. She had too much fun ahead of her to get bogged down with required membership meetings where the People sat and voted on weighty issues like shunning wayward and sinful folk. No, she didn't think she was ready for that kind of responsibility. And, if the full truth were known, she sometimes resented the People for ousting Sadie the way they had when all the girl had gone and done was fall in love with the wrong boy. Sure, Sadie had known better, but putting her under the Bann for life was so awful harsh, wasn't it? Unforgiving too. Mary Ruth wasn't certain she could set herself up as a holy example amongst the People . . . not the powerful way she longed for Elias's hugs and kisses, though Mamma would have a fit if she knew. With Hannah and Ezra courting on their own, the temptation would be stronger for her when with Elias, especially when the moon was as bright and beautiful as it would be tonight.

"If you won't ask Hannah for a clean dress, what 'bout Leah?" Aunt Lizzie suggested.

"Gut idea . . . just might solve the predicament," Mary Ruth said and reached for her aunt, gave her a grateful hug, and hurried out the back door in search of Leah.

Lizzie could see Ida needed to give extra attention to Lydiann, who was awful fussy following supper, so Lizzie stayed to clean up the dishes, then dropped off Hannah, Mary Ruth, and Leah at the barn singing over at Abram's brother Jesse Ebersol's place. It was right nice to see Leah participating in the activities with the young folk again; Lizzie's heart was truly glad.

When she returned from the trip, she took her time unhitching the horse and carriage, in no hurry to head toward the house. The evening was pleasant, and what with having taken the girls to the singing, she was feeling a slight bit sorry for herself. Not like her, really. She knew she ought not to allow her thoughts to stray back to her own courting years, but Abram had told her rather falteringly on several occasions that Leah had been asking questions of him, wanting to know about her father—namely who he was. If Lizzie had her druthers, she'd just as soon never say.

Straightening now, she looked toward the woods and her log house, put there by Abram and his brothers back when she was in such a bad way, expecting Leah and scarcely but a girl herself . . . not knowing anything about her baby's father. At least, not back then. And now didn't it beat all for Leah to be so interested in knowing?

Just what *was* she to tell Leah? She certainly couldn't bring herself to make known the whole story—how she'd run around something terrible as a teenager, thumbing a car ride with a complete stranger, an *Englischer* at that. Oh, the idea of revealing such a thing to precious Leah made her feel queasy with embarrassment. She almost wished to roll back the calendar, thinking it might've been better to leave things as they had been, with Leah thinking Ida was her one and only mamma.

If I could relive the worst of my youth, what would I do differently? she wondered, shuddering at the sudden thought. If she had not had her hair cut or her face made up on New Year's Eve back when—and drunk far too much moonshine—dear sweet Leah would never have been conceived. Truly, the Lord God had wrought a miracle of life and joy out of her great sin.

Feeling glum, she found herself heading toward the Ebersol Cottage, hoping she might offer to help Ida with something, anything at all, as an excuse to stay. At the moment she could not face her own empty house.

She discovered Ida giving Lydiann a bath in the middle of the kitchen in the big galvanized tub. "Here, let me do that for you." She knelt down to splash her little niece while Ida rose and went to sit across the room in Abram's hickory rocker.

"I'm all in," Ida admitted, fanning her face with her apron.

"You just rest there, sister." And to Lydiann, she said, "Now, ain't that right? We'll let your mamma be for a bit while you get all soaped up and clean." She couldn't help it; the baby talk came flying fast out of her mouth as she enjoyed bathing the adorable toddler.

Soon Abram clumped indoors to wash his hands. He made over Lydiann, still sitting in four inches or so of water that had been warmed by the kettle on the wood stove. Lydiann tapped a wooden spoon on the water's surface, making more and more bubbles.

"Well, now, Ida, looks like we've got ourselves a tidy

youngster," said Abram, standing near the tub and watching.

"Soon it'll be Ida's turn in the bath, jah?" Lizzie said, glancing at Ida, who was grinning at her wee daughter, lathered up from head to toe.

"I should say so," Ida replied. "Goodness knows, I must smell like a pig, what with the awful heat this week."

Lizzie offered to tuck Lydiann in for the night, but the girl cried up a storm when she went to pick her up. "Aw, you wanna play longer?" She set her back down.

Abram chuckled. "You're spoiling the child; that's plain to see."

"She's only two once, ain't?" Ida said, beaming with love from the rocking chair.

Going to sit on the bench, Abram leaned back against the table, his elbows spread behind him. "You's oughta guess who I ran into this morning," he said.

"Who?" Lizzie said.

"Peter Mast." On any given day, Abram would have avoided all discussion about the Masts, quickly looking at the floor if they were mentioned in conversation, as if merely hearing the name caused him distress.

"Did he speak to ya?" Ida asked, leaning forward.

"Not a word." Abram shook his head. "'Tis the oddest thing, really."

"Jah" was all Ida said.

Lizzie had an idea—maybe not such a bright one, but she shared it anyway. "Has anyone thought of taking some fruit pies over to Fannie Mast?"

Ida clasped her hands and brought them up as if praying.

"I've considered doing so any number of times as a goodwill gesture."

"A peace offering?" Abram frowned, clearly not sure if this was something to ponder, let alone pursue.

"What if you sent the twins over to deliver the pies?" Lizzie suggested.

"Certainly not Leah," Ida said.

Nodding in agreement over that, Abram rose and wandered into the dark front room, and Lizzie heard him sink down into a chair.

"Well, what do ya say?" she asked Ida, who came and threw a towel over her shoulder and lifted out Lydiann. The toddler's soft bottom looked as shriveled as a prune.

"It would be nice to get things smoothed over with the Masts, but I'm sure Abram will want to think on it some more," Ida said as she wrapped Lydiann, bawling and squirming, in the towel before marching out of the room and upstairs.

A couple of tasty pies just might begin to repair the breach, Lizzie thought, removing her wet black apron and going to hang it up in the utility room. If so, how foolish of them to have waited all this time.

Chapter Eight

The next day was a no-church Sunday, a day set aside not for Preaching service but for rest, reading the Good Book, and visiting relatives and friends.

Mary Ruth held the reins while Hannah sat to her left, silent as a rock. "Dat and Mamma must've thought this over for a gut long time, us goin' to Grasshopper Level with pies for the Masts," Mary Ruth muttered.

"Two long years Mamma's been thinking of what to do, I 'spect," Hannah said softly.

"Aunt Lizzie baked till late last night is what I was told. Must've been a hurry-up job."

"While we were at singing, maybe," Hannah replied.

Mary Ruth scratched her head. "By the way, did you happen to see who Leah rode home with last night?"

"I thought 'twas Gid, though I can't be certain."

"Won't Dat be happy if it was?"

Hannah made a little sound, then spoke. "Mamma prob'ly will be, too, seein' Leah's been hurt so awful bad . . . the way Jonas did her wrong."

"Wasn't all Jonas's fault, don't forget. Takes two, ya know." Mary Ruth felt she had to remind Hannah.

"Wouldn't *any* parent be pleased to have Smithy Gid as a son-in-law?"

· "Can you see Gid and Leah as husband and wife? Honestly, can you?" asked Mary Ruth.

Hannah sighed. "Maybe so," she said in almost a whisper. Then abruptly she changed the subject. "Mamma's nothin' short of wonderful-gut. She never once thinks of Leah as her niece, now, does she?"

Mary Ruth found this turn of topic rather interesting. They had spoken behind closed doors of Lizzie's being Leah's birth mother after Mamma had shared with them, almost two years ago, the story of their aunt's wild days. Occasionally the twins would rehash their feelings, so great had been their surprise. "Seems to me, Leah is just as much Mamma's as you and I are." Mary Ruth meant this with all of her heart. "I wouldn't want things to change with Leah just because we know the truth 'bout Aunt Lizzie."

"Me neither." Hannah smoothed out her long green dress.

"Anyway, I could never think of Leah as merely our first cousin, even though she is that. The heart ties that unite are so strong, ain't so?" She surprised herself saying as much. "We'll always be sisters."

The tie that binds . . .

Now was as good a time as any for Hannah to bring up the knotty fact they were no longer double courting with the Stoltzfus boys . . . that there was a sort of estrangement between the two of them.

But Hannah said nothing, and they rode on in silence for the last mile.

As the twins pulled in the lane at the Masts' farmhouse, Mary Ruth noticed several of the younger Mast children scampering about. But when the youngsters spotted who was driving up in the carriage, they quickly disappeared into the house.

"Just as I expected," Mary Ruth said. "Now what?"

"We could end up sittin' here till the cows come home if we don't get out and make our delivery," Hannah replied.

"I wish Aunt Lizzie had come 'stead of us." Mary Ruth felt not only embarrassed but put out at having to come here when the Masts had chosen of their own accord to shun them.

Hannah was the one to stand up first, taking hold of the pies neatly placed in Mamma's wicker food hamper. "I'm not afraid of Cousin Fannie. I never did her wrong." With that she climbed down out of the buggy.

Taken aback by her sister's uncharacteristic boldness, Mary Ruth breathed in deeply and stepped out, too. "Which of us is goin' to knock on the back door?"

"Why, both of us. That's who" came Hannah's quick answer.

Mary Ruth wasn't so sure any of this was such a good idea, yet she was shocked at the way Hannah's feet pounded against the ground. Sure was a first, far as she could remember—

Hannah spouting off without uttering a word, using only her feet to do the talking!

Not to be outdone, Mary Ruth knocked on the kitchen screen door, wishing the whole ordeal were over. She could see past the screened-in porch and into the long kitchen, part of the bench next to the table showing. But there was no one in sight, which was downright peculiar on a "visiting" Sunday.

"Your turn to knock," she told Hannah, who promptly did so.

They waited, but the house remained apparently uninhabited. The call of birds seemed louder than before.

"How much longer should we wait?" Hannah asked.

Mary Ruth glanced over her shoulder, looking for any sign of life, but there were no sounds coming from the barn nor, naturally, from the fields, it being the Lord's Day and all. "I say we leave," she said at last.

"But . . . what 'bout the pies?" It was Hannah who was wide-eyed now.

"We'll have 'em for supper ourselves."

"What'll Mamma say?"

Then, just as Hannah was speaking, here came Cousin Fannie shuffling along toward the door like she really didn't want to at all. She poked her head out.

Before Fannie could speak, Mary Ruth said quickly, "We brought you something from Mamma and Aunt Lizzie."

A frown flickered across Fannie's face as she eyed the pies. "I'm sorry, but we can't accept them." She started to close the screen door.

"Oh, but Aunt Lizzie wants you to have them. She made them special for you and Cousin Peter," Mary Ruth explained,

feeling awkward having to beg someone to accept such delicious gifts.

But Fannie soundly latched the screen door, then backed
away, shaking her head before turning and walking to the
kitchen.

"Well, I declare!" said Mary Ruth, tugging on Hannah's
sleeve. "Come along, sister. They don't deserve Aunt Lizzie's
pies!" With that they hurried to the buggy and got in. The
horse pulled them slowly up to the widest section of the barnyard, then circled around to come back down the lane.

Mary Ruth spotted two small heads peering out the back
door. "Look," she whispered. "Isn't that Mandie and Jake?"

"Sure looks like them to me," Hannah agreed.

"So . . . we've been out-and-out refused. Well, isn't this a
fine howdy-do!"

"Something to talk about at supper tonight," Hannah
said.

"Won't Mamma be irked?"

Hannah nodded. "Irked and offended both."

"It's really too bad our families can't make amends." Mary
Ruth was certain both Mamma and Dat would have a reaction to this. Aunt Lizzie, too.

"What if we give them one more chance—try 'n' break
the ice, so to speak," Hannah suggested.

"And do what?"

"We could both write to Rebekah and Katie one last
time . . . see what comes of it. See if they'll reply."

"What a waste of time and stationery. But go ahead, if you
want."

"I say, best ask Mamma what *she* thinks." Hannah seemed

to make a to-do of crossing her arms and sighing.

"Well, now, why are you upset at me, Hannah? I'm not the one ignorin' your letters." Mary Ruth paused. "Whoever said twins had to be baptized into the church the same year, anyway?" There—she'd said exactly what was on her mind.

Hannah began to sniffle, which turned into a full-blown sob in a hurry. Mary Ruth had no desire to offer one bit of comfort. If Hannah wanted to cry her eyes out right here on the road, in plain sight . . . well, let her.

Half a mile later, she spotted Luke and Naomi Bontrager riding in their enclosed carriage. "You best dry your eyes," she cautioned. "Here comes the bishop's grandson. Word might get back that you looked mighty sour today."

Hannah turned to face her, quick as a wink. "What do I care? Truth is, the bishop himself already knows what you're up to!"

"What do you mean?" Mary Ruth didn't want to believe her ears.

"Bishop Bontrager has been askin' why you aren't joinin' church with me."

"And what're you sayin' to that?"

"Seems to me that's your problem."

Mary Ruth bit her lip. Luke and Naomi were smiling and waving now as they approached on the opposite side of the road. "Wave back," she whispered to Hannah.

Meekly Hannah did so, and Mary Ruth called to them, "Hullo, Luke and Naomi!"—waving and grinning for all she was worth. *Can't make things any worse . . . might actually help some*, she reasoned.

"Couldn't you offer a smile with your wave?" she asked Hannah.

"Didn't feel like it," Hannah said when the other buggy had passed by.

Mary Ruth knew she could easily say the wrong thing if she opened her mouth just now, so she pressed her lips shut.

Hannah, however, couldn't seem to drop the argument of Mary Ruth joining church. "'To him that knoweth to do good, and doeth it not, to him it is sin.'" Hannah stated the pointed verse oft quoted amongst the People.

Without a shadow of doubt, Mary Ruth knew Hannah was altogether peeved at her about rejecting baptism this year. It was beginning to cloud nearly everything, even something as innocent as a ride in the family carriage. *I won't cut short my rumschpringe!* she thought. *I'll join church when I feel like it.*

◆

On Sunday, July 17, Leah met up with Naomi Kauffman Bontrager in Deacon Stoltzfus's barnyard. She, along with Mamma, Aunt Lizzie, and the twins, had been milling about with the other women folk, waiting for the ministers to arrive before Preaching service.

"Hullo, Leah, nice to see ya," Naomi greeted Leah warmly, taking both her hands and squeezing them gently. "I've been wishin' we could talk."

They strolled away from the large group of women and young children. "Everything all right, Naomi?"

There was a distinct dampness to the day, which put a bit

of a wave in Naomi's hair—the wispy strands at the nape of her neck, at least.

"Oh, jah, things are fine." Naomi's eyes lit up. "I've been meaning to tell ya my news. I'm in the family way. Come this December, Luke and I will have us our first wee babe. Close to Christmas . . . when your mamma's baby is due."

"This is gut news and I'm ever so happy for you." She kissed Naomi's cheek. "Luke must be awful excited, too."

"He's holdin' his breath for a son, naturally."

"Maybe you'll get *two* boys," Leah replied, recalling that twins seemed plentiful on Naomi's mother's side. In fact, there was a set of triplet boys.

"I s'pose I wouldn't mind several babies at once. Whatever the Good Lord gives us will be all right."

"I'm glad I heard directly from you," Leah said as they walked back toward the women. She was truly happy for Sadie's former girlfriend, and hearing the news from Naomi got her thinking of her own future and the possibility of many children. After all, Mamma was expecting this baby in her midforties. Leah counted the years, thinking ahead. *If I were to marry Gid by next year, I'd have plenty of childbearing years ahead of me. . . .*

But she knew it was better not to think in terms of what might be . . . or worse, *what might have been* where Jonas was concerned. No, she would trust the Lord God, just as she had promised to do at her baptism. She would honor the Almighty One all the days of her life, and He alone would lead her. If God willed that she should marry and have children, then so be it. If not, she would try to be as cheerful and content with her lot as Aunt Lizzie.

Thinking of her aunt, she spied Lizzie chattering with the deacon's wife and had to smile. *Aunt Lizzie's a sly one, she is . . . talking to Ezra and Elias's mother, of all things!*

It was fairly common knowledge among Dat, Mamma, and Aunt Lizzie that two of the Stoltzfus boys were awful sweet on Hannah and Mary Ruth. Mamma had confided this to Leah, who, in turn, had mentioned something to Dat in the barn last week. Dat, bless his heart, had tried to act like he didn't know too much about it, but Leah could see the helpless smile of delight on her father's face. Since they all knew who was who and what was what, it was best they keep quiet now and allow the courting process to take over. Could be, as soon as a year from this fall, Hannah might be wed.

As for Mary Ruth, she'd most likely missed out on also marrying then. Much better to take her time and be sure than to rush into something and be sorry later, thought Leah. She guessed she ought to think likewise about her courtship with Smithy Gid, because he was visibly smitten . . . and, truth be known, she was falling for him, too.

Could it be Hannah and I will marry during the same wedding season? she wondered, spotting Gid's shock of light brown hair above the throng of men preparing to go inside the barn for the Sunday meeting. Her heart skipped a little as he caught her eye and then turned discreetly, pretending not to have seen her. The People's way . . .

Mamma might faint if she knew how fond Gid is of me . . . how often he says he loves me. I have yet to tell him, though. I must be ever so sure.

Chapter Nine

Lorraine Schwartz had been so deeply moved by the previous Sunday's sermon that she readily agreed to go with the Nolts to the midweek service. She had not a hunch how Henry would take this, but she was altogether eager to attend the Mennonite house of worship again, and she told him about it just as he was sitting down for supper on Wednesday night. "I hope you won't mind if I go out this evening for a few hours." She went on to say what she was planning.

He was slow to speak, evidently tired. "Are you trying to keep up with your son?"

She hadn't thought of it in that light, but now that Henry had mentioned it, she assumed Robert's quest for the spiritual might have influenced her, as well. "Why don't you come along?" she suddenly suggested. "You might be surprised and enjoy yourself."

"My desk is piled high with paper work." The tone of his voice caught her off guard; he was insulted.

"Are you all right with this, Henry?"

He looked across the table, his brow creased. "Go, if you must."

Fortunately their suppertime talk took a turn when Henry admitted he was toying with the idea of expanding the clinic, perhaps offering an internship to a medical student and building on to make room for more patients.

This was news to her, but she liked the idea. Henry, though he was close to his forty-fifth birthday, had aged considerably in the past year—virtually before her eyes. She speculated it was due to keeping himself busy with an overabundance of patients, more than enough for one country doctor, and she sometimes worried about his frequent lethargy. Even so, he had much to teach anyone interested in medicine.

Henry's need to extend himself to new blood coming up in the ranks surely had something to do with his sons' lack of interest in the medical profession—Derek having chosen a soldier's life and Robert, more recently, the Lord's work. She was almost certain Robert's abrupt fork in the road had affected Henry more than he realized.

"Any hope of Derek getting leave time for Christmas?" she asked, changing the subject.

"He'll have off two weeks, I would presume."

"Have you written him lately?"

"I did a week ago," said Henry.

Good, she thought. Her husband was keeping in touch with their younger son in spite of Derek's stubborn silence.

Henry shook his head and reached for his coffee. "Deep down, our boy *does* have a beating heart."

She was glad to hear this from Henry's lips and watched as he drank his coffee. Slowly she finished off her carrot cake and ice cream. If only Henry might consent to go with her to church, even a single time, she believed the pockets of stress under his eyes might soften and the spring in his step might return.

Hannah could scarcely wait to show Mary Ruth the letter from Grasshopper Level. They were already in their cotton nightgowns, each having brushed the other's hair, when Hannah asked her twin to "guess who'd written."

Mary Ruth shrugged. "I'm too tired to care, really." She slipped under the sheet and snuggled into bed.

"Well, listen to this," Hannah said. "It's a letter from our cousin Rebekah Mast!"

"What?"

"I saved it till just now."

Hopping out of bed, Mary Ruth hurried to peer over Hannah's shoulder. "Quick, read it to me."

> *Dear Cousin Hannah,*
>
> *This is the last letter I'm planning to send to you! I haven't even told Mamma I'm writing, but you need to know she's awful peeved you and Mary Ruth would come here. We don't need no pies and no letters, neither, from you Ebersols.*
>
> *If I sound upset, I am. After all, your sister Leah got our brother Jonas shunned by talking him into joining church over there in your neck of the woods. I won't say everything that's on my mind, but we wish to goodness he'd never laid eyes on her!*
>
> *Please don't bother to answer this letter. We have nothing*

88

to say to each other. Only one good thing came out of this awful mess—Sadie and Jonas have found some true happiness out west. That's all I best be saying.

So long,

Rebekah Mast

"Well, I declare!" Mary Ruth said a bit too loudly.

"Shh! You'll wake up the whole house." Hannah shoved the letter into the envelope and stuffed it in her drawer. "What a horrible cousin."

"You can say that again." Looking mighty gloomy now, Mary Ruth headed back to her side of the bed.

"I didn't think Rebekah had it in her to be so rude."

Mary Ruth pulled up the sheet and muttered, "No doubt Becky's echoing what Cousins Fannie and Peter are sayin' and thinking 'bout us."

Hannah put out the oil lamp on the dresser and crawled into bed. "I knew she was bossy and liked to talk a big talk, but this . . ." She almost wished she'd never bothered to open the envelope, especially not at night. Now the cutting words would encircle her thoughts, and she needed her sleep. Tomorrow she planned to help Leah mow all the yards— front, back, and side—then burn the week's trash. That alone would take nearly the whole morning.

"Don't worry yourself over Becky Mast," said Mary Ruth, reaching over and stroking her hand. "Just consider the source."

"Jah, I s'pose."

They lay quietly for a time; then Mary Ruth spoke again. "Aunt Lizzie and I will be canning quarts and quarts of pickles

89

tomorrow. Who's gonna look after Lydiann?"

Hannah shared with her what she planned to do, laughing a little. "Maybe Dawdi John will come over and look after our baby sister."

"That's not such a gut idea, do you think? Not as quick on her feet as Lydiann is gettin' to be." Mary Ruth had a point there.

"Jah, he may be hard-pressed to keep up with our baby sister; it's a good thing Dawdi John's hip has improved with Dr. Schwartz's help."

Hannah was anxious for sleep to come.

Mary Ruth yawned and turned to face her. "Do you ever wonder who it was Lizzie must've loved enough to give up her innocence before marryin'?"

"I hate to admit it, but I've thought about the same thing. . . ." She didn't want to speculate, but she guessed Leah's birth father must surely be the son of one of the Hickory Hollow ministers. And, if so, well . . . wouldn't it be interesting to know just who? "Best be sayin' good night now," she said, hoping to turn off the chatter.

Ida found herself standing in the hallway where she had stood that first morning twenty years ago now—here, at the top of the stairs, where the window looked out to the southeast, to the Peacheys' fine-looking spread of land. Tonight, though, she did not care to admire the smithy's acres and acres of corn and grazing land. No, she was looking up, high overhead. The stars captured her attention this night.

Bless the Lord, o my soul: and all that is within me, bless his holy name. She paused to rest her hands on her middle. O

Father God, place your hand of blessing on this babe of mine, growing so restlessly within, she prayed silently.

Here she stood, suffering twinges in her stomach on the very spot where so long ago she had accidentally overheard Abram telling young Lizzie what she must do about *her* baby. Lizzie had begun to soften from the near-rebellious state she was in when she and Abram brought her home to live with them. Ida recalled, too, that Abram had repeatedly questioned Lizzie to no avail that same day. "Your baby's father . . . who is he?" Her sister could only weep, not once mentioning the young man's name.

Surely she'll want to share the truth with Leah someday, Ida thought, still staring at the sky strewn with stars. But deep inside, in that near-sacred place where a woman frets silently over her dear ones, Ida was fearful. Nervous for Lizzie and Leah both, for what such a revelation might do to the good solid relationship they enjoyed. But, most of all, she worried for Abram. If Leah were ever to know her blood father, would Abram lose his rightful, even special place in Leah's eyes? She could only imagine what hurt this could cause him and the girls. All of them, really.

She moved away from the window, wincing as she caressed her stomach . . . her unborn child, wondering if Leah's natural father even knew he had a daughter. She ambled down the hall, stopping at the first bedroom to look in on Leah, sound asleep, then on to Hannah and Mary Ruth's room, where they, too, slept peacefully, like two small kittens nearly nose to nose.

Checking, observing, loving . . . her beloved family of girls, minus one. Would the hands of time turn things around for Sadie? Would the grace and goodness of God—the blessed Holy Spirit—woo her to Him faster than the People's shun? She prayed it would be so.

How she loved her girls, all of them equally, and she prayed as she walked the hallway, speaking to the Lord silently, imploring Him for each one's future. Ida longed for them to walk uprightly, to know the Holy One of Israel not only as their heavenly Father, but to embrace the atonement of His Son, the Lord Jesus.

Bring peace to this house . . . to my heart, she prayed without speaking. At last she headed back to the bedroom where Lydiann slept in a wooden crib in the corner and Abram lay sound asleep, not knowing she had been walking softly and praying earnestly. Not knowing that all too often, of late, the wee hours were filled with sharp pain, and sleep was far from her.

Chapter Ten

July stepped gingerly into August, and soon after September came in on wild turkeys' feet, surprising the local folk with much cooler temperatures and buckets of rain. The unsuspecting gobblers wandered brazenly out of the woods, becoming unwelcome visitors to the cornfield, as if daring someone to shoot them before small-game hunting season.

Mamma observed her forty-fifth birthday on the second day of September without much ado other than a card shower from the women folk. Leah said the hydrangea bushes near the house had seen fit to mix their brilliant hues with some deep bronze on cue for Mamma's special day, the first hint of long and lazy autumn days leading the way for the harvest and silo filling.

October's gleaming red and yellow apples rapidly turned to applesauce, cider, and strudel, and the musty scent of wet leaves led smack-dab into November's wedding season and the glory of deepest autumn.

It was the Sunday evening before Thanksgiving Day when Leah consented to ride along with Smithy Gid to visit his ailing uncle Ike. She was glad for the heavy woolen lap robe protecting them, since the open carriage provided no shelter from twilight's falling temperatures.

Gid held the reins with one hand and steadied his harmonica in the other, playing one tune after another as they rode along. In between songs, he whistled, as cheerful as she'd ever known him to be.

We're practically betrothed, she thought but instead quickly brought up the subject of his uncle. "Has a doctor seen him for his pneumonia yet?"

"Aunt Martha wants to call in the hex doctor, but Uncle Ike won't hear of it. Seems they're at a standstill, but I'm sure my uncle will have his say-so."

Leah thought on this. "What do *you* think of powwowing, Gid?"

"I don't rightly know. Pop says there ain't nothin' wrong with having the hex doctor have a look-see when somebody's sick, but *Mamm,* now, there's a whole 'nother story."

"She goes to the medical doctor, then?"

"I believe Mamm would rather die than have white witchcraft goin's-on in our house. And that's just how she says it, too."

White witchcraft? Leah pondered that. Seemed her own mamma lined up with Miriam Peachey on this matter. Dat, now, he didn't seem to care one way or the other—neither did Dawdi John. Aunt Lizzie, though, liked to have had a fit when Leah mentioned it some time back in regard to the day she was born. "Was there an Amish midwife or hex doctor on hand?" she'd asked, to which Lizzie had replied, "No midwife . . . not the powwow doctor, neither one," turning an indignant shade of peach when Leah mentioned the latter.

"What do the ministers say 'bout powwowing?" she asked.

Gid shook his head. "They'd prob'ly say they have more important things to think about."

Seemed to her the brethren ought to have an opinion one way or the other. Still, such a topic would never be preached on in any Sunday sermon.

Recalling that Jonas used to write her about certain Scriptures not being used in sermons here in Gobbler's Knob, she thought of asking Gid what he thought of *that*. But she kept her peace, not wanting to touch on the past—good or bad.

The road from Quarryville was particularly deserted this evening. Most folk were indoors keeping warm on such a brisk night, Robert Schwartz assumed. He wanted to surprise his parents by arriving early for Thanksgiving but had been just as eager to attend the Oak Shade Mennonite Church before heading northeast to Gobbler's Knob.

The minister had begun by speaking slowly to the congregation in an almost conversational tone. As time passed, though, his discourse had become swift and strong in its delivery, and Robert had been enthralled by the message, "Finding God's Plan for Your Life."

"As sons and daughters of Christ Jesus, we have an obligation to seek out His will and live it," the preacher had instructed. "We must delve into the Word of God for answers. What would God have *you* do with your remaining days on earth? Will He send you forth into the field, for it is white unto harvest?"

White unto harvest. The words had seeped into Robert's

heart, taking hold. To think what he might have accomplished for God in the weeks and months leading up to the invasion at Utah Beach in Normandy. The Allied air forces had dropped all those bombs . . . twenty thousand tons on France alone. Too many of his buddies had died on those bombing missions. And he'd lost his sweetheart, a true flower of a girl, though an unbeliever. *If only I'd known the Lord then*, he thought sadly as he remembered Verena.

Tonight he had gladly received the preacher's fervent words. They, along with many months of Bible study at the Mennonite college, had converged in an overwhelming epiphany, clinching his decision to become a country preacher. Truly, he wished he might have known God on some significant level during the war. What comfort and support he might have offered to his comrades and others had he been a believer then. Certainly the chaplains weren't the only ones imparting spiritual consolation during those horrendous days and nights. He recalled there had been a few Christian boys who had shared the Good News among the young, yet hardened soldiers. He would have joined ranks with them had he known then what he knew now. To think he might have saved a life or two, or more . . . for God. Instead, he had aided in the death of many enemies of the Allied forces—a martial victory, true, but a defeat for eternity, nevertheless.

Now, on the drive home, the words of the seasoned minister continued to resound in his thinking. He felt nearly euphoric as he drove the forsaken back road. Something was compelling him to follow through, to get his license to preach despite his father's disapproval, which was ongoing and would surely be voiced during the coming holiday. Still, his spirit had been touched in a way unlike any he had ever felt in the village church where his parents had infrequently attended through the years. There parishioners dutifully congregated Sunday mornings to hear a social gospel that trumpeted Jesus' humanitarian accomplishments, with few references to the true and living Word of God. If Robert was not mistaken, the small edifice with its numerous stained-glass windows was coming up here fairly soon on the left side of the road.

I'm here to answer your call, O Lord, he prayed, gripping the steering wheel as the road narrowed and the dense woods closed in on either side.

They had been talking about the fact that neither of them was well versed in the Holy Scripture when Leah first heard a siren in the distance. The wail came closer as Gid's horse pulled the courting buggy back from Uncle Ike's farmhouse toward Gobbler's Knob.

"Ach, Gid," Leah said, clutching her throat. "Someone nearby must be hurt."

The ambulance was approaching fast behind them, and Gid skillfully reined the horse onto the dirt shoulder and stopped while the shrill siren pierced their eardrums.

"Wanna follow and see if we can be of some help?" Gid asked after the ambulance had sped by.

"Sure, if we can catch up."

The accident, as it turned out, was less than a mile away, but by the time they arrived, the ambulance had already arrived and left. Two patrol cars blocked the road in both directions, so Gid parked the buggy a distance away, leaving Leah holding the reins. "I'll be back right quick." He jumped out of the buggy. "Will you be all right here alone?"

She said she would, but up ahead the sight of a car criss-cross in the road, its headlights shining across the mowed cornfield, frightened her no end. A lame horse, which looked to be awful young—more like a pony, really—was being led limping off the road by one of the policemen.

Then she noticed a young Englisher sitting in the backseat of one of the police cars. Could it be he was the driver of the car? Had he caused the accident, maybe startling the young horse?

Heart pounding, she stood up for a better look and saw the splintered remains of what looked to be a pony cart. On the east side of the road, a farmhouse stood way back snuggled against tall trees. She wasn't so sure in the dark, but she thought this might be the homestead of Deacon Stoltzfus and his large family.

She did think it peculiar that, by now, none of the family had come running down the lane to offer assistance. Then it dawned on her that maybe—hopefully not—one of their children had been riding in the crumpled pony cart, in which case the deacon and probably his wife and some of the youngest children would have gone along in the ambulance, leaving the oldest girls to look after the rest. The older boys, Leroy, Gideon, Ezra, and Elias, most likely were out riding around with their girlfriends, unaware of the dreadful accident.

A lump caught in her throat. *Dear God, please help whoever was hurt here tonight*, she prayed.

The distinctive ripeness of late autumn closed in around

her, and when a sudden wind came up, Leah felt its eerie chill and drew her shawl near. Oh, she wished Gid would hurry back and tell her what on earth had happened.

"The pony and cart shot out from the lane onto the road, you say?" the police officer quizzed Robert.

Pointing to the concealed treed lane, Robert explained, "Over there, leading down from the farmhouse. The cart appeared out of nowhere, right in front of me . . . before I could ever stop." He felt sick with the memory of the youth lying unconscious in the road, broken and bleeding. "My car hit it broadside."

The policeman filled out an accident report, scrutinizing Robert's driver's license, then inquired about his father. "Is Doc Schwartz your old man?"

"That's right."

The policeman looked him over. "Say . . . aren't you the son who fought in the war?"

He felt his shoulders tense. "I . . . well, sir, God must have been watching out for me overseas." That's all he could say about the past when the present—and possibly the future— was staring him hard in the face.

Returning his attention to the accident report, the officer added, "The lad's Old Order Amish, so I doubt there will be charges filed against you, although it's clear you weren't in the wrong. If this goes the way most accidents do involving them, you'll never hear boo from anybody. The Amish practice non-resistance."

Nonresistance . . .

Robert swallowed hard, hoping the boy would survive the

accident for both the boy's sake and his family's. He had certainly put into practice every first-aid technique he'd ever learned from his father in tending to him—his body crushed and bleeding—trying his best to save the kid's life.

"You were driving the speed limit or less?" he was asked.

"Yes, sir." He waited as the policeman finished filling out the accident report, feeling a desperate coldness steal over him. Robert shuddered in the darkness as the reality of what had happened here sunk in. "Can someone please phone me later? I'd like to know the boy's name and where I might visit him," he said.

A visit to the hospital was the least he could do; he wished he could do more. No doubt there would already be Amish friends and relatives gathering at the hospital, as was their custom. They would not want the boy and his family to suffer through the dark night alone.

"Someone from the station will be in touch with you, Mr. Schwartz." The policeman's voice startled him. "Take care, son."

"Why . . . thank you," he heard himself say. Robert's words, though sincere, sounded hollow and distant even to his own ears.

Due to the lateness of the hour and the heavy cloud cover, the road leading home was even darker now as Robert headed down the final stretch. His memory haunted him as he replayed the accident scene again and again. The shattered pony cart, the moaning boy lying in the road, the mournful neigh of the wounded horse . . .

"O Lord in heaven . . . please let the boy survive. Please, let him live," Robert implored. He slowed the car to a near crawl as he rounded the bend and saw the yard light on at his parents' house. *How can I begin to tell my family what has happened this night . . . what I have done?*

"It was a terrible mess up there," Gid told Leah when he returned at last, somewhat out of breath. "If somebody didn't die in that wreck, I'd be mighty surprised."

"Anyone we know?" She was unnerved.

Gid seemed dazed as he took the reins from her, sitting there for the longest time without speaking. And then finally he did. "*Himmel,* this slaughter on the roads—cars and carriages—just keeps . . . happening." His voice faltered.

Leah was shaking. What if one of her own kin was in such an accident? The People reckoned tragedies as being God's sovereign will, yet she shuddered to think of losing a sister to death.

"The pony cart belonged to young Elias Stoltzfus," Gid said at last. "He was severely injured tonight . . . if not mortally."

Leah gasped. *Not Mary Ruth's beau!* Suddenly she was panic-stricken at the thought of her own sister. *Was she riding along with Elias tonight?* she wondered. *Was she?*

"Was there anyone else in the cart?" Leah managed to ask.

"I don't know."

"Are you certain it was Elias who was hit?"

Gid nodded slowly, his expression sad.

If the boy did not survive, many of the People would

gather as a compassionate community for the wake at the Stoltzfus house, offering to help in any way possible. Leah determined that if the worst were to be, she would volunteer to help with the milking and whatnot. Anything to assist and by so doing lessen the immediate pain of loss.

Leah arrived home, where she was relieved to learn Mary Ruth was safe. Hours later she witnessed firsthand how much Mary Ruth cared for Elias—the whole family did. When they saw the tall figure of Leroy, the oldest Stoltzfus boy, on the back step, face drawn, eyes red . . . coming to deliver the death message, Mary Ruth burst out sobbing and fled from the kitchen.

Her heartrending cries were heard all through the house, and the pitiful sound struck Leah at the core of her very heart, for she knew too well something of the sting of Mary Ruth's loss.

Leah, Hannah, and Mamma offered their sympathy as best they could, but Mary Ruth would not be comforted. Her weeping continued as Leah sat on the side of the twins' bed, stroking Mary Ruth's hair while Hannah lay next to her twin, her slender arm wrapped around her. Mamma, after a time, kissed each of them good night, then slipped off to her own room, sniffling every bit as much as Leah recalled her doing the weeks following Sadie's shunning.

Miserable and helpless to know what to say or do, Leah decided now was a good time to pray—not the familiar rote prayers of their childhood, but one that came directly from her heart. The kind she knew Mamma and Aunt Lizzie often prayed, and the kind of earnest prayer she herself had offered in the woods, following her heartbreak over Jonas.

Sitting in the darkness, she silently pleaded for divine comfort for her grief-stricken younger sister, as well as the brokenhearted Stoltzfus family.

Chapter Eleven

Restless and unable to sleep, Mary Ruth tiptoed down the stairs after midnight, leaving the warmth of her bed to hurry outdoors. The night was as still as the animals resting in the stable area of the barn. Deftly she reached for the sides of the old wooden ladder and climbed to the hayloft without making a sound, wanting to sit alone in the midst of the baled hay.

She anguished at the memory of her last conversation with Elias in the barnyard following Preaching service yesterday. He had asked her to go "on a lark, for some fun before going to the singing." Ezra, it seemed, had gotten first dibs on the courting buggy and was planning to spend time with Hannah again, just the two of them. So Elias had wanted to use his pony cart.

If Ezra had included Elias and me, she thought, *my dear beau might still be alive!*

Now in spite of Elias's fondness for her and hers for him, he was gone forever, soon to be buried in the People's cemetery not so far away. Her own beloved.

Too exhausted to ponder further what might've happened

if things had been much different this night, she pulled the long black shawl about her and wrapped her arms around her knees. Sassy, the new pup—short for Sassafras—soon found her. The droopy-eyed pet comforted Mary Ruth by licking her salty cheeks, remaining by her side as she wept till close to dawn.

Hannah stared at the new handkerchief she had quickly made for Elias's grieving mother. Somehow, she hoped to find a way to slip it to the poor woman, though seeing the crowd of mourners gathered at the Stoltzfus house, she didn't know how or when that might be possible.

Just now, though, standing in the backyard with the other women of her family, waiting to enter the farmhouse, Hannah couldn't shake the fear of death knocking on her own door, coming too soon, before she was ready for it. She'd long struggled this way. Like Elias had been, she felt she was much too young to die, though if such a thing should happen, even prematurely, the People believed it was the divine order of things. Hannah had been taught this from her childhood, and being a baptized church member now, having made her kneeling vow back in September with Ezra, she felt she, too, must embrace the Lord God's supreme plan for each of His children. Yet she still battled the horror of death—when it was to come and how it might happen . . . and, most of all, how difficult it might be to get to the other side. She felt her neck grow exceedingly warm with the worry.

Just what *did* the Lord God heavenly Father want with

young Elias up in heaven when there was so much left for him to do down here? She guessed there must be some mighty important work waiting for him in Glory Land—maybe something that required lots of time. *Jah, maybe that's why he was taken so early.*

Robert was reduced to sitting in the backseat, a passenger in his father's car as he and his parents traveled down the road to the Amish funeral on Tuesday morning. Not able to sleep or eat since the accident, he had thought of staying home and would have preferred to, but his mother had slipped into his room after breakfast and attempted to console him, reminding him the mishap was simply not his fault. "Any driver might have hit the boy. It was impossible for you to see him," she'd insisted. Then she had encouraged Robert to "come along with us, in spite of the accident. Share your sadness with the Amish community. The entire Stoltzfus family will be there, I am sure."

And they were, all thirteen of them—eleven remaining sad-faced children, some teenagers, and their somber parents. Robert had gone immediately with his father to the hospital, following the accident, but he had not had the chance to see Elias. Sadly the young man had been pronounced dead on arrival, and Robert could merely offer his condolences to the solemn parents. How very taxing that had been. He instantly deemed himself a murderer, however unintentional the act. Most difficult for Robert was knowing full well that if he had never gone to the Quarryville church meeting and had driven straight home from college in Harrisonburg, Virginia, he might have been home this morning reading or watching television, and young Elias would have been alive.

How does this nightmarish thing fit into God's plan? he agonized. What exactly would the dynamic Mennonite preacher have to say about the circumstances Robert so unpredictably found himself in? The policeman at the collision scene had been correct in his assessment; no charges had been discussed with Robert nor filed. He had been driving well under the speed limit, so there was no question of a reckless driving charge. He felt he should be somewhat relieved, but he was nothing of the kind. A sense of despondency encompassed him, and he was miserable with the knowledge that, however blameless, he was responsible for snuffing out a young life.

Staring out the car window, he was aware of the blur that became one Amish farmhouse, then pastureland, cornfields, and another farmhouse, and so on, one after another. He had survived the horrors of war on foreign soil only to come home and accidentally kill an innocent civilian.

Stunned with grief and struggling to sit through the long funeral in the house of worship—*house of sorrow,* Mary Ruth thought—she attempted to keep her hands folded, yet every so often she noticed she had been unconsciously wringing her handkerchief. At one point Hannah leaned close to her and whispered, "I believe that's the driver of the automobile."

She sighed ever so deeply, her breath coming in ragged gasps as she fought tears and looked over at the man Hannah assumed to be Robert Schwartz. The mere thought of a car plowing into Elias's vulnerable pony cart made her wince; it was next to impossible for a person to survive such an impact. She battled the urge to despise the Englisher. *Who does he think he is, coming to the funeral?*

Somehow, as the service progressed, she was able to deny her tears, having spent all day yesterday and Sunday night, too, wearing herself out in distress over her beau. Through sheer will, she had managed to go with Leah and Aunt Lizzie to the Stoltzfus farm early yesterday morning to help with some of the cooking, cleaning, and tending to the small children, just as other church members had.

Presently she was in desperate straits, trying hard to listen to the first sermon, thirty minutes long and given in Pennsylvania Dutch, followed by Scriptures read in High German, which she did not understand. Who of the People did? Most of the old-timers perhaps, but none of the youth.

She was suddenly stirred, then and there, wishing she might comprehend the words Preacher Yoder read from the Old German *Biewel*—wanting to know what was being said at her beau's funeral, for pity's sake!

During the second sermon, she noticed Robert Schwartz sitting tall and stately, yet weeping silent tears that coursed down his solemn face. Strangely, he made no attempt to brush them away. Mary Ruth found this curious, never having seen a grown man shed tears in public, let alone at a large gathering. She felt compelled to glance his way every so often but only with her eyes, never moving her head.

Goodness knows what he must be feeling, she thought, but her heart was bound up with fond memories of dear Elias, as well as her own great sadness. How could she ever forget how he'd made it a point to put off joining church to run around a bit longer? What did this mean for his everlasting soul?

The People were admonished to live righteous lives, as

one never knew when his or her "day of reckoning" might come. The second minister spoke on this subject for nearly an hour, urging young people to think carefully about joining church. "Do not put off the Holy Ordinance. It has the power to seal your eternal fate."

Mary Ruth felt a quiver run up her spine as the minister continued preaching. She wondered, just then, if what had befallen Elias was connected in any way to his decision to postpone church membership "till another year," as he'd said. But no, she couldn't allow herself to be that superstitious.

She *did* wonder if Elias had died in his sins. Since he was not baptized at the time of the accident, were the ministers right? Was her beloved standing *outside* the gates of Glory?

During the brief obituary reading in German by Preacher Yoder, Mary Ruth considered the idea of wearing her black mourning garment for a full year, as if she were Elias's widow-bride. She knew Mamma would not approve, but at this moment of determined loyalty to her beau, she didn't rightly care what anyone thought.

◆

While the coffin was being moved outside so the People could view the body, Leah noticed Dr. Schwartz and his wife, Lorraine, walking toward their car. It seemed they were scarcely able to put one foot in front of the other, so downtrodden they and their son Robert looked. She had recognized him from seeing his pictures several places in the Schwartz house, as well as on the wall of the clinic waiting room.

Watching them cross the yard together, arm in arm, she

felt a deep measure of sympathy and wondered if Dr. Schwartz would say something to her about this awful sad day come Friday, when she was scheduled to do some cleaning at the clinic. She wouldn't be so rude as to bring up the topic of Elias's death herself. Still, she wondered how the Schwartz family would manage to cope.

When she turned back toward the house, she noticed Mary Ruth hovering near the coffin, now situated on the front porch for the final viewing before burial. She wondered if her sister was out of her mind with grief, as sometimes happened to couples if one or the other was taken early. Then she knew for sure Mary Ruth was suffering unspeakably, for her sister leaned down and touched Elias's face—her last chance to see him ever so close. But when she bent lower and kissed him, Leah cried. *She's saying farewell*, she thought, wishing she, too, might have had that opportunity, though keenly aware how tragically different a situation *this* was.

Later, in the *Graabhof*, her father stood next to Smithy Peachey, black felt hat in his rough hands, as they glanced now and then at the coffin-shaped hole in the earth. Small grave markers were scattered here and there in unpredictable rows within a makeshift fence. For a moment the wire barrier made her feel captive to the People, and she thought of Sadie and her endless shunning.

Leah's gaze drifted to the brethren—the ministers and grown men, farmers all—who set forth the unwritten guidelines for living. *The* Ordnung *rules our very lives*, she thought, missing her elder sister anew. The faces of the men looked pale in spite of their ruddy, sunburned complexions, she noticed, and women and girls dabbed handkerchiefs at their eyes, trying not to call attention to themselves. Yet how could they stop their tears when the deacon's red-haired young son—once spirited and smiling—lay lifeless in a simple walnut box?

Four pallbearers used shovels to fill the grave once the coffin had been lowered into the previously dug tomb by the use of long straps. Deacon Stoltzfus stood near his remaining sons, their jaws clenched, lower lips quivering uncontrollably; Ezra, especially, looked ashen faced. Elias's mother, grandmothers, aunts, and many sisters clustered together, some of them holding hands and crying, but none of them wept aloud. It was not the People's way to wail and mourn conspicuously, and Leah was glad for that. The sadness she felt for these dear ones spilled over into her own spirit, and she hung her head as if in prayer.

Once the grave was nearly filled, the pallbearers ceased their shoveling and Preacher Yoder stood tall and read a hymn from the *Ausbund*. The People did not sing on this most sobering occasion, and every man and boy in attendance removed his black hat.

Leah could scarcely wait for the sunset, hours from now, that would bring an end to this heart-wrenching day. The prevailing gloom triggered the familiar helpless feeling she had often wrestled with in the black of night as she lay quiet as death itself, wishing for sleep to come and rescue her from her memories of Jonas. Of course, there was far less of that these days than before she and Smithy Gid had begun spending time together. If things went as she assumed they might, she and the smithy's son would be husband and wife come next year; she felt sure Gid was looking toward that end. As for herself, she understood fully why her father had been adamant about Gid being a "wonderful-gut young man," not to mention his first choice as a husband for her. What was to fear?

Hannah put her hand over her heart, taking short little breaths as the soil was mounded. The burial complete, she felt like she might break into a sob, and just then Mamma reached over and found her hand, holding it for the longest time. Listening intently, perhaps too much so, she was scarcely able to draw a breath as Preacher Yoder admonished the People, "Be ready when your time comes."

She could only hope that she would be . . . if or when her number should be called. *How can I or anyone be ready for that day?* she pondered, not knowing in the slightest.

She felt she should talk to Mamma about her worries. After all, she'd heard her mother praying beside her bed several times—typically in the late-night hours, when Mamma surely must have assumed her girls were fast asleep. Honestly it seemed maybe both Mamma and Aunt Lizzie knew more about the Good Lord than they were ever allowed to let on, and it was time for her to ask a few important questions. With Elias's funeral taking up much of this day, she hoped to find some time soon to talk quietly with Mamma before Thanksgiving. They wouldn't be observing the day as an all-out holiday the way the English did, nor with prayer and fasting as Plain folk in Ohio did. They were taught to be grateful for every day as it came, though they did gather as families around a bountiful feast table, especially because it was their season of weddings. Attending this funeral of her sister's beloved at such a normally joyous time was the most difficult thing Hannah had ever done.

The afternoon crept along ever so slowly for Mary Ruth, particularly during the shared meal. About three hundred mourners had returned to Deacon Stoltzfus's home, passing by the location of the actual calamity there on the road at the end of the long dirt lane. Mary Ruth had refused to look; she'd kept her head tilted back, eyes on the stark tree branches lining the way.

She observed Ezra sitting at the table with his younger brothers. His face was swollen, and the stern set of his jaw betrayed something of his pain, making her flinch. Their custom of eating a meal with the family of the deceased created a strong sense of comfort and belonging for all of them, to be sure, yet she was painfully aware of the hole in the very middle of her heart. Elias had brought energy and excitement into her life. His keen attention had given her even more reason to spring out of bed each morning and, if she were truthful with herself, was equal to her pleasure in book learning.

But now . . . what was she to do? She'd completely missed joining church with Hannah this year, deciding to put it off because she and Elias wanted to enjoy rumschpringe longer. Much longer, truth be known. Now it surely seemed as if Hannah and Ezra were the wiser.

Mary Ruth felt herself sinking into a gray despair such as she had never known.

Chapter Twelve

Dejected and in urgent need of prayer, Robert left his father's house and drove to Quarryville for Wednesday prayer meeting the night following Elias's funeral. At the church, he prayed silently before the service began, pouring out his great woe to God. When he raised his head, anticipating the beginning of the meeting, he was aware of a number of Amish youth gathered there—serious, distraught young people more than likely searching for consolation on the heels of the startling death of Elias. Yet their attendance was highly unusual, to be sure.

Following the singing of hymns, the pastor invited those with a testimony of grace to stand and "give a witness." One church member after another praised the Lord publicly, expressing the ways they believed God was at work in their hearts.

When a short lull ensued, Robert felt compelled to stand. Turning to face the people, he directed his solemn remarks primarily to the Amish youth. He began by sharing his anguish and then faltered. "I humbly beg ... your forgiveness . . . for having been the driver of the car last Sunday night. I pray you might find it in your hearts—all of you here—to forgive me for accidentally killing your own Elias Stoltzfus." Shuddering as he spoke, he was aware of sniffling and then a single sob. Unable to go on, he sat down, fighting back tears. His feelings of guilt over not having been charged with involuntary manslaughter or even a lesser charge continued to preoccupy his thoughts, although Reverend Longenecker had kindly pointed out when he had met with him privately before the service that Robert's guilt was unfounded. Nevertheless, the minister's words had not lessened the fact Robert sincerely wished the Stoltzfus family had not let him off scot-free.

When the minister stood behind the pulpit and began to pray, not a sound was heard except his earnest voice. "Our Father in heaven, we come this night, carrying our burdens to you, O Lord. . . ."

Mary Ruth volunteered quickly when Mamma asked for someone to take one of two batches of graham-cracker pudding over to the Peacheys' the Thursday following Elias's funeral. Glad for an excuse to clear her head in the chilly air, she headed across the cornfield to the neighbors', low in spirit and dressed in the black garb of a mourner. Spying Adah's younger sister driving into the lane, she hurried to deliver the pudding to Miriam, then returned to help Dorcas unhitch the horse from the carriage.

"Are ya doin' all right, Mary Ruth?" asked Dorcas, who

reached for and squeezed her hand.

"No . . . not so gut. Not at all, to be honest."

"I'm ever so sorry for ya, truly I am." Dorcas let go of her hand and looked around like she wanted to say something private. "Have ya heard tell of the meeting last night in Quarryville?" she asked.

Mary Ruth had not.

Dorcas leaned closer and whispered now. "You could go 'n' see for yourself."

"How's that?"

"'Cause there's another gathering tonight. I wish I could go again, but maybe *you* could. Might help ya some."

She urged Dorcas to tell her more and was surprised to hear the Englisher who'd hit and killed Elias had stood up in the meeting and made a sober apology. "Ever so odd it was, yet awful sad, too. I mean, we Amish just wouldn't think of holdin' a grudge against someone, yet there he was, talkin' like that. I tell ya it made us all cry. Every one of us."

Mary Ruth didn't bother to ask who all from Gobbler's Knob had gone, but she assumed from what Dorcas was saying that a sorrowing bunch of the youth had made the trip, seeking for something more than the Amish church could offer.

◆

By Thanksgiving night, the very evening following Robert's apology, the Mennonite meetinghouse had filled to capacity simply by word of mouth—the local Amish grapevine was evidently lightning quick. Robert was surprised to see an even larger group of Old Order youth there to mourn their friend Elias and hear of God's goodness and grace—some for the first time, he was certain.

When Reverend Longenecker asked Robert to stand and give his testimony, he did so with confidence. Later, when the minister gave the altar call, ten more Amish young people came forward to open their hearts to the Lord Jesus.

The first Saturday after Elias's death, Leah happened to overhear Mary Ruth squabbling with Dat out in the barn. "I need to take the family buggy tonight," she was insisting.

"Where to?" Dat asked.

"Quarryville."

"What's down there?"

"A gathering of young folk, is all."

"Amish youth?"

"No."

Dat drew in an audible breath. "I forbid you to go, then."

She wondered if he, too, might've heard all the talk—the reports of a throng of Amish young folk finding God at the Mennonite church. "Well, I'm goin', anyway. One way or the other, I am!"

"Just 'cause you're in the midst of rumschpringe . . . doesn't mean you should be back-talkin' your father!" Dat shot back and rather loudly at that.

"Well, if I'm old enough to run around with boys, shouldn't I be allowed to speak my mind 'bout *some* things?"

Leah felt terrible about standing there behind the wall of the milk house, just off the main part of the barn. Yet she hardly knew how to make her presence known. And, truth be told, she wasn't sure she wanted to.

Mary Ruth didn't wait for Dat to give his answer; she simply ran out of the barn, crying as she went.

Leah scarcely knew what to do or say, though she hurt something fierce for both Dat and Mary Ruth. She also felt awkward to know how to get herself out of the milk house without Dat spotting her and wanting to know what the world she was doing sneaking around like that, listening in on a private conversation.

So she set about cleaning out the place once again, sweeping, then rinsing down the floor, stopping only when she happened to realize Dat had come in and was standing there staring at her, for who knows how long, waiting.

"Your sister's bent on havin' her own way, as you already know. Might be best, next time—should there be a next time—to cough or sneeze or something, Leah. Eavesdropping is out-and-out deceitful. Best be more respectful from this time forth."

Before she could speak, he turned and left, his work boots making powerful clumps against the ground. She was glad he'd left, in a way, because she would not have been able to defend herself, nor did she want to. Truth was, she felt nearly as innocent as the dogs—King, Blackie, and Sassy—who'd also been privy to Dat's wrath and Mary Ruth's foolhardy determination.

Put out with herself and, if she dared admit it, with Dat, too, Leah hurried to the house, her father nowhere in sight. She could hear Lydiann wailing her lungs out. "There, there," she said, running upstairs to rescue the napped-out tot. "Did you get left up here all by your lonesome? Did Mamma forget 'bout ya?"

Such a thing was no way near the truth. Mamma had probably gone to the outhouse. Hannah, meanwhile, was redding up her and Mary Ruth's bedroom, and Mary Ruth was right now running pell-mell down the lane, heading toward the road. Just where she thought she was going was anybody's guess. Leah *was* concerned about her grieving sister and wished she might help in some way, do something to ease not only the tension between Dat and Mary Ruth, but lessen the ache in Mary Ruth's heart.

"Let's go downstairs and see what Dawdi John's doin'," she whispered to Lydiann. The tiny girl's eyes were wide and bright from awakening, though tears still glistened from her attention-getting cries. "Your grandfather hasn't seen you yet today, so it's time we go over and visit, ain't so?" She continued to coo as she carried her sister down the stairs, through the front room, and over to the small attached home built onto the main house. The Dawdi Haus was a refuge for elderly or single relatives. For Leah, it was a comfort to be able to go and sit with Mamma's father in his cozy front room, situated close enough to the cook stove in the tiny kitchen to keep it warm on even winter days.

"There, now." She set Lydiann down near Dawdi.

"Did you come to see your ol' Papa?" He reached for her and Lydiann held up her chubby arms.

"That-a girl," he said, putting her on his knee and bouncing her gently. "Here's a horsey, a-trottin' and a-goin' to market . . . to market."

Her sister giggled, and Leah sat down across from them,

watching with pleasure the joy Lydiann brought to Dawdi—
to all of them, for that matter. Soon, within another full
month, there would be a baby sister or brother for them to
hold and love . . . for Lydiann to grow up with, too.

How nice for all of us, 'specially Dawdi, she pondered,
knowing he was slowing down more all the time, even though
his health had greatly improved and his good days seemed to
be very good.

She pondered whether to ask the question she was almost
too curious about—and how to ask it without causing a stir.

"Dawdi," she began, "I sometimes wonder . . . I mean,
what do you know 'bout my father?"

A serious look on his face, her grandfather replied, "Well,
now, I've been workin' with your father all morning, Leah."

"Ach, you know what I mean, don'tcha?" she said.

He grew more somber. "I know you've had yourself some
difficult times, getting adjusted to who the mother was that
birthed you. Guess you feel like you have two mammas,
ain't?"

"Sometimes, jah, I s'pose I do, though I can't say I think
on that so much."

He tilted his head, gazing lovingly at Lydiann. As he did,
Leah noticed his beard was thinner than she'd remembered
and whiter, too. "I wish it could stop right there. Wish you
could be content with simply knowing 'bout your first
mamma, Lizzie, and the woman who raised ya as her very
own. Seems to me the rest of it, well, ain't all that important."

"Is there more to Lizzie's secret than she's willin' to share?
I don't know . . . she seems almost closed up about it."

Dawdi said softly, "Or is it something else altogether?"

Her heart quickened and she sat there in the tiny room, not taking her eyes off Dawdi, hoping this might be the moment of revelation. "Do *you* know who my blood father is?"

He began to shake his head back and forth, slowly at first, and then faster. Then he stopped abruptly and looked straight into her face . . . into her heart, too, it seemed. "I just never thought you'd care a speck 'bout Lizzie's wildest days. 'Tis long forgotten . . . why dig up the shameful past?" He sighed loudly. "And 'tis hurtful, I must say, dear girl."

"For Lizzie, too?"

"Above all."

She considered this moment here with Dawdi and the soft babble of Lydiann as the moment when she felt she understood something of her grandfather's love for herself and for Lizzie. No matter which woman she claimed as her mother, Dawdi John Brenneman was her devoted grandfather, and nothing she could do or not do, know or not know, would change that. Dawdi John was her flesh-and-blood grandfather for always, and what he might know about her paternal origins no longer concerned her. She had asked and not received the information she desired.

She must simply wait for it to unfold before her, as surely it would in time.

All day Mary Ruth waited for the tension to diminish between herself and Dat. At the noon meal she found the strain even harder to bear, as her father refused to ask her to pass the potatoes and gravy, even though they were clearly in front of her. Instead, he asked Hannah or Leah, making it seem as if she wasn't even present at the table.

Is this what it's like to be under the Bann? she thought.

She could not get used to the fact her own father did not come close to understanding her. Not only did he not understand or attempt to, she felt he was too harsh in his stance.

When dusk fell and she was still wishing to attend the nighttime church meeting, she asked Dat once again if she might borrow the family buggy. This, after supper dishes were cleared off the table, washed, and put away. She attempted to soften her voice and her approach, though she felt as if she might boil over with eagerness. "I'll take gut care, Dat, honest I will. If you'll just think 'bout letting me go . . ."

"You should not be goin' alone after dark," Dat said.

"I could take Hannah, if you'll let her come along." She wondered momentarily how that would set, since Hannah was already a baptized church member.

"What's the urgency to go all that way?" he asked.

She refused to confess the rumors that Plain teenagers were getting religion. "I'll know better once I get there," she said best as she could muster. "Ach, just say I can go."

"Why not stay home, help your mamma bathe Lydiann and whatnot?" He wasn't budging.

"Please, Dat, won'tcha let me take the buggy and Hannah, too? We won't be gone long."

He turned beet red and pulled hard on his beard, making his lower lip protrude. "I'm not in favor of it; no way, no how." He stared at her, a frown crossing his brow. "But . . . I s'pose 'tis better to have ya goin' in my family carriage than out runnin' round with empty-headed boys all hours."

He was referring to Elias's reckless buggy driving, no doubt, before it got him killed. But she kept her mouth closed. Stunned that she was actually allowed to go, however reluctantly Dat had granted permission, she did not voice her gratitude. She took off running to the barn to get the horse and carriage hitched before he could change his mind.

Mary Ruth had unconsciously retained the image of tall young Robert Schwartz from Elias's funeral, and when she saw him sitting on the men's side of the meetinghouse, her anger was rekindled. Yet she was strangely conscious of his demeanor, his compelling and kind, yet sad eyes. The minister introduced the young man as having a zealous testimony of God's forgiveness and grace before asking him to rise and stand behind the pulpit. Already this was not at all like an Amish preaching service.

Beside her, Hannah fidgeted, glancing at Mary Ruth, probably wishing she hadn't come along now that they were settled into the seventh row on the left side with the other women. Surprisingly there were numerous youth present, a good many of them from their own church district.

When Robert read his sermon text in English, she wondered how this could possibly be. She had never known a gathering where the Scripture was read, and so freely, not from the High German but in a language understandable to all present. And to think that *this* young man was the preacher tonight!

" 'Wherefore lay apart all filthiness and superfluity of naughtiness, and receive with meekness the engrafted word, which is able to save your souls. But be ye doers of the word, and not hearers only, deceiving your own selves.'" He read the text from the epistle of James, chapter one. The doctor's son went on to say it was "high time for men and women to stand up and be counted for the Lord. We are called to do His work. But in order to make our bodies a living sacrifice to this high calling—to be used of Him in the harvest fields of souls—we must first present ourselves to the Most High God. Do not wait until it is too late to 'Give of your best to the Master. Give of the strength of your youth.'"

Mary Ruth intently listened to words and phrases from sections of the Bible she was completely unfamiliar with, and she hungered for more.

The engrafted word, which is able to save your souls . . .

The young preacher continued. "We—all of us—are lost, and we're inclined toward sin and the self ruin that follows. From our birth onward, we yearn to be set free. We long for someone to take away our burden of sin and sadness. Our sin-sick souls crave to be reborn, renewed."

She felt a strange tugging in her heart, something ever so new. She had been taught there was no assurance of salvation in this life. A person had to die first and then only on the Judgment Day could the words—"Well done, thou good and faithful servant," or "Depart from me, ye workers of iniquity"—ever be spoken.

But evidently the Bible stated your soul could be saved here and now, while you were still alive and breathing; the verses just read confirmed this clearly.

124

She had thought of asking someone about the Scriptures that had been read in High German at Elias's funeral. Now that she was here, inside a church *building*, of all things—her first time ever—she wished there was someone to help her understand.

"O Lord," the young speaker began to pray, "look into our shattered hearts this night. Heal our brokenness and soothe our sorrow. Let us understand fully the price you paid for our salvation, for each of us assembled here. You have redeemed us for yourself with your precious blood spilled on Calvary's tree, and we are forever grateful. In Jesus' blessed name. Amen."

Those gathered in this most reverent place began to sing softly a hymn Mary Ruth had never heard before, yet the words tugged at her heart. "Fightings and fears within, without . . . O Lamb of God, I come, I come." The heartfelt song so perfectly described this night and clinched her longing for the Lord Jesus.

◆

All the way home, Mary Ruth chattered to Hannah, who wasn't at all interested in discussing "forbidden Scriptures," as her twin put it. "But didn't the preacher's words stir up something in you, sister . . . didn't they?"

"The young man speaking tonight killed Ezra's brother" was Hannah's harsh response. "That's all I could think of, though it's not my place to judge. I'm surprised it's me thinkin' this and not you!"

Mary Ruth was suddenly outraged, though she'd felt the

selfsame way as Hannah at Elias's funeral just days before. "I happen to believe Elias died as a result of an accident, pure and simple. An *accident*. Why do you question the sovereignty of God?"

Hannah shook her head, glaring at her. "The young preacher-man *slaughtered* your beau with his automobile, that's what. Such modern things are of the world and are therefore a sin. That's how I see it. So should you."

Mary Ruth felt as if she might burst out crying again, reliving the shocking news of that horrid night, but she wouldn't give in to the grief she had endured. Besides, Hannah had redirected her thoughts with her comments. Truly, Elias's death was a woeful thing and the reason she would wear her long black cape dress and apron for as long as they felt right to her. Yet tonight she had stumbled onto something amazing: the renewal of life and the spirit. Hers. This renewal was something altogether foreign to her, yet she yearned for it like someone dying of thirst yearns for water.

"You saw him, Hannah. . . . Did Robert Schwartz look like a man who would intentionally run his automobile into a pony cart? Did he sound like it as he read the Word of God?"

"Ach, you talk nonsense," Hannah said. "What's got into you?"

She ignored her sister's barbed remark. "Best keep your thoughts to yourself, 'cause I have no intention of staying home tomorrow night. If the meetings continue on, I'm gonna be there."

"Best count *me* out. I made my vow to God and the Amish church. Ain't no room for Mennonite gatherings in my future."

"I'll go with or without you, then," Mary Ruth said, surprised at Hannah's outburst; wasn't like her twin to give voice to such frustration and so strongly, too. She, on the other hand, had been venting her thoughts far too often. "If I have to get the Nolts to drive me in their car, I'm goin' back. I'm empty in my soul, Hannah, ya hear? The Amish church can't even tell me Elias is in heaven. I want to know God the way the doctor's son described Him. I may not always have known it, but I've been lookin' for this my whole life."

That hushed Hannah up quicklike, for which Mary Ruth was ever so glad; she'd had about all she could take. The hour was awful late, and she felt nearly too limp to attend to the reins. Yet such a hankering she had to know and hear more of God's Word.

I will return tomorrow night, she promised herself. *No matter.*

Chapter Thirteen

Mary Ruth stood in the shadow of the springhouse, waiting for Dat to head to the barn. She knew he was indoors talking up a storm to Mamma, probably saying how the twins had come dragging in mighty late last night. Maybe, too, he was letting off steam about the many Gobbler's Knob young folk "out lookin' for the Lord God in all the wrong places."

She wouldn't put it past her father to say something like that. Then Mamma might speak up and say how she felt, or simply nod her head and remain quiet this time.

It certainly didn't matter to Mary Ruth whether or not Mamma voiced her opinion. Truth was, she felt strongly enough about what she'd heard at the church in Quarryville to convince her entirely. Scarcely could she wait to speak to Dat, who was just now hurrying out the back door and making a beeline for the barn.

She waited a bit, then took out after him, willing her feet to walk not run. *Slow down, Mary Ruth . . . take your time.*

Once inside the barn, she sought out her father, noting his disheveled appearance—hair mussed and oily from a week of hard work. He pushed his tattered black work hat onto his head, securing it with dirty and callused hands.

She called to him and, getting his attention, hurried in his direction. "I best be talkin' with you, Dat." Quickly she began to share those things she'd heard from the Mennonite pulpit and had been pondering overnight.

As soon as her comments focused on the assurance of salvation, a change came over her father's countenance—a hardening in his eyes, a frown on his face.

"I have no time for such talk!" he replied.

She fought hard the urge to holler out her aggravation in the stillness of the barn. "Don't you see, there are Scriptures to help us get to heaven? We can *know* we're goin' there! We've been kept in the dark all these years."

Dat was just as adamant. "It smacks of pride for a person to say they've received salvation. You know the story of creation by heart, Mary Ruth. The all-powerful, all-knowing God fashioned all things, both on the earth and in the heavens. Then the evil one, Satan, was cast out of heaven for the ultimate sin of pride, and tempted Eve into thinking she could be 'better than God,' which is exactly what you're sayin' when you claim salvation."

Here Dat paused a moment, then went on. "Must I take you to the bishop himself to discuss these things you know already?"

She decided then and there, Bishop Bontrager ought to be told the truth of the Holy Scriptures. After all, he was the chief authority and responsible under God for the Gobbler's Knob church district. "That's a wonderful-gut idea," she shot back. "We could open the Bible to the selfsame verses preached on last night."

Dat's eyebrows came together in a dark ripple. "Then you knew all along where you were headed—to the Mennonites." He shook his head in disgust. "You cause strife in our midst, daughter."

She felt the hot stain of embarrassment on her cheeks, yet she would not submit; she had absolutely nothing to lose. She must fight for what she believed the Lord God had allowed her to hear and witness in a strange church, because in the span of a single night, her world had been altered more than she could say.

As much as she respected her Amish upbringing, and as much as she missed her dear Elias, Mary Ruth now realized she must follow her heart to higher education, that one thing the Lord had implanted deep within her.

"Dat, I don't mean to cause trouble. I've waited a full year—and more. Why should I wait any longer to go to high school? I'm old enough to do as I please; anybody knows that."

"We had this all worked out, Mary Ruth. You agreed to stay home with your mamma and help . . . till you married, whenever that time came." Dat's voice sounded nearly breathless.

"But all that's changed . . . don't you see? Everything's different now."

"Just 'cause Elias died?"

"Since my beau was . . . *taken* from me." Mary Ruth was angry and sorrowful all mixed up together. "Nobody knows this, but Elias and I were goin' to be wed . . . one day."

"I'm awful sorry 'bout his death, daughter. Truly, I am."

"Oh, Dat!" she sobbed. "If you mean it, then won'tcha give me your blessing to get my education? This is the only thing I really want now in life."

A long silence ensued. Sadly she knew pursuing the dream would eventually lead her away from her parents' church. Unknowingly she had been searching for something deeper her whole life . . . for true wisdom. Losing Elias had uncovered the emptiness in her spirit, and the obvious lack on the part of Bishop Bontrager and the brethren to fill it.

When Dat did not respond to her fervent plea, she spoke again. This time with an even more fiery edge to her words. "Blessing or not, I'm goin' to get my high school diploma . . . as soon as I can get myself enrolled. Even if I have to do it by correspondence or whatnot, I must follow God's bidding."

"How on earth can ya know such a thing?" Dat asked.

"Can't explain it, really. All I know is the Almighty put it there . . . my desire to teach young children." She paused, contemplating what she must say next. "And I want to read and study the Bible."

"Study, ya say?"

"Jah, and no wonder the Quarryville church has room only to stand at the back. The place is packed, and you and Mamma . . . you should go and see for yourself. *Hear* the words of the Lord God preached in such a way as you've never known."

She knew her father faithfully read Scripture, but he did not pause and ponder any of it or ask questions of anyone about what he read. Usually he did so silently in High German, seven chapters at a time, and, when asked, he would read in Pennsylvania Dutch to the family. But at no time would he have admitted to formally studying the verses. That was thought to be haughty and high-minded . . . and far from the ways of the People.

No wonder Mamma had been opposed to the library books once hidden beneath Mary Ruth's bed. Was she worried Dat might discover Mary Ruth also desired to study the Holy Bible, perhaps in English? Begin poring over it the way she did every other book?

"Mamma reads the Bible for herself, even says some of the verses over and over again. I know she does." Mary Ruth said it too quickly, and she worried she may have mistakenly pulled her mother into the center of the storm.

"Ain't your concern a'tall." Dat turned away, removing his black hat and raising it ever so high off his head, as if preparing to shoo a fly, but there was no fly in sight. Downright mad he was, and she knew it.

Then, nearly as swiftly as he'd lost his temper, he somehow managed to regain it and pushed the hat back square on his mashed-down hair. He turned to face her. "I'm tellin' you this here minute, if you are so *schtarrkeppich* as to insist on your way—to ignore my rightful authority as your father—I'll have no choice but to go to the brethren about this matter."

"What can *they* do?" she retorted. "I'm not baptized."

"No . . . but Hannah is, and the two of you are bound by unbroken cords of blood and spirit." He was surely grasping at straws.

She felt put upon, as if she'd done something terribly wrong against her twin. *Bound by unbroken cords . . . well, for pity's sake.* Baptism was up to the individual, not a mandate of the People.

Dat shrugged, then walked away.

She could see it was no use trying to continue the heated debate; Dat's mind was made up. Now she would have to follow his wishes or suffer the consequences—rumschpringe or not.

Still, she could not squelch the hankering to know more. She despised the feeling of having been kept from things that truly mattered—essential truths found in the Holy Bible. After all, there must be some important reason why folk called it the *Good* Book. Mary Ruth didn't rightly know how she would get to Quarryville again, but one way or another she was going tonight. If she had to run down the road to the Nolts' place, she would.

◆

Leah was out searching and calling for a wayward cow, up in the high meadow and clear back toward the woods on the north side. She couldn't help but think as she wandered the field that the cow was truly the smart one. The day was awful pretty, what with the skies as blue as one of her for-good dresses, and not a single cloud. Such late autumn days wouldn't stay nice like this much longer. It was highly unusual for the twenty-seventh of November to be this mild.

We're having us a fine Indian summer, she thought, tramping through the tall grass, wearing shoes for the first time that autumn on feet swollen from months of going barefoot.

At long last Leah located Rosie under a stand of trees, the

boughs void of leaves now but still sturdy enough to provide a bit of shade. Munching away and minding her own business, the cow appeared to be content this far from the bank barn. "I'd say you went explorin' today, didn'tcha?" Leah slapped Rosie's hindquarters playfully. "Let's go on home now."

On the walk back, Leah spoke coaxingly to King and Blackie, who ran together more often now that the pup, Sassy, had come to live with them. *Three's an odd partnership,* Mamma liked to say. Leah was seeing it firsthand, for the younger pup preferred to stay close to home, begging for handouts at the back door. It was easy to see Mamma was spoiling that one.

"When will the first snow fly?" She reached down, petting King and Blackie both as they went. Then she had to direct the cow away from the temptation of going belly deep in a clear creek nearby. "Can you sniff the air and forecast a change in weather like Aunt Lizzie does?"

She had to smile. Her blood mother, bless her heart, was the sweetest, dearest Aendi she had, and there were plenty on both sides of the family. Leah was looking forward to seeing more of Mamma and Lizzie's sisters again over in Hickory Hollow come next Saturday. It had been a good long time since Dat had actually consented to take the family to the old Brenneman homestead, where Dawdi John and Mammi— gone to heaven—had lived and raised their brood of children. This visit they planned to see Aunt Becky and Uncle Noah Brenneman, the man Dat had often tried to avoid at all costs, before the truth of Lizzie's past had finally come to Leah's ears.

"Nearly time for milkin'," Leah said, nearing the corral and following Rosie into the barn. She was eager for winter weather, because once the windmill started clanging its tinny song and strong gusts of cold air swept up from the distant hills, piling snow up high against the north side of the barn, Dat wouldn't need her so much outdoors. No, Dat was awful kind that way, and he was beginning to be even more considerate these days, now that he suspected Leah was seriously seeing Gid.

Funny how that is, she thought, preparing the cows for milking. *When Dat's happy, everybody else is bound to be, too.*

She wondered how things would go when the smithy's son asked Dat for her hand. That day couldn't be too far off, and she felt almost breathless with excitement. She looked forward to long winter days of quilting, when she would once again be included in the community of women folk, something she enjoyed more than ever.

Is it because I am soon to become a wife? She didn't quite know why her attitude toward work frolics was changing. Scarcely could she wait to see what pattern and colors would be used in sewing the next quilt. This one, she knew, was meant to be given to Deacon Stoltzfus's wife for her birthday, come Christmas. Everyone knew the reason behind the gesture was to bring a bit of cheer to the grieving woman. She had looked awful peaked last Sunday at Preaching service, Leah recalled, her heart going out not only to Elias's mother but to the whole family.

When Dat came shuffling into the barn, she greeted him. "Just in time for milkin'," she said. But he surprised her by heading right back outside without saying a word.

Something's awful wrong, she thought, hoping it wasn't more bickering with Mary Ruth. Still, she couldn't help wondering, because just before she'd gone looking for missing Rosie, Hannah had dashed through the barnyard, running hard down the lane after Mary Ruth, hollering, "Come back, sister. Won'tcha please come back?"

She pressed the cow's teat, milking by hand as she always did, and was nearly startled at the strength of the first spritz of creamy milk. "Good girl, Rosie," she said softly. "Glad *someone's* content round here."

Robert Schwartz held the obituary in his hands—a paper memorial. He had cut out the small square of newsprint last Wednesday, tucking it in his personal possessions to take back to college. Something tangible to forever remind him . . .

He sat in the dark, in the formal front room, where he could contemplate the events of the last week without interruption. Life-altering days when opinions and perceptions had radically changed. How could one twenty-four-hour period be so drastically different from the next?

He replayed the entire week from Sunday to Sunday in his head. Visions of Elias's body sprawled pitifully out on the road . . . recollections too painful to ponder. Elias's mother at the funeral, how she looked as if her knees might give out, leaving her too weak to stand. The Deacon Stoltzfus, as he had been reintroduced to Robert prior to the service, had worn a solemn face, sitting erect with his sons, the weight of the world on his back. Robert had recognized the invisible burden, because he, too, carried one linked to all the misery of the day.

He had heard the sniffling of one young woman in particular. She was surely not more than a teenager, likely Elias's own age, perhaps younger. A girl with a look-alike sister, possibly a twin—both with strawberry blond hair—had struggled through the endless funeral service, even leaning, at one point, on the shoulder of the other girl. *Elias's sweetheart*, he had surmised at the time, for no other woman, apart from the mother, had appeared to be as distraught.

Robert had noticed the same girl and her sister at the Quarryville church. On the final night of meetings, just last evening, he had spoken with her briefly as she made her way out the door with Dan and Dottie Nolt and their son. Dan had introduced her to him as "Elias's former bride-to-be, who came along with us tonight." He wanted to say how very sorry he was, say the accident was the worst thing that had ever happened to him, but any words of sympathy he might have offered remained locked behind his lips. He could not recall the few words he'd said in response to Dan's brief introduction, but he remembered offering his hand and shaking hers quite gently, lest it break, requesting forgiveness with his eyes.

Thinking back, he suddenly realized there would have been no spontaneous meetings at all—no rejoicing of the heavenly hosts when dozens of grieving, repentant Amish young people came to the Lord Jesus—had he driven home last Sunday night without incident. *"Things happen for a reason,"* one of his professors often stated with conviction. *"Therefore the sovereignty of God can be wholly trusted. You can throw your life on His mercy. . . ."*

Contemplating these things in the quietude, he was startled when his father wandered into the darkened room and sat on the leather chair, put his feet up with a sigh, and merely sat silently for more than a full minute. Robert felt obliged to be the first to speak, and he began by simply saying he wondered if the whole village of Gobbler's Knob hadn't turned out for the funeral of Elias Stoltzfus . . . as well as the revival meetings that followed.

His father frowned disapprovingly, changing the subject to the weather. Not to be daunted, Robert rose and offered to pour some freshly brewed coffee. To this his father agreed. Robert hurried from the parlor, toward the kitchen, glad for some common ground, inconsequential as it was.

Chapter Fourteen

Ida, now at the end of her eighth month of pregnancy, had not slept soundly for three nights straight. She shared this in passing with Leah, who had come in from the barn. "Catch your breath a bit, dear," she said. "And I will, too."

Leah settled down nearest the window with a cup of tea. "Soon we'll be using the one-horse sleigh to get to and from Preaching and market and all."

Ida sighed, glad for this rare quiet moment. "And we'll soon have us another sweet babe to hold and warm us in the midst of our winter. I'm ever so eager. Can't help but thinkin' this one might be Abram's first son."

"Oh, Mamma, really?"

She didn't want to make too much of it, Leah having been Dat's longtime sidekick for these many years. But if she were forthright, she'd have to admit this baby was mighty different from his sisters. He kicked harder and poked deep into her ribs at times. He jumped and leaped and ran in place all night long, chasing sleep away. "What shall we name him if he's to be a boy?"

"Well, the name Abram *does* come to mind." Leah smiled broadly.

Ida had thought of that, too. "Well, now, 'tween you and me, I think there's room for only one Abram under this roof." She paused momentarily before continuing. "What would ya think if we named the baby Abe?"

"It sounds similar to Abram, for sure. Like a wee chip off the old block." Leah glanced up at the ceiling like she was thinking it through. When her gaze drifted back down, she offered another smile. "I think Abe's a right fine name. So why not see what Dat says to it?"

"Jah, Abram might enjoy namin' his boy." She went and poured herself some hot tea, stirring two teaspoons of honey into the steaming brew. Ida knew Leah was right. It was fitting to include Abram in all the excitement of a new little one. He'd gotten somewhat lost in the shuffle with the previous births, except for the day Leah came into the world.

She sipped her tea and recalled the autumn day, suddenly feeling compelled to tell Lizzie's first and only child the events surrounding the day of her birth. Rather impulsively, she began. "I understand from Abram you're quite curious 'bout your birthday—your very first one, that is."

Leah's hazel-gold eyes brightened instantly. "Jah, Mamma, what can you tell me?"

"Only as much as I know," she said. "That October day was a busy one, what with potato diggin' in full swing. As I recall, the sun was warm and the skies were clear, although we'd had the very first frost of the season—quite heavy, in fact. That morning I thought of all the weeds blackened by the killing frost, not one bit sad 'bout that. But . . . the flowers, well, I was awful sorry to see their perty heads all wilted overnight.

"Lizzie and I had awakened quite early. She'd come down from her log house to eat breakfast with us here, and after a bit we decided to make some apple dumplings, then redd up the kitchen.

"Several hours after I'd gone to help Cousin Fannie with her fall housecleaning, Lizzie's labor began. There was no way for Abram to get word to Grasshopper Level 'bout Lizzie without leaving her alone, and she was fairly terrified, puttin' it mildly. He hollered for the smithy and Miriam, but the Peacheys were out diggin' potatoes clear on the other side of their barn. So poor Abram, if he wasn't beside himself, wonderin' what the world to do.

"Then things began to happen awful fast, and there was no time to call for the Amish midwife, not the doctor, neither one. By the time I arrived home, late in the afternoon, you had already made your entrance into the world."

Stopping to catch her breath, Ida felt again some of the surprise and excitement of that day. She drank a little more of her tea. "Abram was the one who came to our Lizzie's rescue, bless his heart, and helped with your birth. He delivered his little niece—you—and we raised you as our own second daughter. And, 'course, you know all the rest." She felt she might cry now as she remembered Abram's account of the special day.

"Dat, you see, was the first to hold you and speak softly to you—'welcome home,' he said—and kiss your little head, covered with the softest brown peach fuzz. Oh, how Abram loved you, Leah. Right from the start he did. Honestly, I believe he fixed his gaze on you like no other man might have, maybe 'cause your own birth father was nowhere to be found . . . or, far as we knew, even known." She reached over and covered Leah's hand with her own.

Leah was still now, eyes wide. "Oh, Mamma, no wonder Dat took me under his fatherly wing. No wonder . . ."

"Jah, 'tis for certain. And not only that, but Dat had it in his head that he'd spared your life back when, after Lizzie first knew she was carrying you, which was prob'ly true, too. It was during that time your outspoken uncle Noah was bent on sending Lizzie away to end her pregnancy."

Leah clasped Ida's hand. "Mamma, why is it Dat has never wanted to talk 'bout my birth to me?"

She'd wondered if Leah might press further. "I daresay he may be embarrassed, really, recounting all the day entailed, ya know. . . ."

"I just thought there was more to it, that's all."

She shook her head. "You now know all I know, Leah. If it's your first father you're thinkin' of, well, I don't know a stitch more than I've already said."

Leah glanced out the window and Ida slipped her hand away. "You mustn't ever think you weren't longed for or dearly wanted by Lizzie . . . and Dat and me. Just 'cause, well, you know—"

"Because Lizzie didn't have a husband? Is that what you mean?"

Neither of them spoke for a time. The warmth from the wood stove encircled them like a sheer prayer veiling as both women brought their teacups to their lips.

Ida set her cup down and leaned on the table, studying

Leah. "I'd like you to know something," she said at last. "You comin' into the world, the moment you did . . . well, it turned my wayward sister round right quick . . . away from the lure of worldly things. She had a change of heart even while she was expecting you. You gave her purpose to live a holy and upright life. She nursed and tended to you—with plenty of help from me—and began to seek after the Lord God and His ways." Here she couldn't help but sigh, remembering. "Lizzie became nearly childlike in her faith. Truly, the grace of God was upon her. She wanted to learn how to pray . . . and I taught her, just as Abram's mother had taught me long ago."

"So Lizzie wasn't content with the memorized prayers of the People?"

"She had a yearning to share from her heart is the best way I can explain it. She wanted to learn to listen more to the Lord, as well."

Leah's eyes widened at that. "Ach, Mamma, whatever do you mean?"

She wondered how to describe the deep longing in both her heart and Lizzie's. "I s'pose at one time or 'nother, most all of us yearn after the Lord Jesus in a way that may be difficult to understand." She hoped her comments might whet Leah's appetite to walk with the Lord God heavenly Father in a similar manner.

"I promised, at the time of my baptism, to uphold the Ordnung." Leah fiddled with the oilcloth on the table before going on. "You're not sayin' you go beyond what the brethren teach at Preaching service in the prayers you speak of . . . are ya?"

"To honor the unwritten code of behavior amongst the

143

People is all well and good, but it's equally important to obey God's Word, the Holy Bible."

Leah looked up just then, catching Ida's eye. "Aunt Lizzie taught me to talk to God from my heart, as she likes to say. After Jonas and I . . . after we didn't end up getting married, when I was ever so brokenhearted, Lizzie helped pick up the pieces of my life by showing me the way to open up my spirit to the Holy One."

"I pleaded with her to do so," Ida admitted. "I felt this was something you and she could share—mother and daughter, ya know."

Leah got up abruptly and came around the table. She sat next to her and leaned her head on Ida's shoulder. "Oh, Mamma, I don't know what I ever did to deserve two such loving women in my life. You and Lizzie . . ." She brushed away her tears. "I'm mighty grateful . . . and I hope ya know."

Drawn anew to Leah, she patted her girl's face. "The way I look at it, God must've loved Lizzie and me a lot to give you to *both* of us. Such a dear one you are."

At this Leah straightened and reached around her and gave a gentle squeeze. "I'm all the better for it, Mamma."

"All three of us are," Ida declared, getting up to warm her tea.

"In case you're wonderin', it makes no difference when it is that I find out who was my first father. I've decided to be patient in this and simply wait till Lizzie's ready to share with me . . . and not before."

You may have to wait forever on that, Ida thought but did not voice it.

———◆———

Leah hurried to the cellar to help Mamma run the clothes through the wringer between Monday morning milking and breakfast. Hannah and Mary Ruth were already working in the kitchen, and Leah was glad for that. She could stay put near Mamma, aware of an extra-special closeness on this dawning of a new day, wanting to continue the conversation from last night.

"Why don't the ministers teach us to pray the way you and Aunt Lizzie do?" Leah asked when it appeared they might be alone for a while longer.

Mamma glanced toward the stairs. "'Tis best you keep such things to yourself."

"Why's that?" She felt strangely intrigued, as if sharing something forbidden.

"The brethren need not know of this." Mamma looked a bit worried now. "There are different ways of lookin' at things, far as I'm concerned. If a body wants to speak directly from the heart to the Almighty—not use the rote prayers—then who's to stop him or her?" She nodded her head. "This happens to be one of those big issues that, sad to say, is downright niggling. Divisive, even, amongst the People."

"*Hinnerlich?*"

"Oh my, ever so troublesome, jah."

She wondered what other things Mamma might be referring to; the not knowing caused even more of an urge to question. Still, she was obedient and held her peace, trusting God to bring things to light in His own timing and way.

When lunch had been cleared away, Mamma sent Leah over to Miriam Peachey's with a large casserole of Washday Dinner, consisting of a hearty layer of onions, an ample coating of sliced new potatoes, tomato juice, and sausages.

"Mamma heard you were under the weather," Leah said, handing the meal to the smithy's wife, her someday mother-in-law, Lord willing.

Miriam's face warmed with the gesture as she accepted the tasty offering with a smile and a joyful "Denki!" then asked, "Tell me, how's your mamma now?"

"Oh, she has her energy back and is doin' all her regular work—and keepin' up with Lydiann, too," Leah assured her.

Miriam nodded her head and thanked Leah once more. "I'll return the favor next week."

"No need to, really. Mamma's feelin' wonderful-gut. Has some trouble sleepin' at night but that's all." Leah turned to go, noticing Gid in his father's blacksmith shop, running the blower, stirring up the coals to make the forge hotter. She wouldn't bother him by going over to say a quick hello when it was obvious how occupied he was just now.

Returning home, she found herself imagining how busy Smithy Gid would be as her husband, managing his black-smithing obligation to his father, as well as his work with Dat, which would take Gid back and forth between the Peachey and Ebersol farms. Not to mention his own work hauling and splitting wood for the cook stove and mowing and keeping things tidy outdoors, wherever he and she might end up living. She wondered if Aunt Lizzie might possibly move down to the Dawdi Haus to care for Dawdi John at some point, making it possible for Leah and Gid to live as newlyweds in the little log house half in and half out of the woods. No one had ever suggested such a thing, but she smiled at the idea, thinking how much fun it would be to get her pretty things out from her hope chest, making a home at last for herself and Gid . . . and, eventually, their children.

She wondered if Lizzie had ever stopped to think about her own future, back when she was Leah's age. *Was she at all like me when she was young? Did she think some of the same thoughts as I do now?* She tried to imagine Lizzie Brenneman wandering outside as a young girl, talking quietlike to a favorite dog—like Leah often did to companionable King—or looking up at the black night sky, speckled with bright stars, and wishing she could count them, so many there were.

Just who will I be? Leah wondered. *In the future, will I be satisfied with the choices I make now? Who will I become in the eyes of the Lord, and will He be pleased with me?*

———◆———

Nobody knew it, but the night Leroy Stoltzfus had come into the kitchen to tell the news of Elias's accident, Mary Ruth had felt her heart turn nearly hard as a stone. She could scarcely hear what Leroy was saying—only the words *Elias died tonight* had broken through.

It was as if she had willingly stopped up her own ears somehow. She didn't know for sure if the tuckered-out feeling she had just now was a delayed reaction to the funeral, this being the eighth day since the shocking news had come. She felt heavy inside as she headed upstairs and sat on her side of the bed, on top of the colorful handmade quilt made by Mamma and Mammi Ebersol years before.

She ought not to have been surprised when, nearly thirty minutes later, Leah tiptoed near, settled on the floor near the bed, and leaned her head against the mattress, her hand resting on Mary Ruth's. "You can cry for Elias all ya want, but I won't have you up here cryin' alone."

Tears continued to seep out of the corners of her eyes, spilling down the bridge of her nose. "Oh, I miss him so . . . I just can't say how awful much."

"Mary Ruth, honey . . . I believe I understand," Leah replied.

She knows 'cause she lost Jonas . . . just not to death, thought Mary Ruth, at least glad of the latter for poor Leah. "But I can't begin to know how *you* must've felt, Leah . . . you-know-who doin' what she did."

They fell quiet, the two of them there together, both acquainted with similar sorrow.

When Mary Ruth got the strength to speak again, it was a whisper. "Would you help me talk to Dat 'bout getting my education? He's ever so fired up these days."

A flicker of a frown creased Leah's brow. "Well, I don't know."

"Please, sister? See if you can gain some ground for me."

Leah sighed. "All right, I'll do whatever I can."

"You'll go and speak to him, then?" She wanted to get up, she felt that much encouraged, but she sat there without moving, still exhausted.

"I'll do what I'm able." This was Leah's promise to her.

"That's ever so gut and I'm grateful." She gripped Leah's hand. "I don't like shouting matches," she declared. "Not one little bit."

"Then why do it?" came the quick reply. "Dat wants only what's best for you."

"I s'pose I'm too quick to say what I'm thinkin' is all. You know me—everyone knows how much I like to talk. Gets me in hot water more than I can say; more than I *should* say. And sometimes the talkin' gets mixed up with the thinkin', and that's when I have the most trouble."

Leah smiled sweetly. "Seems to me you could do more thinkin' and less, well . . . *you* know."

"I'll keep that in mind."

To this they both smiled. Mary Ruth felt more hopeful and cared for when Leah was near and she told her so. What she did not say was that she had run off to Dottie Nolt, mad as all get out, and discovered another sympathetic ear down the road. No, it was best Dat or anyone else not know she was talking to the "enemy," so to speak, though the Nolts were the nicest, kindest Englishers she'd ever known, and she sincerely liked them. Still, if Dat knew they'd invited Mary Ruth to come live with them, well, he'd raise the barn roof—for sure and for certain.

Chapter Fifteen

Leah was out helping Dat split wood the morning after her heart-to-heart with Mary Ruth when she got up the nerve to say something about her grieving sister's zeal for education. "I know you've already talked this out with Mary Ruth some time back, but she's more determined than ever to attend high school."

Dat avoided her gaze, raising his ax clear behind his head and back, then bringing it forward to meet the log. "She oughta know better than to put you up to this," he grumbled when he'd sliced through the piece of wood with a single blow.

"I just thought—"

"How can you, Leah?" he interjected. "Why must ya think your sister will benefit in any way from stubbornly lusting after the world?"

"She'll probably do it, anyway. Why not give her the go-ahead just as you allowed both of us girls to work outside the home?" she replied softly.

He leaned hard on the ax, the blade next to the soil. "If I

let her attend public high school, she might end up like . . ." He stopped short of uttering Sadie's name.

Leah had scarcely felt like speaking up in defense of something she herself did not believe in, yet she'd dared to, knowing of Mary Ruth's torment over wanting something she could not have. Leah was stuck, it seemed, loving Mary Ruth and wanting to honor Dat and do the right thing.

He looked at her, eyes blazing. "I say if you're to be Mary Ruth's mouthpiece, then tell her this for *me*. Tell her she is no longer welcome in this house if she chooses to disobey her father!"

Oh no, Dat . . . no. This was the worst thing for Mary Ruth, because surely now she *would* leave; she was just that stubborn. Without Elias alive to keep her linked to the People and her Amish roots, she would most certainly fly away to the world.

❖

Leah tried to get Mamma to sit down and rest in her big bedroom. She had asked Hannah to play with Lydiann for a while, hoping to coax Mamma off her feet and into bed. Terribly distressed at the news of Mary Ruth packing her clothes, Mamma began to weep.

"Maybe she won't like high school," Leah suggested, doubting it herself.

"No . . . no . . . no," sobbed Mamma. " 'Tis wrong, ever so wrong, to push her out of the nest too soon like this."

Feeling awkward about hearing Mamma voice her disapproval of Dat's decision, Leah hovered near. Mamma was standing in defiance, looking out the bedroom window. "Best talk to Dat 'bout all this," whispered Leah.

"I'll talk all right!" Mamma turned and suddenly fell into Leah's arms. "Oh, what's to become of us? First my eldest daughter, now Mary Ruth."

"Preacher Yoder says all is not lost till it's truly too late. 'As long as there's breath there is hope,' he says, ya know."

"Life and hope, jah. I just don't want to see Mary Ruth sent away like this. We all love her so!" She began to cry again. "What'll dear Hannah do, bless her heart? They're close twins, for goodness' sake."

Leah felt like sobbing, too, but she needed to be stronger than poor Mamma. Wordlessly she helped her mother over to the bed to stretch out a bit, then closed the door and tiptoed down the stairs to the kitchen, where she would start supper soon. First, though, Leah must tend to sad Hannah, check on Lydiann . . . and pray fervently for God's grace and mercy to fill this too-empty house.

———◆———

Leah, Lydiann, and Aunt Lizzie piled into the second seat of the buggy the Saturday of the planned visit to Hickory Hollow. Mamma and Dat sat up front. Hannah, having volunteered her companionship, stayed home with Dawdi John, who was suffering a head cold and a sore throat. Leah was fairly sure the real reason Hannah had stayed behind was to steal away to the Nolts' for a good long visit with Mary Ruth; that way Dat wouldn't have to know about it and neither would Mamma, who was beginning to worry Leah and Lizzie both.

Lizzie had made a fuss about Mamma making the long trip today, but her pleas had fallen on deaf ears. "I don't need pamperin'," Mamma said in response to Lizzie's entreaty.

Besides that, Dat didn't look too kindly on Lizzie interfering with the set plans for this brisk, yet sunny afternoon. "I'll see to Ida. You see to yourself," he snapped, startling Leah.

All during the ride to Hickory Hollow, Dat sat stiff and aloof, holding the reins. Leah felt awful sorry for Mamma and wished she could be sitting next to her, patting her hand if need be. Dear, dear Mamma . . . two of her girls were gone from the house . . . and the Fold.

Of course, none of them knew for sure if Sadie had ever gained acceptance into an Ohio church community, so Leah guessed she ought not to jump to conclusions. Still, they all assumed Bishop Bontrager would have heard something if Sadie *was* a repentant member of a "high" church, one with a more relaxed discipline—in short, just plain more worldly.

Leah pondered this while taking in the sky and trees, now bare of leaf and stark as could be against the wispy clouds and fiercely blue sky, hinting of gloomy gray days, blowing snow, and icy winds. Soon heavy snows would put everything into slow motion once again.

She shivered suddenly, eager for Mamma's newborn babe, knowing full well the great joy an infant could offer a wounded soul. In the eyes of her heart, though, she could not imagine ever holding her own baby, hard as she tried. "Oh, that'll come, surely it will, once you and Smithy Gid are husband and wife," Aunt Lizzie had assured her the other day when she'd confided this.

Once I am a wife . . .

The words still seemed somewhat foreign to her, yet she knew her heart was ready to both give and receive love again. *"Once you're married, you'll forget you ever loved Jonas,"* one quilter had cheekily whispered in her ear during a break for coffee and sticky buns.

Leah didn't see how she'd ever quite forget the relationship she'd had with Jonas, maybe because he had been her girlhood love. But, in due time, Mamma had recently insisted, Leah's injury of the heart would mend "a hundred percent."

◆

When they neared Cattail Road, tired from traveling, Dat announced they were coming up on Hickory Hollow.

Leah liked the sound of the small place and wondered how it got its name. She knew what a hollow was—a holler the People called it—but just why was the nearly invisible dot on the map named Hickory? Was it because of the many hardwood trees growing nearby, most originating from the walnut family? She'd heard her father speak of a farmer there who made hickory rockers as a hobby. Dat had purchased several rocking chairs some years back from the older gentleman. Whatever the source of the name, Leah was eager to lay eyes on the well-forested landscape once again.

Once they arrived, Dat jumped out and hurried around the carriage to help Mamma down, seemingly more compassionate toward her than at the outset of the trip.

Now for some good fellowship, Leah thought, breathing a relieved sigh at having safely reached their destination, as well as at Dat's improved mood. They all could use a carefree afternoon, what with Mary Ruth gone to live with Englishers.

During the ride up, Aunt Lizzie had talked softly to Leah, who was glad to cradle sleeping Lydiann in her arms. "Noah and Becky will be mighty glad to see us," Lizzie had said. "'Specially Lydiann, I would think."

"Much too long since we've visited, ain't?"

Lizzie had nodded. "We ought not to be so distanced from relatives."

Immediately Cousins Peter and Fannie Mast came to mind. Leah shook herself, not so much physically as mentally. She dared not allow herself to think about the Mast family.

Now she leaned down and kissed the tip of Lydiann's tiny nose. Her little sister's eyes blinked open. "Lookee where we are now. You slept nearly all the way, dear one."

She continued to hold Lydiann close for a moment, till the wee girl awakened. Then she rose and got down out of the buggy herself, still carrying her sister.

"What a nice December day!" Lizzie commented as they followed Becky and Noah into their Dawdi Haus, filling up nearly all the places for sitting in the small front room.

Aunt Becky served hot spiced cider to each of them, except for Lydiann, who seemed glad to sit off away from the others at the small kitchen table, drinking a cup of chocolate milk. Leah pulled out a chair to be near Lydiann, noticing Lizzie and Mamma's sister-in-law, Becky, was moving slower, even limping on occasion. Uncle Noah, with his long graying beard, was, too.

Goodness, they look older than I thought they might. She wondered how long it would be before Dat and Mamma began to show their age and slow down. Uncle Noah was lots older than Lizzie, for sure, and a number of years ahead of Mamma, too. She observed Aunt Becky, who had seemed to be trying very hard not to stare at Mamma's swollen stomach.

She probably thinks Mamma shouldn't be out in public, thought Leah. After all, there were probably only three weeks left before they'd know if Abram's daughters would be welcoming a brother at long last. *At least two of us will be on hand to help Mamma with the new one.* Leah was thinking of Aunt Lizzie and herself; naturally Hannah and Lydiann would be nowhere near the birthing room. Just then she wondered if Dat would ban Mary Ruth from the house even on the joyous day of Mamma's delivery.

Mamma's voice drew Leah back to the moment. "A new baby will help keep my *Mann* and me young longer," she said right out. "Ain't so, Abram?"

Dat appeared sheepish now and said nothing.

Leah found his lack of response intriguing. "Well, now, that's the truth," she whispered playfully to Lydiann, reaching over to tickle her head as the toddler reached up and grabbed Leah's fingers with an unexpectedly strong grip.

"*Schweschder* . . . Lee—ah," Lydiann surprised her by saying.

"Jah, that's right. I *am* your sister." She laughed softly. Wouldn't Mamma enjoy hearing about Lydiann's sweet words? She would be sure to tell her on the ride home to Gobbler's Knob.

◆

After sitting and talking about the weather and whatnot, as well as asking about both Hannah and Mary Ruth, Aunt Becky brought out a small tray of crackers and several kinds of cheeses, along with sliced apples. "Help yourself," she said, tottering about the room while balancing the tray in one hand. Her wooden cane had made its appearance, but no one said a word about it.

Uncle Noah and Aunt Becky talked of their own friends and relatives, including one Ella Mae Zook. "The dear woman's known for her mint tea and mighty lovin' heart," Aunt Becky said. "She's even got herself a nickname."

"Oh? What's that?" asked Mamma.

"Some folk nowadays are callin' her the Wise Woman."

Uncle Noah grimaced and made a peculiar sound in the back of his throat. "What women don't go 'n' think up. . . ." Leah thought she heard him mutter.

But the real news from Hickory Hollow that day was about Sadie. "I hear Sadie's in the family way," Aunt Becky said, grunting as she sat down.

Mamma's face at once brightened and then instantly sagged. Dat right away turned and stared hard at the window. Leah didn't know if he was struggling with the mention of his firstborn's name or just what.

She kept waiting for someone, anyone at all, to make a reminder that there was to be no mention of Sadie's name in the midst of the Gobbler's Knob folk by Bishop Bontrager's decree—and Dat's own wishes. Of course, the Bann did not include Hickory Hollow.

"When did ya hear?" Mamma managed to say.

"Just yesterday," Aunt Becky replied.

Right then it seemed Mamma and Becky Brenneman were the only two in the room and communing on some cherished level.

"Who told ya?" Mamma asked, eyes wide.

"A cousin of a friend of Ella Mae's."

"Anything I can read for myself?" Mamma said, shocking Leah and evidently Aunt Lizzie, too, as Lizzie's hands flew to her throat.

Aunt Becky shook her head. "No. Sorry, Ida."

"Simple hearsay, then?"

"Either she's expecting a baby or she ain't," Aunt Becky replied, accompanied by a severe stare from Uncle Noah.

"No more!" Abram's head was bowed low, as if in prayer. Raising his face to them, he spoke again. "Best leave things be."

Glancing around the room at Dat and Mamma . . . and Aunt Lizzie, too, Leah saw pain mirrored on their faces. She felt the urge to speak up like Mary Ruth had been doing lately. Trembling, she had to will herself to remain silent and simply let the news of Sadie's first baby as a married woman sink into the hollows of her mind. Seeping slowly, surely into her splintered heart.

Chapter Sixteen

Ida went about her washday routine the Monday after the Hickory Hollow visit, washing and hanging out clothes with help from Leah and Hannah, who took turns tending to Lydiann throughout the morning hours. Ida refused to give in to the jagged pain that wracked her middle. Surely this was nothing more than the result of too much brooding over Mary Ruth moving out so awful sudden ... and the disquieting news of Sadie being with child—and lo, at the selfsame time as Ida again. *Same as when I was carrying Lydiann.* What was it about her firstborn and herself? Was it the tie that binds, as Lizzie so often referred to regarding mothers and daughters?

It wasn't wise to waste time wondering or worrying when she had plenty to accomplish, just as she did every day but Sunday. Her "vacation" was nigh upon her, and that would be all well and good once her baby arrived. She knew instinctively this was to be her last child, just as Lizzie seemed to always know when the weather was changing and rain or snow was headed their way. For her own sake, she must not dwell on either Sadie or Mary Ruth any longer, though it was mighty hard not to, especially when Mary Ruth showed up later that afternoon, long after the noon meal.

"I need to speak with you, Mamma," she said, her pretty face close to the screen door.

Ida hurried to the back door. *What'll Abram say if he catches her sneaking round here?* She didn't care so much to be finding out.

"'S'okay if I come in?" Mary Ruth was *rutsching* around, squirming to beat the band.

"Well, jah, all right," Ida said, not going all the way to the door, but motioning quickly to her.

They scampered like frightened cats upstairs to what was now Hannah's bedroom. "I *had* to see you," Mary Ruth said. "Even if it means I get a tongue-lashin' from Dat." Then she began to cry. "I want, more than anything, to share what's happened to me. I just never thought . . ."

"Now, now, dear girl," Ida said, cradling her. "I know your heart's taken over, that's all. We all struggle so at one time or 'nother."

"Then you *do* understand, Mamma? You don't hate me for what I must do?"

She shook her head. "Believe me, there is not a speck of anything but love in me for you and your sisters. Never doubt that, Mary Ruth."

"I hope Dat will allow me to visit sometimes, see the new baby, too. I'm not under the Bann, for pity's sake." Mary Ruth was sitting on the side of the bed where, till now, she'd always slept.

"That, you're not." Ida felt all in now, wondering whether or not to say what she wanted to. And then she did, surprising herself. "This should never have happened—you bein' sent away. Your father is of the old school, so to speak. And, well, s'posin' I am, too, 'cause I'm married to him. He's mighty determined not to let his opinions slip to the side—not 'bout higher education nor spending time with Mennonites, neither one."

They looked at each other, basking in the love only a mother and daughter can know. "So then, I'm bein' shunned by Dat alone?"

"Sad to say, but seems so. No reason for it, really . . . you aren't baptized yet."

Mary Ruth hung her head. "I can't put aside my hopes and dreams—and my newfound joy in the Lord Jesus." She began to share the arrangement she had with Dan and Dottie Nolt. "They want to help me with my studies; then next semester—beginning in January—I'll start school at Paradise High School."

"These plans of yours, they've been simmerin' inside ya for ever so long." Ida knew this was true. Oh, the light of adventure filled every part of her talkative girl.

"I'm ever so happy in one way . . . and awful sad in another."

"Jah, I 'spect so, but there's nothin' to be done 'bout it, now, is there?" she said, feeling the tightness in her stomach again.

"'Tis awful nice that I live within walkin' distance of you and Dat." Mary Ruth's pretty blue eyes glistened and filled with tears once more. "I can only hope and pray Dat will see the light of God's Word, that he'll understand I must follow the Lord's call. Honestly, Mamma, I've found such *life* at my

---

doubt be as troubling to Mary Ruth as it was to her. It was pointless to reveal too much, lest she discourage her daughter's boundless joy, profoundly registered on her lovely face.

Hannah didn't like the thought of winter setting in here before too long; the cold and bleak season had always reminded her of her own mortality. She found herself wondering what it had felt like for Elias to die so suddenly out on the road. Had he endured excruciating pain? Was that the thing that killed a person ... took a soul from this world to the next?

As for winter, the season was good only for missing the smell of air-dried clothes on the wash line, the sun beating down on her back as she tended the roadside stand, the sound of birds—the same songbirds Mamma loved. But the worst of it was Mary Ruth leaving home in the month of Christmas, of all sad things. And just as Mamma was close to her delivery date, leaving only Hannah and Leah to help with Lydiann and soon another baby sister or brother. Not much for tending to children, Hannah supposed she best get used to holding babies, what with Ezra Stoltzfus having dropped some strong hints about getting married sometime next year. Here lately, though, she didn't know for sure where he stood on the matter ... or where *she* did. He hadn't gone to the singing last night, hadn't let her know he wouldn't be there, either, and he hadn't contacted her to go riding with him next Saturday after dark. Most likely he was still taken up with mourning the loss of his brother. Understandably so.

Still, something in the back of her mind wondered her about Ezra. He might need a lot more time to get back on his feet. She would wait till he felt more sociable again. But that wasn't her biggest worry.

She was far more concerned over her twin's peculiar comments about their visit to the meetinghouse last week. Seemed mighty odd to hear Mary Ruth go on so about the Scripture readings. In the deep of Hannah's heart, she feared she and her sister might lose the closeness they'd always had growing up. Mary Ruth's passionate interest in "salvation through grace," as she put it, was the worst of it.

Curling her toes, she flinched at the thought. She ought not to have gone, for had she refused, Mary Ruth might never have gone herself. But she had succumbed to her twin's persuasion—Mary Ruth ever so good at pleading, making things seem urgent and all. Hannah wished she'd stood her ground and stayed home. Of course, riding along to Quarryville meant she was on hand to assist Mary Ruth in case there was trouble with the carriage or the horse. Other than that, she had not enjoyed her experience at the strange gathering and had even felt guilty for being there. Her first, and hopefully last, breach of the Ordnung. Yet according to Mary Ruth, Dat had not put his foot down about their going. He'd even given a halfhearted blessing, though not knowing precisely where they were headed.

Quickly she set the table while a kettle of oyster stew simmered on the cook stove. She couldn't help but wonder how much longer Mamma would insist on leaving an empty spot where Sadie had always sat at the table, as if for someone deceased. Mary Ruth's place was empty, too, and not to be filled by another family member. The family had shrunk down to near nothing—the pain of it especially evident in Mamma's eyes at mealtime. Wouldn't be long and Leah's place would also be vacant, once she married Smithy Gid, which she surely would do. Made no sense to be a maidel if a nice boy like Gideon Peachey was asking.

When Mary Ruth returned to her new home away from home, she felt nearly wrung out with the effort she'd put forth to steal in and out of the Ebersol Cottage. She could imagine the fury in Dat if ever she was caught visiting Mamma or her sisters—Aunt Lizzie, too.

For now she could put that worry behind her. She found Dottie in the kitchen peeling yellow delicious apples for drying. Not eager to expend additional energy telling of her visit with Mamma, she asked if Carl was awake from his nap.

"If he isn't, he oughta be," Dottie said, her hair tied back in a ponytail that made her look younger than her years. "Why don't you go and wake him, if you'd like."

Mary Ruth agreed. "I'll check and see if he's stirring. If he's awake, I'll keep him company for a bit."

Dottie nodded her consent. "He'll be glad to see you. I think he's becoming very attached."

He'll mistakenly think I'm his big sister before too long, she thought, wondering if that was such a good thing, being that she didn't know how long she would be living here.

In Carl's nursery, she tiptoed to the pint-sized bed and was delighted to see the beautiful boy lying very still but smiling up at her with shining eyes. "Well, hullo, sweetie," she said, standing over him. "Do you want to play with Aunt Mary

Ruth?" She smiled at the name she'd just assigned to herself.

"Ma-ry," he said, sitting up.

"That's right." She helped him escape from under the tucked-in sheet and blanket.

Together, they found the box of blocks and began to pile them up in a tower, only for Carl to take absolute glee in knocking them down with a swift sweep of his small hand.

Later she took him downstairs to Dottie, and while Carl sat in his high chair and fed himself pieces of orange and banana, Dottie began to tell of the "miracle that occurred when Dr. Henry Schwartz called with news of a baby boy."

Mary Ruth listened with eagerness, thankful for the obvious hand of the sovereign Lord on the Nolts' home, especially because they had longed for a child for a good long time before Dr. Schwartz's phone call had come. "God knows our hearts' cry—our deepest desires" was all Mary Ruth was able to express for the lump in her throat.

◆

Intuitively Gid recognized there was something downright gritty about early December that made him contemplate the future and prospects for having a family of his own. Fields had already turned brown and the mouth-watering apples had been picked—a few rotten ones languished on the ground, and red fox, scavengers at twilight, came searching them out, devouring them in quick *chomps*. Farmers were twiddling their thumbs following the corn harvest, looking ahead to the first farm sale of the season and finding excuses to gather in the barnyard, smoking pipe tobacco and chewing the fat, watching teenage boys play cornerball while waiting to bid on a piece of farm equipment. Such happenings turned Gid's thoughts to hearth and home, helped along by the scent of cinnamon pervading the kitchen as spicy pumpkin pies appeared supper after supper on the family table.

Perhaps it was the nearness of Christmas that got him thinking, as well. Complete with the annual program at the one-room school, as well as the feast day, the Lord's birthday was the most celebrated of all the holidays among the People, no doubt because it centered around kith and kin. Second Christmas, observed January 6—known as Epiphany by some—was also a time for families to gather and eat and play games indoors and out. Seemed to him every young man *his* age had already married and was expecting a baby come next summer. Even Adah had settled down and married Leah's cousin Sam in the past few weeks. Dorcas, his younger sister, would follow in Adah's footsteps in another year or so, most likely.

As it was, Gid would have to go through another long and cold winter without a mate to warm him, since the wedding season was all but past. If Leah would have him, they would wait till next autumn to marry.

These were a few of the reasons he felt urged to ask Leah to be his wife while they rode together in his open carriage on a courting Saturday night. A wistful winter night of nights, chilly enough for a woolen lap robe and his protective arm around his dear girl.

What with all Smithy Gid's talk of plans to help his uncle butcher hogs next week, Leah hardly felt much in a romantic mood, yet she listened intently as he talked of sharpening knives and scouring the enormous iron kettle.

"There'll be plenty of youngsters there," he told her, "takin' turns working the sausage grinder, ya know."

She knew all right from her own childhood days. Several times Dat had allowed both her and Sadie to miss school for a butchering day, saying the event was "mighty educational," so she'd had ample experience in just what butchering a hog entailed. Everything from heating the water to scalding in the black kettle situated in the washhouse, to hanging the carcasses up and, later on, squaring the middlings and trimming the hams and shoulders. Sadie had always said the stench was awful, and she didn't see why she had to watch when she much preferred to stay home with Mamma and cook or clean or sew.

For Leah, the whole process was intriguing; she especially liked watching the men hoist up the large hams and shoulders, hanging them from the smokehouse crossbeams till they were completely cured and flavorful. Sometimes she'd chase after the younger girls, who collected the silken pigs' ears, and she giggled as the little boys took the tails for souvenirs of the day, pretending to fasten them to one Dawdi or another. Naturally for the women there was the fun of visiting and planning the next work frolic, while men talked of divvying up the meat, daydreaming, no doubt, about the tender sausages, tasty fried bacon, and home-cured baked-ham dinners their wives were sure to prepare.

Sadie said the best part was knowing the rendered lard

would make for yummy doughnuts. Thinking of that, just now, helped put Leah in a sweeter mood as Gid slowed the horse's gait.

"I've been thinkin' an awful lot." His tone was gentle as could be. "What would ya say 'bout becomin' my wife . . . come next year?"

She'd honestly wondered if Gid might ask her tonight, but she hadn't expected the important question to come on the heels of the hog-butchering talk. "We *have* been seein' a lot of each other lately," she said.

He paused before continuing. "If you agree, we could marry in late October next year. Be one of the first couples to marry during the wedding season."

She was glad to be snug and warm under the lap robe, her hands hidden from Gid's touch. That way his words and his eyes did the talking, and his fingers couldn't cloud her thinking, putting pressure on her to say jah.

"Would it be all right if we pray privately 'bout this? Ask almighty God to bless our union?"

He nodded, seemingly taken back a bit by the unexpected reply. "No need to hurry up with your answer," he was kind enough to say—kind as he always had been for as long as she'd known him.

It wasn't that she thought she needed time to consider Gid as her husband-to-be, her betrothed. She honestly couldn't stop thinking about recent talks with Mamma, who seemed to want to speak to the Lord about most everything. *So why not pray about her response to a possible mate?*

She assumed it best if she not say what was going through her mind. Clearly Gid was eager to move on now, discuss something else. She hoped he wasn't miffed. It was just that most couples who'd spent time courting this long would probably go walking in the woods somewhere, hand in hand, watch the moon from a high vantage point, then talk of their wedding day. She had no idea what she and Gid would talk about for the rest of the evening, now that she hadn't answered with a quick reply to his heartfelt question.

Settling back, she breathed in the fresh and crisp night air, glad Gid had simply begun to play his harmonica, sweet and low, surprising her with his unruffled repose. One tune after another, he played, seeming to her as a kind of loving serenade to a nervous sweetheart.

As he played, she thought back to all the years of his unwarranted faithfulness to her, years of uncertainty. Yet he'd responded with sheer loyalty, patiently waiting for her, and now he was asking her to be his wife, the mother of his children, making it possible for her to do that thing she was called to be and do. What Amish girl would refuse such a true and sincere gesture? Gid loved her immeasurably; she knew that beyond doubt.

A stir of affection for him welled up in her. When he stopped playing his cheerful tune, he clicked his cheek to send a signal to the horse to speed to a trot, and she brought her hand out into the cold air and touched his arm. "Gid, I don't need more time to think on your question."

He waited without speaking, eyes fixed on her.

"I would be ever so glad to be your wife." At that very moment she truly cherished her own words.

Chapter Seventeen

If any former blemishes had been evident on the rolling front yard and surrounding landscape of her father's house prior to the thick blanket of snow, the present winter scene was so breathtakingly perfect that Leah found herself staring at the Ebersol Cottage as she made the turn into the lane leading to the barnyard and back door.

She had stolen away in the predawn hour of Christmas Eve day to Grasshopper Level, choosing the faster of Dat's two driving horses. At the Masts' orchard house, she dropped off a basket of goodies and fruit for little Jeremiah and the twins. Once there she got out of the carriage and made her way through the ice and snow to the back stoop, depositing the bright basket with its red ribbon on the top step.

Only Aunt Lizzie was aware of her "splendid idea," as she'd put it, to spread cheer to relatives who'd shunned them for much too long. Not even Mamma knew of the furtive trip, and Leah hoped to keep it that way. Together, she and Lizzie had made a big batch of peanut-butter balls dipped in melted chocolate, several dozen sand tarts, candied dates, and crystal stick candy at Lizzie's house yesterday. They'd had a laughing good time doing so. The best part of all was there were still plenty of sweets to go around, even having shared a considerable portion with Cousin Peter and Fannie's family.

Dat would more than likely devour a half dozen or more himself before the weekend was over. Unhitching the horse and buggy in the barnyard, she was glad to bring such happiness to his heart with the surprise. This, along with the fact she'd purposely let slip her intention to marry his choice of a mate, come next year.

Their neighbors down the road, including the Schwartzes and Nolts, had already taken axes to the dense woods and found attractive trees to chop down and set in a prominent place in their houses. Tonight, following Christmas Eve supper, most English families would carefully decorate fir or spruce with strung popcorn, colorful glass balls, bubbling lights, and tinsel strands.

The Ordnung did not allow for a tree to become an idol in the way of the Englishers. Instead, the People would happily celebrate the birthday of the Son of God tomorrow by attending Preaching service and sharing a common meal. Since Christmas fell on Sunday this year, much visiting would go on throughout the week. Folk would look into the faces of dear family members and friends, enjoying their precious nearness while sharing feasts at noon on Christmas Eve Saturday and sitting around the wood stove afterward to tell stories and recite poetry, giving and partaking of homemade candy, cookies, and other sweets. Dat would also read aloud certain passages from the Good Book to all who gathered there. Others would wait till Monday to celebrate, being Sunday was church.

Leah *had* seen the Nolts' tree twinkling from their front windows in the two-story clapboard house where Mary Ruth now lived and worked. They must have been eager to put it up and decorate before Christmas Eve this year, maybe because Mary Ruth was living there, and, too, because young Carl would enjoy all the merriment.

As for the Schwartz family, Leah had observed the enormous tree the doctor and his two sons dragged from the forest across the street just yesterday, when she dusted the furniture and washed the floors for Lorraine. She was certainly glad not to have been formally introduced to the younger Schwartz boy, Derry, whom Sadie had said such horrid things about— though Leah might have *had* to meet him if she'd stayed much longer at the Schwartz abode. Fact was, Leah had purposely finished up her duties in a jiffy, having clearly recognized Derry as she watched the threesome tugging on the nine-foot tree from the dining-room window, hoping against hope to avoid either shaking his hand or looking him in the eye.

Miraculously she had. She'd called rather softly, "Happy Christmas," over her shoulder to Lorraine, not wanting to draw a smidgen of attention to herself, then hurried out the door. Too nervous to look back, she found herself rushing down Georgetown Road, heart in her throat. She was most afraid she might not be able to temper what things came flying out of her mouth if she encountered Sadie's former beau.

Thank goodness she's nowhere near Gobbler's Knob, Leah thought, awful anxious for Dat's farmhouse to come into view.

But now, as she slipped into Mamma's toasty-warm

kitchen, she spotted the pretty presents wrapped and waiting on the sideboard for the family to gather on the day after Christmas, when they planned to celebrate with the Peacheys. After the Monday meal, following Aunt Lizzie's desserts of nut loaf, apple pie, and hot-water sponge cake, they would exchange simple gifts, fewer than any other year before. Mary Ruth's absence would add to the pain of Sadie being gone yet another blessed Christmas. But Mamma, great with child, was the next best blessing of all. Leah could scarcely wait to hold the newborn babe, coming so close to the Lord's own birthday.

Henry had been soundly stunned to see Derek arrive home the day before Christmas Eve, in time to select a tree. The boy had nearly frightened Lorraine to death as he stomped his army boots up the snowy front walk and burst into the house unannounced, wearing a pressed uniform and tossing his hat onto the coat-tree in the foyer as if he owned the place.

For months, Henry had written letters requesting, nearly pleading, for Derek to return home for the holidays. *Your presence would cheer your mother greatly*, he had penned in his most recent note. It appeared his persuasive efforts had paid off famously; their wayward son was seated at his mother's Christmas table of lace and fine china as Henry said a traditional grace, offering thanks for the bounty with which they had been blessed this year.

When Henry raised his head, he noticed Derek had neither closed his eyes nor bowed his head, and his hand held the fork, poised to dig in.

Has he learned nothing from his time in the military? Henry wondered. For a moment he wished he might have saved his time, ink, and stationery. But as the day wore on, things seemed to lighten up and Henry had a change of heart *and* mind, especially as he observed Lorraine smiling and even laughing from time to time, less in her hostess mode than usual and more relaxed overall. In fact, Henry observed, the day almost seemed as pleasant as many Christmases before it—this as they sat together exchanging gifts in the shadow of the fine Christmas tree ablaze with lights. From the radio, Bing Crosby crooned "Here Comes Santa Claus," backed up by the Andrews Sisters.

After gifts were opened and bows and wrapping paper lay scattered on the floor, Lorraine spoke softly, saying she wished to share a short reading. "From the New Testament . . . Luke's account of the birth of my Lord and Savior."

Henry happened to catch Derek's dismayed look. The boy stood abruptly and, without excusing himself, left the room. Heavy footsteps were heard echoing from the hall, and when the back door slammed, Lorraine jumped.

Robert pulled out a pocket Testament from his sports coat. "Here, Mother," he said. "Don't worry over Derek . . . I have an idea the Lord is at work where his heart's concerned."

More ill at ease than he had been in some years, Henry braced himself for the Scripture verses Lorraine appeared determined to share.

Until this moment, Mary Ruth wouldn't have admitted to missing her parents and sisters dreadfully during the past weeks, but she felt an overwhelming sadness as she helped redd up the kitchen for Dottie. She felt sluggish this Christmas Day, slow to gather up scraps of wrapping paper and odds and ends of boxes from the front room. "I'd be happy to take the trash out," she called to Dottie, who was putting Carl down for his afternoon nap.

Meanwhile, Dan was out back gathering up dry cut wood from the timber box to add to the embers in the front room fireplace as Mary Ruth headed for the front door. Scarcely had she tossed the rubbish and closed the top on the trash receptacle than she heard a pounding of feet on the road. Looking up, she noticed a dark-headed young man running in a military uniform of some sort, though she couldn't be sure, as she'd never before seen a soldier.

She wouldn't have stood there watching, but the young man's angry movements caught her attention—the fierce way he swung his arms as he ran, as if ready for a fighting match.

Mary Ruth felt so curious beholding this peculiar sight, she didn't catch the sneeze that crept up on her, calling attention to *her*, and for that she was perturbed.

Immediately the stranger halted in his tracks, his dark, dark eyes inching together as he frowned hard. When he spoke, she instinctively stepped back. "Hey . . . I know you, don't I?" The frown faded and a smile took its place. "Aren't you Sadie's little sister?"

At once she was no longer startled, because she recognized him as the boy who'd stopped by the vegetable and fruit stand years back; this same fancy fellow with the handsome features had handed her a letter for Sadie on that day. Just why was he carrying on like a madman out there on the road, and on Christmas Day yet?

"Jah, I'm Mary Ruth." She took a step forward to show her confidence. "And who are you?"

He blinked his eyes, holding her gaze. "An old friend of Sadie's."

She shook her head. "If you say your name, I might just recognize it."

"Name's not important. Truth is, I'm home for the holidays—a wounded soldier." Here he leaned down and began to roll up his left pant leg. "Let me show you—"

"No, no, I believe you." She noticed his short hair cut on the side above his ears, beneath his uniform-style hat, so what he'd said was probably true. "Sorry you got yourself hurt."

"Maybe you could help me . . . so I won't have to go all the way down the road to visit Sadie, after all." He pushed his trouser leg back down where it belonged and leaned hard on the other good leg, his right hand on his hip now.

"Just what did you have in mind?" She stood her ground, no longer frightened by him, though she still wondered what business he had with Sadie.

"I've been thinking . . . wondering how she's doing. That's all. Is she well?"

His question sounded strange. *How would I know?* "My sister's not ill, far as I know." The words popped right off her tongue. Besides, if Sadie were still living here in Gobbler's Knob, what would she want with a fancy Englisher . . . and on Christmas?

"Well, I haven't seen her in a while. Thought I might

catch her outdoors milking cows, maybe . . . present myself to her as a sort of surprise."

She sighed. "Oh, well, if it's my sister you're after, you best be savin' your steps, 'cause she's married out in Ohio."

He ran his hand straight down the middle of his hat, smiling at her in a way that suddenly made her feel uncomfortable. "Isn't that a pity. She was the prettiest Amish girl I ever laid eyes on." Then, stepping back, he added, "But now that I'm here talking to you, I think you've got my Sadie beat all to pieces."

My Sadie . . .

Something sprang up in her that instant, and she felt she best return to the house. "I oughta be goin' now." She turned to leave.

But he followed on her heels. "Wait! No need to be afraid. Don't you know who I am, Mary Ruth?"

She stopped walking and turned around and looked him over. Now that she was beginning to put two and two together, this was probably the boy who'd put her big sister in the family way—the young father of Sadie's dead baby.

He limped toward her a bit. "You mean to say she never told you about me?"

Her mind leaped to a final conclusion. "So . . . you must be. . . ?"

"That's right. I'm the old man, and I mean to lay eyes on my son or daughter." He breathed in and rubbed his knuckles against his chest, displaying a sickening conceit. "Boy or girl, which is it?"

Silently she prayed; she felt she needed God's help lest this man standing before her begin to thrash his arms yet again, directing his anger toward her. And, come to think of it, his limping was downright deceitful, because she had seen him *running* to beat the band before she'd ever let out her sneeze. "I take it . . . you must not know what happened. Oh, it's awful sad, really."

"Well . . . *what?*"

Filling her lungs with air, she told him. "Sadie's baby died 'fore it ever had a chance to live."

"Stillborn, you say?" To this he appeared rather stunned, but gradually his surprise turned to obvious relief. Without so much as a good-bye, he walked away, leaving Mary Ruth standing there.

Ach, what a wretched soul! How on earth did Sadie ever fall in love with such a boy? she wondered. She could not comprehend in the slightest. Encountering him as she had, she hoped and prayed the Lord had heard her sister's cries of repentance. Surely by now dear Sadie had called out to God for help and forgiveness. *Dear Lord Jesus, please be near and dear to my Ohio sister this day,* Mary Ruth prayed.

Chapter Eighteen

The day following Christmas, Leah insisted on Mamma resting after the big noon meal. Even though their close neighbors, the Peacheys, along with Adah and husband Sam, had come to share the feast, Mamma excused herself at Leah's urging and went to lie down.

Leah followed her to the upstairs bedroom, watching as she sat on the bed. "Here, let me help you," Leah said, getting a blanket out of the chest at the foot of the bed. "Are ya in need of more warmth?"

"No, no . . . I'm just fine now, denki." Mamma leaned back and sighed, closing her eyes. "Will ya see to our guests while I nap?"

Leah nodded. "Of course. You have nothin' to worry 'bout." She leaned down and kissed Mamma's cheek, then quietly slipped out the door.

Downstairs, she found Miriam and Aunt Lizzie playing a game of checkers while Dat, Smithy, and Sam sat around the wood stove, rocking slowly and talking low. Adah was playing peekaboo with Lydiann, and Hannah and Dorcas were visiting quietly in the corner of the kitchen.

Meanwhile, Gid sat on the floor near the wood stove, reading *The Budget*, pausing to chuckle every so often at one humorous story or another. "Listen to this." He held up the paper, and Dat and Gid's father both leaned in to hear better. "Some folk over in New Holland had a letter the other day sayin' they were gonna be getting a buggy full of company for supper, but it says right here they don't have any idea who it'll be." Gid looked up, a grin on his face. "So they're lookin' forward to seein' just who's coming . . . and wonderin' if their guess is correct."

"That *is* funny," Dat agreed.

Smithy Peachey nodded, rocking harder now. "Seems to me whoever wrote oughta have had the courtesy to say who they was!"

"You'd think so, ain't?" Dat glanced at Leah, a quick frown on his brow. He motioned for her to come over, and Leah was glad to tell him Mamma was resting.

"She's all right now. Don't worry."

She went and sat on the floor on a round braided rug next to Gid as he read silently from the Sugarcreek, Ohio, newspaper. After a time he whispered, "Here, Leah, read this." He pointed to a report from Lititz.

I went downtown and got myself a nice haircut last Tuesday, the Amish scribe had written. *That afternoon Barbara Zimmerman and myself answered jah to several questions asked us by our old bishop. Then, quick as a wink, he changed Barbara's name from Zimmerman to Wert. I'm awful glad she said yes, and she's ever so glad I got me a haircut!*

Leah couldn't help but think next year around this time

her name would be Leah Peachey. When she glanced at Gid, he smiled and winked at her. Leah's cheeks flushed and her heart did a little flip-flop, and she wondered if he might give her his Christmas gift outside. Gid was pretty good at thinking of reasons to take her outdoors today. Still, Dat was the only one who knew anything of their engagement, except maybe the smithy and Adah. Neither Mamma nor Hannah suspected anything, she didn't think, though she could be wrong.

Aunt Lizzie looked her way and Leah ducked her head, hiding behind *The Budget,* hoping Lizzie wouldn't see what was probably written all over her face. Truth was, Leah was awfully fond of Gid and was enjoying herself this sweet Christmastide.

"Best be headin' out for milkin'," Gid said just loud enough for the two fathers' benefit.

That was Leah's cue to get up and go along with him. After all, there was no need for Dat to leave his best friend and nephew, nor the warmth of Mamma's kitchen, anytime soon. This, then, was her gift to her father . . . so Gid could present *his* to her.

After Mamma's long nap and once Leah and Gid had finished the milking, they all sat down again for a light supper of leftovers. Mamma kept her hand on the meat platter, ready to dish up well before anyone might request seconds. That was Mamma, Leah thought, always eager to serve her family and others.

The meal over, Aunt Lizzie, Hannah, and Dorcas cleared off the table while Mamma and Miriam settled into chairs near the wood stove and Sam and Adah bundled up and went out for a walk, like newlyweds so often do.

Dat and Smithy headed outside to get the toboggans out of the barn and ready for some snow fun. Gid and his sister Dorcas and Leah and Hannah carried the sleds back behind the barn, to the banked bridge connecting the lower level to the upper. Gid and Dorcas were the first to go flying down the slope amidst squeals of delight from the girls.

With Leah at the helm, Leah and Hannah piled on the second toboggan, and they had themselves a turn. In nothing flat, Gid got the idea to race the sleds down the hill. They did that three times, with Gid and his sister winning each run.

"Ach, it ain't fair. You've got more weight with Gid on." Leah pointed out the reason.

"Jah, that's why," Dorcas said, smiling at Leah.

"Try it with Gid alone," Hannah suggested, "and the three of us girls."

"If all of us can even fit on one," Leah said, laughing.

In the end, the girls beat Gid soundly. And when a stiff wind blew up out of the north, Dorcas and Hannah said they were cold and headed for the house, leaving Gid and Leah alone once again.

"I wanted to tell you, Leah . . . you've made this the best Christmas for me." He leaned down and kissed her cheek.

She reached up and hugged his neck, but he didn't let her go quickly; he held her close, his rough cheek against her cold face. "Next year we'll be husband and wife," he said. "Lord willin'."

"A blessed Christmas to you, Gid," she replied, happy to be nestled in his strong arms, grateful for his present—a pretty wall hanging of a special calendar that could be used over and over, the days marked in with a calligraphy pen. She could hardly wait to start filling it in.

"Once we're published at the Preaching service next year, I'll show you the pine chest I plan to make for you—an engagement gift soon to come."

She was overjoyed. What a happy day of days!

Gentle snowflakes fell as Leah took Hannah along to deliver the birthday quilt to Elias's mother after supper. She had been hoping for this chance to take the one-horse sleigh down the snow-packed road, to get all bundled up again in earmuffs and mittens, hot bricks at her feet.

Hannah was more talkative tonight than usual, perhaps because she missed Mary Ruth something fierce.

They stopped in at the Stoltzfus family's, staying longer than planned because the deacon's wife wanted to warm them up with hot chocolate topped with whipped cream, also offering a plateful of oatmeal-raisin cookies for them to nibble during the ride home. "Share the rest with your whole family," she insisted.

There are fewer of us Ebersols all the time, Leah thought while standing with her back to the wood stove, sipping cocoa. She glanced at Hannah, noting her sister seemed rather aloof, her face too pale. Soon enough Leah understood as she spotted Ezra . . . his back to them at the kitchen table.

He never even turned round when we came in, she thought, suspecting something was terribly wrong between him and Hannah. But she said nothing, waiting for Hannah to mention his peculiar behavior later on the ride home—if at all.

"I have an idea," Leah said now, hurrying the horse just a bit. "Let's stop by and wish Mary Ruth a happy Christmas. What would ya say to that?"

"Oh, sister, could we?" Hannah's eyes glistened in the moonlight.

"We can . . . and we will!"

She wanted Hannah to end the day happily, and seeing Mary Ruth was sure to put a smile on her face. Besides, Leah was lonesome for Mary Ruth . . . as was Mamma—possibly the reason their mother had looked so gray around the eyes and all washed out earlier. If only Dat had been more patient, even merciful toward Mary Ruth, Christmas could have been far less somber this year. Mamma would've had her spirits up, for sure and for certain.

With this in mind, Leah strained to see the bend in the road and the corner lot where the Nolts lived . . . where Mary Ruth now resided, a boarder to Englishers, of all things.

Hannah choked back sad tears, downright grateful to be with Leah tonight, though the evening was freezing to the bones. She'd actually thought she might become ill back there in Ezra's mamma's kitchen.

Ezra. What on earth had made him change so? His brother's death—could it be? Was he so angry at God he was taking his rage out on her?

She had no idea what to think. Ezra was downright

185

standoffish and hadn't been showing his face at recent singings. Was he staying away to avoid seeing her? She hoped not. For her, it was hardly worth going to the barn singings anymore—a waste of time to ask Lizzie to take her and drop her off. There was only one reason to go at all: in hopes of being asked to ride home with Ezra in his courting buggy.

Deliberately Hannah turned her attention to seeing Mary Ruth again, though she also felt a bit distanced herself when it came to her twin. It wondered her, as she and Leah rode in the sleigh, what Leah might make—if she knew—of the things spoken about at the Quarryville church that had added fuel to the fire for Mary Ruth. Her recent switch to the Mennonites, along with her renewed determination to get an English education, had set things off the beam between Dat and her twin.

Sighing, Hannah felt her breath literally freeze in midair. To think their father would send Mary Ruth away because of her stubbornness—and during rumschpringe, no less, when Amish parents typically let their youth run free, if not wild. It made not a bit of sense. *Has to be more than that,* thought Hannah. *Dat's ire is up about Mary Ruth going to high school!*

She settled against the buggy seat, reflecting on this day— the love and the laughter of the earlier time with family and the Peacheys—wishing she had brought along the embroidered pillowcases she'd sewn for Mary Ruth. She felt strangely empty, like a tall glass half full.

The lights from a Christmas tree brightened the window at the Nolts' house as the horse pulled the sleigh into their driveway. "Ach, is it such a gut idea to stop so late like this?" she asked Leah.

"Mary Ruth's bound to be homesick tonight," Leah answered. "C'mon, a visit will do us all good." She paused. "But we best not tell 'bout the fun we had tobogganing with Peacheys, jah?"

Hannah nodded. She struggled with guilt at having spoken out so boldly to Mary Ruth after going with her to Quarryville that single night. "I wouldn't think of adding more sadness to her," she mumbled as they picked their way over the snow and ice to the back door. *Not one little bit.*

Hannah embraced Mary Ruth in the entryway of the Nolts' fine house. "Oh, how I miss you, sister!" she whispered.

"I miss *you*," Mary Ruth said, clinging to her.

Leah wrapped her arms around both twins, and the three of them stood hugging and weeping.

After a time Mary Ruth showed them into the front room, where the tree stood alight with shimmering tinsel strands and tall bubbling lights. They spoke softly to each other, Mary Ruth doing most of the talking, as usual. "How's Mamma feeling?" she asked.

"She had to rest awhile following the noon meal," Leah offered, "but she was back up again before supper and had herself a right nice time." Then Leah began to share the news of Naomi and Luke Bontrager's baby boy, born six days ago.

Mary Ruth asked, "I wonder who could get word about Naomi's first baby to our sister?" Leah knew she meant Sadie but had politely refrained from mentioning the forbidden

187

name. After some discussion, none of them felt the urgency to force the issue.

There was an awkward pause, and then Hannah spoke up, "The smithy's whole family came to our house today." She seemed eager to change the subject. "Adah and Sam sure are an awful cute couple."

Leah nodded, eyes fixed on the sparkling tree while Mary Ruth sat with her hands folded against the black of her mourning dress and apron.

Hannah recalled Adah and Sam's wedding, where Leah and Dorcas had stood up as bridesmaids, along with Adah's same-age cousin, Rachel Peachey. What a joyful day it had been. Leah herself had been absolutely radiant—almost like a bride.

Suddenly Hannah felt sorry all over again for Mary Ruth, having lost her beau to death. *I shouldn't have mentioned Adah and Sam*, she thought, chagrined.

Quickly Hannah said, "If I'd known we were goin' to stop by here, I would've brought the present I made for you. Aw, that's too bad."

Leah shook her head, her hazel eyes shimmering with tears. "The idea to surprise you popped in my head on our way back from taking the birthday quilt to Deacon Stoltzfus's wife."

"Oh jah . . . and how nice of you," Mary Ruth said, filling in as both Hannah and Leah brushed tears away. "S'pose Mrs. Stoltzfus was awful glad to have it."

"She was," Leah spoke up. "I hope it brought some cheer to the house, 'cause it was awful hard seeing them . . . all of them lookin' so forlorn."

"How did Ezra seem to you?" asked Mary Ruth.

The reference to his name sliced through Hannah's heart. "He ain't himself a'tall," she managed to say.

"Well, and no wonder," Mary Ruth said softly. "I ran into his older brother Leroy the other day at Central Market in downtown Lancaster. He told me how worried he was . . . that Ezra's not so sure anymore 'bout staying Amish. Feels the Lord God took away his best brother."

They were silent for a time and then Leah said softly, "We'll pray Ezra changes his mind and doesn't get himself shunned."

Hannah stiffened at her sister's words but said nothing.

"He'll need time to grieve, of course." Mary Ruth reached for Hannah's hand. "I say you're right, Leah. We'll pray."

Standing up, Hannah went to the Christmas tree and stood before it, hoping not to hear further talk of her beau. Her eyes were dazzled by the brightness and vivid colors. "How can ya think of stayin' on here, sister?" she asked finally. "Livin' with Englishers 'n' all? Can't ya make things right with Dat and come on home?" Tonight would be the perfect timing for such a thing, she thought. "It's so near to Christmas, after all."

She was surprised to find Mary Ruth at her side just that quick. "Jah, but it's not in my heart to leave behind my new-found faith. It's the Lord's birthday we celebrate."

"You don't need to tell *us*." Leah joined them beside the tree.

"No, I 's'pose not. It's just that . . . I've opened my heart to the Lord Jesus and His ways. I feel brand-new inside, truly I do."

Leah was nodding her head, as if to say she agreed.

Somewhat startled, Hannah stared at the tree. "Seems to me you've embraced the beliefs of Englishers. You're goin' backward 'stead of forward in the faith of our Anabaptist fore-fathers."

"You're upset because I found mercy and grace at a Mennonite church, ain't so?" Mary Ruth asked. "And 'cause I'm living here with fancy folk, too. Isn't that your biggest worry, really?"

Hannah tried her best to share the things that troubled her deeply—possibly living forever apart from Mary Ruth—but her twin was closed up to the Old Ways, it surely seemed. Mary Ruth insisted she'd found a "precious *new* thing," and nothing Hannah could say made a bit of difference.

She and Leah trudged through the snow to the sleigh and horse. Hannah felt awful glum as they rode into the crisp and icy night, back to the Ebersol Cottage. Truth be told, she almost wished they'd gone straight home after the Stoltzfus visit.

Chapter Nineteen

"Leah, come inside quick!" Aunt Lizzie called to her from the doorway.

Leah and Hannah hurried into the kitchen. "What is it?" Leah asked, fear gripping her. She and Hannah followed Lizzie upstairs.

"Is Mamma all right?" Hannah asked softly.

Leah tiptoed into her parents' bedroom, shocked to see Mamma thrashing about, crying out with her wrenching pains.

"This is like nothing she's ever experienced before," Lizzie told them in hushed tones, eyes wide with concern. "She's never uttered a single cry in childbirth . . . never!"

Dat sat off to the side of the room as was customary, though Leah noticed the agitation written on his face as he kept the newspaper raised high to shield his view.

Lizzie asked Hannah, who was still standing in the hall, to wait downstairs. "And, Leah, won't you go 'n' boil some water?"

"Jah," said Leah, her heart in her throat.

"Please close the door behind you," Lizzie said over her shoulder.

Mamma's in trouble! Leah rushed downstairs to put a kettle of water on the wood stove. Swiftly she headed back upstairs to stand at Mamma's bedside. Her heart broke as she watched Mamma struggle so. She wanted to do something to help—take Mamma's pulse, perhaps, while Dat counted the seconds steadily. *Jah, this one thing I can do!*

Tenderly she held her mother's weak arm, feeling the pulse . . . much too slow. Mamma's heartbeat was fading in strength even as Leah pressed her fingers against the white wrist.

"Hannah must ride immediately to get the midwife," Leah said, reliving the night Sadie had travailed with the birth of her dead son.

"No . . . no, it should be the *Hexedokder,*" said Dat, still hiding behind his paper. "We daresn't take any chances."

Mamma tried to lift her head. "No, Abram, not . . ." Her voice trailed off.

"Ida does *not* want the powwow doctor settin' foot in this house," Lizzie insisted, clearly speaking on behalf of Mamma. "Better to call for Anna Mae Yoder, the midwife. She'll know what to do."

"Well, whoever Hannah gets, tell her to make it snappy!" demanded Dat, lowering his newspaper momentarily.

Reluctant to leave Mamma's side, Leah turned and fled the room yet again.

"What's happened . . . to my prayer . . . veiling?" Ida

asked, reaching her right hand up and finding her head bare as she lay in her bed. She felt utterly dismayed at this discovery, her long hair having come loose from its bun. Such prolonged labor . . . never ending it seemed. She tried hard to form the words, make them sound sensible, understandable, yet her lips would not cooperate. Ever so frustrating when she wanted to communicate this needful thing.

"My dear, your head covering's unnecessary just now," Abram said, his face close to hers. She smelled pipe tobacco on his breath, sweet and soothing, and she longed for him to hold her in his arms.

"I'm sinking, Abram. Oh, Lizzie . . . help me. I fear I'm a-fallin'."

"You're right here, dearest sister." It was Lizzie's voice, soft and gentle. "The midwife will be on her way soon. Press on, Ida. Don't give up."

"Find my . . . prayer veiling," she said again, yearning for it. She made an excruciating effort to open her eyes. "Please do this thing . . . I ask."

She was aware of Abram's hand on hers, the gentle dabbing of a damp towel at her forehead. "Ida . . . dear one," he said.

She fell into what seemed to be a deep sleep, suddenly free of stabbing pain. In her stupor, she felt the loving hands of either Lizzie or Leah placing her head covering atop her head, and then tying it tenderly beneath her chin.

"*Da Herr sei mit du* . . . the Lord be with you," said Lizzie and kissed her forehead.

A blissful warm nothingness overtook her, and she was helpless to resist.

Hannah felt she was nearly flying in the family sleigh, hurrying the mare as best she could. After dropping the midwife off at home, she turned right around and rode up the road to the Nolts' place. There she timidly knocked on the door, only to stand on the porch, waiting. In her dire need for a quick response, she remembered it was growing quite late and looked to see if the Christmas tree was still blazing merrily in the front window. She stepped to the side of the door and saw the front room was dark; not a light was on anywhere on the main level of the house that she could tell. Thinking she best hurry, she pressed the doorbell and stepped back, hearing the *ding-dong-ding* of the chime, feeling terribly intrusive and wishing there was a way to alert Mary Ruth without waking up the entire family.

As it turned out, Dan Nolt came to the door in his long bathrobe and slippers. She told him why she'd come at such an hour, apologizing. "Shall I call for Dr. Schwartz?" the man asked with concern in his eyes.

"The Amish midwife is with Mamma now" was all she said.

"Very well," he said. "But if you have any qualms at all . . . the doctor is just around the corner. It would be no trouble at all to summon him."

Hannah wasn't sure what to do; with both Aunt Lizzie and the midwife tending to Mamma, surely all would be well. "Denki, but no," she said shyly. It was terribly unnerving to be speaking about Mamma's care with the head of this English household, of all things!

Soon she found herself upstairs in the grand house, waiting for Mary Ruth in her fine-looking bedroom. Her twin quickly dressed around, anxiety in her eyes. And together the two of them hurried home.

"My friend and sister in the Lord."

Rousing herself, Ida recognized the dim voice as Annie Mae Yoder's. The midwife and her black bag were present at last—Annie Mae would help spare her life and her baby's, too.

Annie Mae examined her and immediately said she would attempt to reposition the baby. "It's breech," she said, placing gentle hands on Ida's abdomen, attempting to begin the forward roll, moving the baby up and out of the pelvic bones. She did this several times, but there was no change in the baby's position, she said.

"The child lies directly across the uterus," Annie told them.

"Horizontal?" Lizzie asked. " 'Tis dangerous, ain't so?"

"Jah," said Annie Mae softly, "the shoulders will lead the way into the birth canal . . . if I can't reposition the baby."

"Well, keep tryin'," Abram insisted.

Annie said meekly, "I fear Ida bleeds too much for that."

Ida, in her haze, took Annie's words to mean real trouble. She'd heard of rare breech positions. But this. *Oh, my dear babe's life is in jeopardy. Father in heaven, help Annie Mae know what to do!*

The intense contractions began again. She held on to the twisted sheet, desperately wanting to control her cries but to no avail.

"My dear Ida, the baby and you . . . both are in an awful bad way," the older woman said when the birth pangs abated momentarily.

"Help my wife live," Abram said. "This I beg of you."

No . . . no, Abram . . . the baby's life is most important. Life for this our son.

But try as she might, she could not verbally express her urgent wish. She squeezed Abram's hand—the simple yet difficult squeeze of her fingers on his calloused flesh.

"She understands you. Now, get on with it!" said her husband.

Ach, Abram, be ever so kind, she thought.

"Work with me, Ida. Help me deliver this child."

"Why not try turning the baby once more?" Lizzie was saying, ever near.

"Ida's hemorrhaging strongly" came the solemn answer. "I scarcely feel her pulse."

In a haze of confusion, Ida did her best to follow Annie's instructions, attempting to be stoic, as she'd always been in the past. In the far recesses of her mind, she strangely recalled that never before had she needed a speck of coaxing or help. Not even with the delivery of twins.

Such a dreadful pain exploded through her, wounding her, lingering longer than before. Deadly. It continued, shuddering its fury within her till she felt she might break asunder. *O Lord Jesus, I call upon your name.*

"Do something!" Abram commanded. "Spare my wife!"

Annie Mae made the offer of ether. "Just a sedative whiff."

"Denki . . . but no. I must hear . . . my baby's cries," Ida managed to say.

"Please let Annie help you, Mamma," Leah urged.

Ida could feel Annie Mae's breath on her cheek now, replacing Abram's. She was aware of the midwife's grip on her weak hand. She felt at once like a small girl again . . . she saw the four-sided Martin birdhouse in Hickory Hollow, where she'd grown up in her parents' big farmhouse . . . the white birdhouse shooting up tall from a yellow daisy-strewn meadow. Martins flew together in family units, going to warmer climes come autumn. Staying together . . .

She felt torn between this world and the next, weary of this pilgrim way, drawn—no, pulled ever so gently, even lovingly—and, oh, she longed to allow herself to simply let go. To fly away to Glory Land, that home of her Lord and Savior where her heart, her spirit, her very being craved to be.

But something held her fast. Her dear baby was on his way. His little body was hankering for life, for air to breathe. This wee boy would grow up without his mamma; she knew this in her bones. He was going to grow under the influence of Abram, to learn to plow and cultivate the soil. *The good earth . . . Oh, this son I am giving life to.*

An image of a pond glistened as a breeze made the sun's kisses sparkle on the surface. Then, away in the distance, a youthful figure came walking toward her.

Oh, Mamma . . . I see you. You're coming for me!

"My darling mother," Leah was saying.

But Ida was confused by her daughter's words, mixed up with her own mother's image near the radiant pond.

"Hang on, Ida," Abram said from the corner of the room.

A surge of energy she had not known in hours filled her completely. She raised her head, leaning on her elbows, and opened her eyes to see Leah and Lizzie on her right and Annie Mae on her left. Dear, dear gray-headed Annie. How many babies had she safely seen into this world?

"Lie back, sweet Ida. Rest now," Annie whispered.

Abram's newspaper closed quickly and she heard him rise from his chair. Once again he came to sit on the bed. His kisses were on her face, her lips, mingled with salty tears. "You stubborn woman," he said. *"Ich lieb dich . . .* still, I love ya so."

The midwife spoke again, encouraging her to birth the babe before giving in to the sinking end. "I'll help ya through this hard valley."

"Oh, Mamma . . . no!" Leah sobbed and the bed trembled.

Leah's tearstained face became less and less visible, but Ida continued to hear the dear girl's voice. Lizzie's, too, now and then. Somewhere along the way, she knew Abram must have slipped out into the hallway. Faintly she heard his voice along with Mary Ruth's and Hannah's, as the sounds drifted in and out of her consciousness.

I bless your name, Lord Jesus. . . .

The bewildering falling sensation came, plunging her down again. Yet she knew she must cling to the thread of life, not let it slip from her grasp until she heard the first birth cries.

My life is in your hands, Lord.

Soon they came. Loud and pitiless, her newborn baby heralded his arrival with a strong set of lungs.

"It's a boy, Ida! Praise be, as healthy as they come," announced Annie Mae.

Thank you, dear Lord. She longed to see her baby, to lay eyes on this miracle of life. Her and Abram's love . . . in the form of a tiny man-child. She looked but saw only blackness.

Then, suddenly, he lay in her arms, nestling against her, moving, searching . . .

"Mamma, can you hear me?" Leah pleaded. Precious girl . . . ever so concerned. Should she be on hand, attending the death of her mother?

Ida nodded, though weakening as the seconds sped by.

Oh, my motherless son . . .

"Don't struggle so, Ida," said Lizzie. "Rest now. Rest . . ."

Ida began to shake her head, back and forth slowly. *No . . . no!* The battle cry continued in her brain. *Someone must care for this baby and his sister Lydiann,* she longed to say but could not.

Hard as she might, she fought to live now, changing her mind. She must survive to care for her only son. She must live for him to suckle, bond, be nourished . . . and he did so as she lay there. Clawing at the walls of life—her happy sweet life—she gasped for her final breaths, her very lifeblood seeping away.

"I love you, Mamma," Leah said, lying down on the bed.

She felt the warmth of Leah's slender body and her loving arms slipping beneath her, cradling both her and the baby.

"I'm here . . . right here with you," Leah said quietly.

Ida could scarcely whisper, "Raise him as your own, Leah. Lydiann, too."

"Oh, Mamma . . . you needn't worry over that just now.

Beseech the Lord God to let you live instead."

Ida felt she might be left hanging in the balance between earth and heaven if she did not know what was to become of her little ones. "Promise me this thing?"

Leah paused; she was silent for too long. Then slowly she said, "I promise, jah . . . to look after Abe, and I'll care for Lydiann till she's grown, Mamma." Leah whispered the words, kissing her face repeatedly. "But only if need be."

Little Abe . . . Lydiann. You'll be greatly loved with Leah. Oh, be safe . . .

The power in the dying was too strong to oppose, yet she labored against it—an unmistakable desire kept her alive and living—till that "acceptable time."

Her baby nursed, making the familiar sucking sounds she cherished. *Stay alive,* she told herself. *Let little Abe have this important start.*

Annie Mae touched her wrist, checking her pulse again. She heard muffled words . . . fading fast away. "I'm so sorry, my sister and friend. May the Lord be with you."

Yet again Ida was keenly aware of her mother's voice . . . closer, it seemed, than before. She felt the cool touch of her mamma's gentle hand, guiding her along. She felt more than she could see, vividly aware of the cross, Jesus' sacrifice made on Calvary's hill for her sins, for all humanity . . . for the People lost in a web of rules and tradition. For her family, for young Lydiann, and now her only son . . . Abe.

Tears slipped down her cheeks, yet she was too weak to brush them away. Leah was seeing to that, darling girl. Lizzie's first and only child, here, caring for *her* in these fragile moments . . . connected to Ida as closely in death as Sadie had been in life. Leah, filling her elder sister's shoes. Beautiful Leah, inside and out.

Sadie . . . share your burdens with the Lord Jesus. She breathed the prayer.

The babe in her arms went limp, resting . . . full of life-giving sustenance . . . for now. He would sleep soundly, she knew.

Bless this child, Lord. Make him a blessing all of his days. . . .

"I'll help you go to Jesus, Mamma," Leah said, wet face against her own.

"Tell Mary Ruth I love her . . . that I wish . . ."

"Jah, Mamma, I will. And I'll tell Hannah, too."

"But *Mary* . . . ach—"

"Mary Ruth knows, Mamma. She's known all along."

Abram whispered trembling words in her ear. "Ida . . . dear wife of mine."

"Oh, Abram . . . be there. When the Lord . . . calls you, be ready." She felt his strong arms beneath her, intertwined with Leah's. "I'll be . . . waitin' . . ."

Breathing her last, she relinquished her grasp on the mortal and utterly gave in to overwhelming love, the purest discerning of it. The Lord Jesus was present, standing next to her own mamma, His nail-pierced hands extended to her. "Welcome home, child," she heard ever so clearly.

And all was well.

Chapter Twenty

More crucial than Leah sitting through the solemn two-day wake with Miriam Peachey and dozens of Ebersol and Brenneman relatives was planning how to care for and feed newborn Abe, keeping her promise to Mamma hour by hour.

She followed Aunt Lizzie's suggestion and gave the baby a small bottle of sugar water the first full day. On the second day she fed him goat's milk diluted with sterile well water, purchased from a meticulous family who shaved their goats for exceptional cleanliness and flavor. Tiny Abe took to it with much eagerness, as if to say, I'm mighty hungry for *life!*

Leah felt honored to look after Abe and Lydiann, tending to them as she might have her own wee ones. She suppressed sorrowful tears during the daylight hours, only succumbing to deepest grief in the privacy of her room after nightfall.

The raw memory of her helplessness and the utter desperation of Mamma's final moments distracted Leah in all her domestic and, now, motherly duties. She would never forget the earnest plea in her mother's sunken eyes, as if calling out to be surrounded by their love.

Ever so near. As close as Leah had ever dared to be, paying no mind to the midwife or Dat when she followed her heart and slipped into the deathbed alongside Mamma. She had felt irresistibly pulled to do so, wanting to help her beloved mother die peacefully.

———◆———

On the day of the funeral Leah sat with Aunt Lizzie and the other women folk and raised her voice in song as best she could, singing the old familiar Ausbund hymns with over two hundred souls gathered in their home. She pondered the strength it would take to carry out her new role. *I must be strong today,* she thought, refusing to cry as she held Lydiann on her lap while Abe slept soundly upstairs in his cradle.

The ache in her throat threatened to choke her midway through the second long sermon. She'd spotted the back of Smithy Gid's head just now, and the unexpected mission of raising Mamma's babies weighed heavily on her mind, accompanied by her great sorrow at their loss. The future, indeed, seemed to stretch beyond her reach.

My help cometh from the Lord, she reminded herself. *Please let it be so, O God.*

As the service drew to a close and the People began making their traditional line to await the viewing, she was keenly aware of her own weakened spirit. It was painfully obvious to her that Peter and Fannie Mast and their family had not cared enough to attend Mamma's funeral service. The news would have easily traveled to their ears over in Grasshopper Level, she knew; nonetheless, far as Leah could tell, Mamma's cousins were nowhere to be seen today. She did not crane her neck in hopes of finding them.

With steadfast heart, she squared her shoulders in reliance upon God, clinging to the hope that one day, Lord willing, the two families might somehow be reunited.

In the week that followed Mamma's death, Leah knelt at her bedside at dawn and dusk, calling on the Lord God heavenly Father for help and strength. But when Hannah came privately to confide her most secret concern, Leah felt nearly powerless to know what to say.

"I hesitate to speak my heart on this," Hannah began, her face ashen as she stood against the bedroom door. "Yet I must say it, or I fear I'll burst apart."

Leah reached for her sister's cold hands. "Don't mince words . . . please, what is it?"

"Don't know how to put this, really."

"Start with a deep breath. It'll come out better that way."

Hannah began again, faltering a bit. "Could it be . . . do ya think Mary Ruth's leavin' home was partly the cause of Mamma dyin'?" she asked. "Did Dat's wrath cause mortal trauma in our mother?"

Honestly Leah didn't think so—at least she didn't *want* to think such a thing. Poor sorrowful Dat needed their kindness, not their finger-pointing. Besides, Mamma had struggled all during this pregnancy, Leah reminded Hannah. "She truly did."

When Leah hinted of Hannah's worries to Lizzie, her aunt

was adamant in her response. "Seems to me Abram has a mighty gut chance to redeem himself by askin' Mary Ruth back home. That's what *I* think."

Leah was surprised. "Do you mean to say you think Dat would actually do that?"

Lizzie stood at the cook stove, wearing her long black apron over a purple cape dress. "Well, why not? 'Tis a mighty big man who looks back on a bad decision and has a hankerin' to make things right."

Aunt Lizzie had hit the nail smack-dab on the head. But just *who* among them was going to bring this up to Dat? Leah shivered a little, contemplating the conflict that was sure to arise.

Holding Abe, who was tightly swaddled in a soft blanket, she went to sit at the table next to Lydiann. She watched as her little sister made broad red crayon strokes on the paper.

"Where's my mamma?" Lydiann looked up at her with big blue eyes.

Right then she thought of Sadie's poor baby, gone to heaven. All those months of her sister's deep grief, her loss . . . never having held her son close as Mamma had so tenderly before her death.

"Our mamma's in heaven." Leah forced a smile.

"I want her *here*," Lydiann said, making a round circle with her crayon.

Leah sighed. This was ever so difficult, yet she must be strong for her youngest sister. "I know, dear one. I miss Mamma, too."

Lydiann put down her crayon and leaned against Leah.

Leah signaled for Aunt Lizzie to take tiny Abe, then lifted

Lydiann up onto her lap. She rocked her gently and whispered, "I'll be your second mamma for as long as you need me."

This brought a little smile to Lydiann's face, though Leah didn't know how much Lydiann comprehended.

Turning, Lydiann clung to her, and Leah rose with the toddler still wrapped in her arms and carried her into the front room. From the window, she drank in the white splendor of snow and ice . . . the stark blackness of tall trees against a merciless gray sky.

The Lord is thy keeper; the Lord is thy shade upon thy right hand. She thought of one of Mamma's favorite psalms.

Then she whispered a promise, "We'll have us a happy life, dear one."

"Happy . . . with Mamma Leah." Lydiann snuggled hard against her.

She hummed a hymn and pondered the future. Just how would the Lord aid her efforts? She knew not the answer. She had only to listen to God's voice one day at a time. *I must not fear the morrow. . . .*

With a kiss on the head, she put Lydiann down, and the two of them wandered back to the kitchen. Abe slept in his cradle not far from the cook stove, where Aunt Lizzie was frying up some chicken.

"There's something I've been thinking 'bout." Lizzie's voice startled her.

"What's that?" Leah turned slightly, watching Mamma's sister at the stove.

"You oughta get out some this week. Goodness' sake, for a girl who nearly grew up outdoors—"

"It's all right, really 'tis. Dat's got himself two hired hands, so I'm not much needed outside anymore. Besides, Hannah's right happy to help Dat some these days, seems to me." She stared down at Abe's smooth forehead, his light tuft of hair. *Liewi Boppli* . . . "As for me, I like bein' with these beloved babies."

"Smithy Gid won't be able to help Abram near as much once the two of you get hitched, ain't so?" Aunt Lizzie was looking down at the frying pan—and rightly so. "Don't ya go sayin' you ain't marryin' him . . . I see how the two of you look at each other."

Leah said nothing. Let Aunt Lizzie say what she wanted. Truth was, she needed to talk to her beau here before too long—needed to share with him the important promise she'd made to Mamma. Pledges, nay, even covenants made to a dying parent could not be taken lightly. She would keep her word and raise Lydiann and Abe as her own. But the more she thought on it, the more the problem increased in her heart and mind. She did not want to hurt Gid, nor herself by parting ways with the man who planned to marry her. Yet she had no idea how to make Mamma's wishes come to pass in light of that.

To soothe herself, she reached down into the cradle and picked up Abe, enjoying his sweetness tucked so close to heart. *What am I to do?*

Following the suppertime meal, Dat took Leah aside before evening prayers. "I know you have your hands busy with the little ones, but when you have a breather tomorrow, could you begin sorting through your mother's things?" he asked, puffy eyes betraying his mournful spirit.

She suspected Dat privately grieved out in the barn, when he was alone with the animals and his somber thoughts, remembering all the years spent as his wife's confidant and lover.

"Jah, I'll see to it, Dat, first thing tomorrow." She touched his arm gently. "You must know ... I miss Mamma, too. Something awful."

He nodded quickly, then straightened and went to the corner cupboard, where he picked up the big German Bible. His voice sounded dreadful this night, a husky monotone. She knew his heart was not in the reading of God's Word.

◆

First, last, and foremost, Leah thought of herself as a compliant sort; except for the years given to her dream of marrying Jonas Mast, she had generally obeyed her father's bidding. But she felt rather bold when Dat asked her not only to go through Mamma's personal effects but to "discard everything but her old Bible ... and her clothing, which can be given away to friends and older relatives." She spoke up, telling Dat there might be certain other things she or the twins might wish to save, perhaps as keepsakes. But observing the unyielding look in Dat's swollen eyes, she held her peace and said no more.

The night of Mamma's passing, she and Hannah had moved both Lydiann's little bed and Abe's cradle into Hannah's and Leah's respective bedrooms. At night Leah was comforted by the soft sounds of Abe's breathing as she tucked him in, and his gurgling as she fed him every three hours or so around the clock. This arrangement also made it possible for Dat to have himself a good night's sleep—if he was able. Thankfully Abe wasn't nearly as fussy as Lydiann had been during her infancy. For this Leah was glad, not so much for herself as for poor Dat, who was obviously aging with each passing day. Without Mamma to seemingly soften his harsher side, Leah worried he might swiftly grow into a cranky old man.

❖

After Dat rose early the next morning, Leah got up and checked on Abe, who slept soundly, then hurried to do the difficult work of sorting through her mother's clothing. She pulled out one drawer after another, folding Mamma's things and making small piles on the bed. Opening the bottom drawer, she discovered a woolen gray scarf and matching knitted mittens, something she hadn't seen Mamma wear in the longest time. *She must've made these long ago, when Dat was courting her.*

Lovingly, Leah slipped her own hands into the scratchy mittens and wrapped the long scarf about her neck, tears clouding her vision. Would Dat rethink his desire to dispose of these precious things? But no. Best to simply give the scarf and mittens to Miriam Peachey or another of Mamma's friends, what with Dat behaving somewhat crossly these days. Better yet, she could slip them to Aunt Lizzie for safekeeping;

that way they could ultimately remain in the family.

She didn't know if she ought to be thinking that way, yet she questioned Dat's demand to discard all that had belonged to their darling mother. She felt even more strongly when her hands discovered a grouping of many letters from Cousin Fannie written to Mamma over the years. And another letter hidden away, farther back in the drawer—this one with Sadie's handwriting clearly on the envelope.

"What's this?" she said aloud.

Did Mamma go against the bishop and keep one of Sadie's early letters?

She could not stop looking at the postmark. She *had* to know.

Going to the dresser, she held the letter under the gas lamp and saw it had been sent in late December of 1947, not so long after Bishop Bontrager decreed Sadie's letters be returned unopened. Dat had laid down the law, as well, saying it was imperative to follow the "man of God on the matter of the shun."

Why would Mamma disregard both the bishop's and Dat's final word on this?

Leah battled right and wrong, holding the envelope, turning it over and noticing it was open already. *Oh,* she groaned inwardly. *I have to know what Sadie was writing to Mamma.*

Hastily she stopped herself and pushed it back, closing the drawer soundly. The notion that Mamma might have been also writing to Sadie crossed her mind. If so, did that mean Mamma's soul was hanging in eternal balance? Had her spirit gone to the Lord God in heaven or not? She shuddered to think Mamma would willingly disobey the Ordnung and risk her everlasting reward. Could it have been a misunderstanding that allowed this letter to find its way into Mamma's drawer?

She felt she knew her mother through and through—Mamma would have confessed such a thing before passing from death unto life. Surely if Mamma viewed keeping and reading Sadie's letter as a sin, she would never have disobeyed. *Niemols!*

Coming to this conclusion, Leah decided if Mamma could read the letter and hide it away—and die peacefully—then why couldn't *she* read it, too? Taking a deep breath, she reopened the drawer and reached for the letter, hurrying out of Dat's bedroom to her own. There she put it away in her bureau, where it would remain till she could take her time to read it—to savor and pore over every word and phrase, hoping for some clue as to what on earth had happened between Jonas and herself.

Chapter Twenty-One

Y ou oughta reconsider this, Abram." Lizzie was glad to have cornered him in the milk house. "Mary Ruth is your daughter!"

"You have no right to order me around!"

She inhaled and held her breath in, then let the words come gushing out. "Ain't it awful clear you were wrong 'bout Mary Ruth?"

His face reddened. "Don't go sayin' I'm responsible for Ida's death 'cause of Mary Ruth's leaving home. Don'tcha dare."

Sighing, she said more softly now, "Seems I don't *have* to, now, do I?"

He slumped and went to the window, looking out through the streaked old glass. "I don't know how a thing like this— Mary Ruth's stubbornness and goin' to live with Englishers— can happen to God-fearin' folk like us."

She was more careful in choosing her words this time. "We let the bishop think for all of us, that's how. The preachers and Bishop Bontrager tell you how to feel 'bout your own dear ones . . . your own Mary Ruth."

Abram muttered something about ministers being chosen—ordained by God. But when he began to cough, he couldn't seem to quit, and she worried he might vomit, so distraught he was.

"I'll leave you be," she said. "I didn't mean to upset you so."

"You best be goin' indoors. Check on that son of mine," Abram said it low but decisively.

He needed some time alone, probably, out here where he sometimes wept so loudly she wondered if he might be making himself ill. But then she, too, was acquainted with such dreadful sadness. Anyone who had lived as long as either she or Abram knew full well the pain of disappointment. She wished she might say he was merely passing through this life, that this old earth was not his eternal home and the treasures of truth were laid up in Glory for him—for all of them. *We've got our eyes fixed on what's all around us,* she thought. *Mistakenly so.*

"Jah, I'll look in on Abe, but Leah's doing a right gut job of taking care of him and Lydiann." She turned to leave, glad to have sobbed away her initial grief, having cried herself to sleep plenty of nights following her sister's funeral. To suffer was a part of living; how well she knew it. Best to simply move on, make the best of life, and trust the Lord, as she had learned to do. And love what family they had left.

Hannah sat in her bedroom with her diary in her lap while Lydiann napped on the side of the bed where Mary Ruth had always slept.

With pen in hand, she began to write, reliving the night of Mamma's death.

Tuesday, January 3, 1950
Dear Diary,

  One week and one day have passed since Mamma breathed her last. For me it is the worst pain I've known. I wish I'd agreed to Dan Nolt's suggestion—calling in Dr. Schwartz might have spared Mamma's life. I feel fairly responsible, but I have shared this with no one. If only I had given a simple nod of my head that night at the Nolts' front door! Oh, what a difference a single choice might have made.

  Leah says Mamma's passing was serene, that she did not seem to fight the final throes of death but embraced it, once she knew Abe was healthy and had cuddled him near. It breaks my heart that my baby brother will never know our mother.

  The night Mamma died, I rode to get Mary Ruth to bring her home with me, thinking it necessary. Dat must not have thought so, for he met us in the hallway just outside their bedroom door. When he greeted me but did not speak to Mary Ruth—not at first—it pained me nearly as much as to think of Mamma struggling terribly in childbirth. Mary Ruth spoke up, though, inquiring of Mamma's condition . . . and the unborn babe's. And she offered a heartfelt apology for having spoken disrespectfully to Dat prior to his sending her away.

  Obviously bewildered, Dat said nothing about my fetching Mary Ruth to the house. Honestly I'd hoped he might've opened his arms to her and welcomed her back. But such was not the case, and we stood quietly, tears glistening, as Mamma's cries became fainter.

  If Dat doesn't feel he caused Mamma great distress in the last days of her carrying wee Abe, I don't understand. Truly, the upset between him and Mary Ruth must have played some part. If my twin still lived here, she would surely have her say; then again, maybe not. Things are awful tense when it comes to Mary Ruth claiming salvation "full and free" while living under a worldly roof . . . not to mention her membership at an English church.

All that aside, I'm beginning to wonder if Ezra will ever attend another singing. He doesn't come to Preaching anymore, either. What's to become of him? I've told no one this, but I saw him on Main Street in Strasburg recently when I went to deliver more embroidered hankies to Frances Brubaker at her consignment shop. Ezra was dressed in blue jeans and had his hair cut like an Englisher—and was smoking a cigarette!

I worry for his dear mother. What she must be going through, losing two sons: Elias to death and Ezra to the world—the flesh and the devil. If Ezra doesn't soon get back on the right path, he'll be in danger of the shun, just as Sadie was.

Along with the guilt I bear for Mamma's death, I also wish to goodness I'd stuck my neck out and talked to her about how to be ready to meet one's Maker. I could kick myself, because I missed my chance forever. Who can I ever share my heart with now?

Oh, I fear I might worry myself sick, and I might, too, if Dat didn't need me helping with the milking and other outdoor chores. Such work helps me a lot, and I do enjoy working alongside Smithy Gid. He has a right gentle way, and it'll be ever so nice when he marries into our family, probably next year, I'd guess. Leah deserves some happiness, and, at long last, I'll have me a big brother. I ought to be counting my blessings more, but it's hard these days. What an awful way to welcome a new year with Mamma gone from us.

Each day I observe Leah going about her responsibilities—

rising before dawn to cook breakfast and on her feet all day long, up several times in the night with Abe. A shining example, for certain. Never does she complain, and I know she must be tuckered out each and every night as we head upstairs to bed. When I can, I help her with Lydiann, but Leah's fulfilling a labor of love. Not only is she a wonderful-good big sister to Abe and Lydiann, she is becoming a tender and loving mamma to them, too. The light in her hazel eyes when she tends to Abe, especially, gives me hope during these dark sad days.

Sorrowfully,
Hannah

Hours before supper Leah hurried out to the barn and found Dat sweeping, looking somewhat dazed. Her heart went out to him, and she wondered if she ought to wait to speak with him later, giving him more time to grieve before she unburdened her soul.

She started to turn to leave when Dat stopped his sweeping. "Somethin' on your mind, daughter?"

She contemplated simply leaving him be but found herself nodding. "Jah," she said slowly. "I was thinkin' I best be talkin' to Gid 'bout my promise to Mamma. But I wanted to speak to you first."

"Well, what's to say?"

Leah went on to tell him she assumed Smithy Gid would urge they now marry quickly, merely going before Preacher Yoder to make their lifelong promises to God and each other. "I'm fairly sure he'll offer to help me raise Lydiann and

Abe . . . the two of us, as a family." She couldn't help but wonder how Dat would feel, this coming from her.

"Gid's a right fine man," Dat began, "but I'll be raisin' my children myself, and no two ways 'bout it."

She wasn't surprised. Dat was fiercely possessive when it came to his family.

"I say you should go ahead with plans to marry Gid when the time comes and let Lizzie or Hannah look after Abe and Lydiann here."

"But Mamma asked *me* to raise them."

Dat sighed loudly. "Your mamma was awful befuddled with the pain of childbirth. I daresay she'd never expect ya to keep such a promise. Besides, you made your betrothal vow to Gid before the one to Mamma, ain't so?" At that he set about pushing hard his wide broom again, making a rhythmic swooshing sound.

Mamma knew my heart, thought Leah. *She trusted me to do the right thing for Abe and Lydiann . . . befuddled or not.*

◆

Before supper Leah hurried over to the blacksmith's shop on the Peacheys' property. She found Smithy Gid and his father both shoeing horses, each mare facing the cement wall. The wide plank-board flooring was dry, having been swept free of snow and other debris. Gid chewed gum as he worked, not tobacco as his father often did, and wore a tan leather apron that covered his legs down to his ankles and *mischdich* black work boots—covered with manure. Unaware she was standing in the corner observing him, he spoke quietly, even gently, to the mare, bringing the animal's leg up between his own, clamping his thighs against it as he positioned the new shoe, hot from the forge, with the end of a rasp. Gid's hair was disheveled as he leaned over, his toes pointing in slightly to better keep his balance.

Glancing at the square-shaped brick forge, she saw the opening, where the blower kept the cinders hot. Smithy Peachey was almost too busy juggling his many Amish clients— and occasionally an Old Order Mennonite customer, too—most of them on an eight-week schedule. Because of this, his father sought out Gid's help several days a week, and Leah was fairly certain he was hoping to pass on his livelihood to his only son.

She waited to let him know she was present till Gid was finished with all four hooves and had accepted the exact amount of money from the farmer. Gid waved a cheerful fare- well as Old Jonathan Lapp led the animal away, an obvious shine on the new horseshoes. The older man hitched his mare to a long sleigh and was gone.

While Gid organized the long tongs, hoof nippers, rasp, and other smithing tools, she moved out of the shadows and, cough- ing a little so as not to startle him, said, "Hullo, Smithy Gid."

"There ya are, girl. How're you today?" His grin was as infectious as ever, and she hoped for a lull between customers.

"Do ya have time to talk?" she asked.

"Why, sure. Always have plenty-a time for my girl." He removed his heavy leather blacksmithing apron and brushed his hands off on his trousers; then he went to get his work coat, which hung on a hook near the wide door, and slipped it on. "Let's walk a bit." Smiling, he reached for her hand and rubbed it between his own.

"I need to tell you something, Gid," she began. "Mamma asked me to raise her babies . . . as she lay dyin', and I said I would."

Smithy Gid nodded his head as if he'd suspected as much.

"I can't go back on my word," she said. "I wouldn't even if I could."

"No . . . no, you oughtn't be thinkin' thataway." He continued. "We could go to the preacher and have us a short wedding as soon as this weekend, if you'd want to. You and I could live in my folks' empty Dawdi Haus, bring up the little ones there as our own."

She figured he'd suggest that. "Just today I talked to Dat 'bout this, and he wants to do *his* part raising Lydiann and Abe."

He turned and gazed at her. "Surely ya know I would do whatever it took to make ya my bride." There was a strange hesitancy in his voice. "But, Leah, I want to have my own family with you . . . make a home separate from our parents. Don't you?"

" 'Course I do, but things have changed now since Mamma died." Breathing deeply, she stared ahead at Blackbird Pond, where they'd played as youngsters. "I just . . ." She felt she couldn't go on.

"What is it, dear?"

She felt his arms around her unexpectedly. "Living apart from Abe and Lydiann just doesn't fit with my promise to Mamma."

"But we're meant for each other," he broke in, fervor in his words. "I love ya so."

She tried not to cry. "Honestly I don't know what to do,"

she said softly. She didn't tell him she'd moved Abe's cradle into her own bedroom, that she knew clearly her infant brother had bonded with her . . . that she couldn't imagine passing the responsibility nor the maternal love off to either Aunt Lizzie or Hannah, as Dat had suggested.

"I've waited this long for ya, Leah. Surely I can get Abram to see the light—to let us raise his little ones in our own house."

"My father won't change his mind on this," she replied sadly. "I know that for sure."

They clung fast to each other, there beneath the lone willow tree, where the recent snow weighed down each slender branch and the pond was frozen over rock hard. Where they, their sisters, and parents had ice skated, built bonfires on the shore, and played hockey on sunny winter days.

"How can I let you go?" Gid caressed her face. "I'd be crazy to."

"Oh, Gid," her voice trembled.

"There must be some other way."

"Surely there is," she whispered. "Surely."

Sitting at the supper table, Gid stared hopelessly at the meat loaf, marbled mashed potatoes, and scalloped asparagus. He could hardly bring himself to pick up the serving dishes when they were passed.

"Something botherin' you, son?" Mamma eyed him curiously.

He would have to make himself eat. There was no sharing

220

his and Leah's problem tonight. Romantic difficulties were never spoken of to parents, though at times, he felt such a tradition was to an extent ridiculous, especially when his older and wiser father might have some powerful-good advice to offer.

Somehow or other, something *had* to give. If it meant talking privately with Abram, he would. He couldn't simply let his engagement to Leah come to an end. Nothing must be permitted to put a wedge between them . . . not even a dying mother's plea!

◆

Robert Schwartz paced the college corridor, eager for posted results of a pre-Christmas theology exam. He recoiled at the memory of both Thanksgiving and Christmas: Elias Stoltzfus's death . . . and Derek's surprise visit. Still, the Plain young man's passing had caused a tremendous religious stir among Elias's own people. God had reached down in goodness and grace, turning the tragedy into a spiritual victory.

Robert wished he could say the same of his brother's brief return home. Christmas Day had been a far cry from his boyhood memories of baked-ham dinners and laughter as the family gathered to decorate the tree on Christmas Eves. Derek had been not only irritable but dreadfully sullen after coming home from a "long walk," as he'd put it, and no amount of persuading on either Dad's or Mother's part could bring him around. He'd wanted "something strong to drink" when he stormed back into the house. After not having seen him for much of the afternoon, their parents spent a miserable evening waiting for the prodigal to return, which did not happen until long past midnight.

Robert had been reluctant to leave Dad and Mother alone, but he wanted to get away and pray for a time. Following supper, he drove to Quarryville and found solace in the stillness of the vacant church, pleading for God's help on behalf of his lost brother . . . and the grieving Amish family who had suffered the greatest loss of all.

Leah could think of nothing else but her talks with both Dat and Gid as she dressed Abe in his tiny pajamas, kissing each little hand as she guided it through the sleeve opening. She was truly glad for Hannah's offer to help with combing Lydiann's hair and getting her ready for bed, though she knew dear Hannah had her share of things to do in the kitchen and elsewhere. *She has a knack for sensing my mood*, Leah thought, grateful for Hannah and missing her other sisters terribly.

The house feels too empty, she pondered, carrying Abe downstairs to warm his milk bottle. *Having Smithy Gid live here surely would fill up the place . . . and Dat wouldn't be so outnumbered.*

Yet she'd seen the look of disappointment in Gid's eyes, and she knew she couldn't take away his rightful place as head of his household. Besides, their own babies would most likely come along soon enough, and how complicated would it be for Gid to assume the fatherly role for his flesh-and-blood children but not for Lydiann and Abe? The problem nagged at her till she was altogether weary of it.

As soon as Abe was nestled in his cradle and asleep, Leah closed the bedroom door and went to the bureau. Taking out Sadie's letter to Mamma, she curled up on the bed and hugged her sister's former pillow as she read.

December 15, 1947
Dearest Mamma,

I hope at least one of the letters I've written ends up being read by you eventually. Christmas is coming soon and the Mellinger children are ever so happy. David and Vera's new baby is already a month old and as sweet as can be.

Jonas loves playing with the little ones, maybe more so than some young men I know. He's been so kind to me, Mamma—you just don't know. I think it's because he wants things to turn out well for me. I suppose I should tell you that I broke down one night and cried out my woes to him—about having a baby out of wedlock with an Englisher and all. He'd offered to go walking with me after supper, and I just couldn't keep the truth inside any longer. You probably wonder how I could tell him such a thing, especially when I wanted to keep it a secret from everyone else back home.

When all was said and done, I did the right thing by sharing with Jonas that I was "damaged goods." He said he wanted to help me, felt sorry for me . . . wanted to make sure I was cared for. That I should be looked after by a kind and good husband. I thought he meant himself . . . and he did. He said he would marry me then and there.

Of course, I argued it might be too soon, what with his having been in love with Leah and engaged and all, but he insisted we get married following my six-week Proving time. We talked a lot about that, too, and how the brethren here seemed to understand my plight, not sharing my sinful past

with the People. Honestly I felt the Lord God must be looking
out for my sin-weary soul. So in my next letter to you, I'll be
writing to say I am a happily married woman. Jonas's Sadie,
I'll be. I know you don't approve, Mamma, but I had to share
these things with you.

I trust you, Dat, and Aunt Lizzie are all right. Don't cry
for me, Mamma. God has a way of leading wayward souls to
Him. Write to me again, please? I miss you so . . . and my
sisters, too.

I know you can't tell Dat or anyone else in the family how
much I love them—if you read this letter, that is—but I surely
do. I hope there might come a day when we will see each other
again face-to-face.

> All my love,
> Your firstborn, Sadie

Holding the letter, Leah stared at it, unseeing. The welcoming curve of the familiar handwriting blurred all too
quickly. Sadie had shared her sinful ways with Jonas, as well
as the news of her stillborn baby, after having resisted doing
so to the brethren here, when and where it was most necessary. How was it so easy for her to do that in Ohio? Had she
fallen for Jonas's dear smile, his gentle eyes?

Not wanting to dwell on this, she let her angry tears flow
freely, pushing the pillow aside. Had Sadie somehow used her
wicked past to purposely play on Jonas's sympathy, kind and
compassionate man that he was? *My sister dared to combine her
sin with yet another—stealing my beloved beau! How could she?*

Reaching over, she pulled Sadie's pillow toward her and
rose, carrying it with her. She thought of pushing it under the
bed where cobwebs and clumps of dust formed faster than she

could keep up, especially now that she was busy caring for a newborn, as well as a two-and-a-half-year-old. Beneath the bed was a good idea, because she would not have to look at the pillow hidden there, recalling the nights she and Sadie had shared their fondest hopes and dreams, lying side by side, their heads resting happily on their pillows.

But no, she'd had enough of those memories. Breathing hard, Leah carried the pillow all the way downstairs to the cold cellar, where she stuffed it deep into the heart of Sadie's old hope chest, giving it a good solid pounding before closing the lid. *I never want to see this again!*

With that she felt she was also willing to live out her whole life long without ever seeing Sadie again.

Back upstairs, she took the letter and began to rip it into as many as pieces as her anger would allow. *I do this for poor Mamma,* she thought, giving in to a rising resentment she'd thought she had long put to rest. *And this is for Dat and Aunt Lizzie . . . for Hannah and Mary Ruth . . . Lydiann and Abe.*

Stopping, Leah realized she was shaking uncontrollably. *I must surely despise Sadie,* she thought, realizing it was true. She continued on, tearing the small pieces into even tinier ones. *This is for Abram's Leah . . . who surely I will be forevermore.*

Chapter Twenty-Two

Before her baby brother awakened for the morning, Leah hurried to pen a note to Vera Mellinger in Millersburg, Ohio, hoping to get word of Mamma's passing to her older sister. Halfway through the letter, after sharing the joyous news of tiny Abe's birth and his good health in spite of the trauma, she noticed her jaw was clenched.

Leaning back against the headboard of her bed, she deliberately tried to relax. *Calm yourself,* she thought, but doing so was a whole different matter. The horrid way she felt about Sadie after reading her letter yesterday, well, she'd just as soon let her older sister continue on in her ignorance, not knowing one speck about Mamma. But such an attitude was cruel, even spiteful, and she knew better than to harbor bitterness. So Leah made herself continue writing, ending with a plea for Vera to write back as soon as she could. *Please tell me how to get word to my sister Sadie.*

She signed off the way Mamma had taught her and quickly wrote her full name. Sealing the envelope, she placed the stamp in the proper place and hurried downstairs to don her woolen cape and snow boots. At the mailbox in front of the house, she pushed the letter inside and looked about her, momentarily glad for the predawn darkness.

The serenity soothed Leah, and she breathed in the icy air, relieved to have accomplished washing and drying the family's laundry two days ago, on Monday's washday. With Hannah and Lizzie's help, she'd hung out the many baby items on the line, though it had been quite tedious in the wrenching cold. Miriam Peachey had come over, bringing a large pot of corn chowder, which everyone enjoyed at noon, especially Dat and Dawdi John. And she'd asked Aunt Lizzie to keep Mamma's old knit scarf and mittens at her house—conceal them, really. Surely Dat would overlook Leah's momentary boldness when he came around—years down the road—and realized how important it had been to hang on to at least one item of Mamma's.

I will lift up mine eyes unto the hills, from whence cometh my help, she thought silently while trudging back to the house.

She knew she must go talk with Dr. Schwartz sometime soon—possibly with Lorraine, too. They must be told that although she wished to keep her part-time job, she was needed nearly twenty-four hours a day here at home. The idea that maybe Mary Ruth might come and take care of Abe and Lydiann for several hours of a Saturday dropped into her mind. But then again, there was the problem of Dat's determined stance—Mary Ruth was not at all welcome in the house. *Nix that idea.* She might ask Aunt Lizzie, though . . . see what ideas *she* might have.

On the way around the back to the kitchen door, she happened to hear her aunt's boots clumping down the snow-covered mule road. "Hullo, Leah!" Lizzie called.

"'Mornin', Aendi!" Leah called back, standing near the back stoop, waiting and shivering, too. *What would we do without sweet Lizzie? Life would be ever so empty without Mamma's sister near.*

Once she and Lizzie were back indoors, she opened the grate on the wood stove and they warmed their hands and feet together. Lizzie asked, "Are ya feelin' all right, honey-girl?"

Leah nodded. "I feel numb when I think of Mamma. But when I'm holding Abe and Lydiann, things tend to change in me . . . some."

"'The Lord giveth and the Lord taketh away.'" Lizzie put her arm around Leah.

Ain't that the truth. She thought again of Sadie's revealing letter to Mamma.

She sighed and went to the window near the long table. "I found something in Mamma's drawer," she began, "when I cleared out her personal things for Dat."

Lizzie came and sat at the head of the table, where Dat always sat at mealtime.

"Seems to me Mamma may have hidden one of Sadie's letters away on purpose." She turned and looked at Lizzie. "What do ya make of that?"

"I shouldn't be surprised, I guess."

She felt the tightness in her chest, wondering if she ought to say what she'd read. Would that be as sinful as Mamma's own disobedience? She didn't know. "So then you must think Mamma disregarded the bishop . . . and Dat, too," Leah said nearly in a whisper.

"Honestly she didn't much care for the do's and don'ts of the Old Ways. She honored the Ordnung as best she could . . . walked a line, s'pose you could say. She read the Good Book from cover to cover nearly every year. She told me she'd shared some of these things with Sadie, Hannah, and Mary Ruth . . . and with *you*, most recently."

Leah clearly remembered the conversation. "But what 'bout *Gelassenheit*—submission to God and to the People? What was Mamma's view on that?"

Lizzie nodded her head. "Sadly that was the biggest issue—the push and pull of it all. Abram wanted to live by the letter of the law, following the bishop's and the preachers' every whim. This annoyed my sister no end. 'Tween you and me, I think when the end came, she was eager to go home to Glory."

"Not 'cause of Dat, I hope."

Lizzie paused a moment, then went on. "She simply yearned to see the Lord Jesus."

"'Best to be in heaven's lap than caught in the world's grasp,'" Leah whispered.

Lizzie patted the bench. "Come and sit. You have a big day ahead."

She smiled. "Every day's thataway."

"You're doin' a wonderful-gut thing, Leah. Never forget," Lizzie said.

Abe's cries were heard just then, so Leah quickly excused herself and ran upstairs to comfort her mamma's precious boy.

◆

The first day of the new school semester, Mary Ruth followed a group of fancy students into Paradise High School. She was happy to ride the school bus with other Mennonite youth, glad she wasn't the only conservative girl on board. Naturally she wasn't nearly as Plain now as she had been, what with her floral-print dress, though long to her ankles.

Thankfully Dottie Nolt had driven her to the school a week earlier, when she had enrolled for the remainder of the year and taken her placement tests. To her delight, she discovered she was ready for *second*-semester tenth grade, even though she'd completed only eight years at the Georgetown School—staying home with Mamma for two years after that. All told, she was well on course to graduate by the time she was nineteen—a full year older than most high school graduates, but that didn't bother her in the least. The main thing was to prepare herself for teacher's college. And, here lately, she believed God was calling her to attend a Christian college someday. She was on her way!

Busy hallways were disconcerting at first, and changing classrooms and having different teachers for each subject was also confusing. After a few days, though, she felt she would become accustomed to the schedule. Still, the sight of girls wearing knee-length wool skirts with bare legs clear down to the tops of their white ankle socks made Mary Ruth feel as if she were in a foreign land.

Getting her locker open was another discouraging situation, but, in the end, the problem had its reward. An attractive boy with brown hair and green eyes noticed her plight and came over to help. "I'm Jimmy Kaiser," he smiled. "You're new, aren't you?"

She nodded, afraid she'd say jah and scare him off, which she certainly didn't want to do, not with those big bright eyes looking right at her.

"If you ever run into a snag with your combination lock, look me up," Jimmy said, pointing toward his own locker. "I'm only five lockers down from yours on the other side of the hallway. Don't be bashful, all right?"

"Nice to meet you, Jimmy."

"Welcome to Paradise . . . *High School*, that is!" Grinning, he turned and hurried away.

Well. She was entirely pleased with the first student she'd met. *Pleased as punch,* she thought. *Does this mean I'm beginning to forget Elias?* She wondered that plenty.

Surely it was a good sign, her experiencing a slight flutter when a good-looking boy like Jimmy made the effort to cross the hall and make her feel welcome.

Another surprise was the first reading assignment given in American literature class: her beloved *Uncle Tom's Cabin.* She knew the book inside and out, perhaps better than the other students in the class because she identified in part with Eliza, the black slave girl, though Mary Ruth had never been abused physically. All the same, the book reopened certain sore spots for her, and she longed to see oppressed people released from spiritual bondage.

That afternoon following school Mary Ruth slipped away to her lovely bedroom at the Nolts' to do her homework, writing carefully the assigned essays and working the geometry problems. When she was finished, she knelt to pray, asking the Lord to help her forgive the brethren, especially Bishop Bontrager, who ruled with an iron hand, much the way Simon

Legree did in Harriet Beecher Stowe's classic novel. The man's shunning of Sadie had altered her family members' lives for the worst, she was sure. She also asked the Lord to forgive her for smooching so awful much with Elias, not having saved lip-kissing for her husband . . . and to guide her life as a Christian young woman.

Following Elias's death, she had initially decided to wear a black dress for a good long time, but recently she'd changed her mind and put aside her mourning clothes. Her newfound joy in the Lord Jesus had turned every part of her life around, including the slightest details. No longer did she part her hair down the middle; she simply brushed it straight back and gathered it into a higher bun, and, like Dottie, she wore the many-pleated formal head covering unique to Mennonite women, with the strings hanging loose and untied. Not quite as Plain, true, but nevertheless not worldly, either.

Getting used to electricity and automobiles had been the easiest adjustment of all, though she knew she would gladly ride in Dat's family carriage if invited.

Perhaps Elias's death had been God's way of giving her a heavenly sign she was never intended to join the Amish church. Truth was, she enjoyed having modern conveniences at her fingertips, and what she was experiencing under Dan and Dottie's roof—and in attending church with them—was pure freedom. For the first time in her life, she could breathe easily, free from bondage, ever ready to honor the Lord in everything she put her hand to do, all the days of her life.

In due time, Leah received word back from Vera Mellinger that Sadie and Jonas no longer lived in Millersburg. Vera wrote that she hadn't heard from them in "quite some time" and said she was "ever so sorry" to hear of Mamma's passing.

Passing. Why was it folk avoided the word *death*? Was it easier to think of a person going from one place to the next, moving forward as their soul surely did at the point of death, instead of lying still in a coffin? The Scriptures taught the passing of the soul from this life into eternity, from "death unto life."

She felt both sorry and thankful having read Vera's letter, and she took it out to the barn, where Hannah and Dat were cleaning out the lower stable area. She regretted Sadie having no way of knowing their mother was dead, yet she was secretly relieved her sister wouldn't be rushing home over the sad news—though Leah did wonder how such news would have affected Jonas if *he* had known of it. But no, she couldn't let herself wonder about that. Too much time had flown to the wind.

Outdoors, she found Hannah wearing old work boots, Leah's own. When Dat was free enough, she handed Vera's letter to him. He stood with his legs braced apart and read it quickly. "Well, if that ain't a fine howdy-do," he said, waving the note once he finished. "She runs off so we can never find her . . . even if it's her own mamma who's died."

Hannah blinked her eyes fast and Leah wondered if she was trying not to cry. But Hannah surprised her by saying, "You did the right thing, Leah, but maybe our shunned sister doesn't wanna be found."

Dat nodded in agreement. "Long gone . . . she is."

"Should I write to Cousin Fannie next? See if *she* has any knowledge of our sister's whereabouts?" She held her breath, unsure what Dat might say to do.

Dat hung his head. "Where the Masts are concerned, we're as gut as dead."

She took that as a no and accepted the letter back from Dat. Heading toward the house, she was eager to check on Lydiann, who was napping, and Abe, who was lying on a quilt spread out on the kitchen floor, the warmest room in the house. She almost wished Dat hadn't sided with Hannah just now, saying Sadie was "long gone." Had he given up on her ever repenting here in Gobbler's Knob?

Mamma's prayers while she lived surely still follow my sister now, she thought.

◆

Abram had seen to it that his work boots were cleaned of caked-on mud and mule droppings before hitching up the horse to the sleigh. It might've been that he'd have made less a spectacle of himself had he simply gone walking to Daniel Nolt's place, but now as Abram reined in his horse in the driveway of the fine house, he sat there, not sure what to do next.

Just why he'd come, he wasn't altogether certain. He knew it had to do with the short letter from Ohio that Leah'd had him read. Something mighty sorrowful about it, he'd decided, and it had prompted him out of his lethargy. Not that he had been digging in his heels about visiting Mary Ruth; no, he just felt it might be the right time to make an attempt to see how his daughter was doing these days.

He got down from the sleigh and let the reins lie loose on the seat; the well-mannered horse would be fine here for a few minutes. Next thing he knew he was standing on the front porch of a stranger's house.

When Mary Ruth came to the door with a bright-eyed youngster in her arms, he was taken aback and found himself sputtering a greeting. She was mighty kind and invited him inside—even brought him some hot black coffee on a fancy tray. They sat and talked in the front room, pretty Mary Ruth and himself, no doubt as foolish sounding as he felt.

"I came to say I was wrong . . . and so were you, daughter," he started the conversation. "But now . . . well, I want you to consider coming home. Wouldja think on that for ol' Dat?"

She was quiet, not responding right off the way she normally did, which surprised him. Instead, she stroked the boy's dark hair, whispering something—he didn't know what—in his tiny ear.

"Your sisters—Leah and Hannah—would be downright happy. And . . . sorry to say, but you haven't properly met your new baby brother, Abe."

"Named after *you*, Dat." Her eyes seemed to light up at the mention of the baby.

"Jah, Leah and . . ." He had to pause. The mere thought of Ida still choked his words.

"Mamma and Leah's choice for a name, then?" She was helping him along. Mary Ruth, ever dear; the daughter who had never lacked for a comment.

He nodded, still composing himself.

"I wished I might've comforted you, Dat, at Mamma's

funeral. . . . Still hurts to think on it." She was silent for a moment; then she continued. "I just felt so far removed from my family. I wish things were better between us."

The punishment *had* been severe; he knew that. "I'd do plenty-a things different . . . now."

"I s'pose all of us would." But in the end, she refused his invitation to move back home. "I'd be a terrible thorn in your flesh, Dat," she admitted. "You see, I started high school— just yesterday, truth be told."

He hung his head. Things were spinning away from him. Nearly every day more things floated out of his reach. First Mary Ruth's odd declaration of salvation, then Ida's passing. He'd even received a fierce tongue-lashing from his father-in-law, of all things. Just yesterday John had given him what for about running Mary Ruth off. To top it all off, John had outright declared he wanted to go back to Hickory Hollow to live with one of his "sensible" grown grandchildren, where he didn't have to look at "the likes of you, Abram Ebersol, day in, day out."

Holding fast to the Old Ways was costing him dearly, but he felt toothless to change. With Ida dead and gone, it remained to be seen just how entrenched he would become over time, unwilling to stand up to Preacher Yoder or the bishop, neither one. Ida had found her strength in the Lord, she'd always said. As for himself, he couldn't see getting down on his knees and speaking words to the Almighty into the air. Lizzie, on the other hand, wasn't afraid to say she set ample time aside each day to do so. "You oughta try it once," she'd told him the day after Ida's funeral, when she'd found him coughing and weeping beside the feed trough as if his life was over. She'd been awful bold and said right out, "Prayer will help ya, Abram. I know this to be true."

Stubborn as he was, he had not followed her suggestion and had no intention of talking to Creator-God that way. Honest to Pete, what was this old world coming to when a man was nagged on mercilessly by his deceased wife's sister?

"I love you, Dat." Mary Ruth interrupted his musings. "I'll come visit, all right?"

"Jah, come see us. Hold your baby brother some, too."

When she reached for him, he didn't hug her back, only grunted. Surely she'd understand it wasn't in him today to be embracing her or anyone else. His heart felt more cold and deserted as each minute ticked by without his Ida.

Be there, his darling had said on her deathbed. *When the Lord calls you, be ready.* Saint that she was . . . Ida had put up with him all these years.

He said his good-byes to Mary Ruth and pressed his black hat down hard on his head. Leaning into the frosty evening, he made haste to return to Leah, Hannah, and his little ones.

On the way, he recalled Ida's funeral and burial service. So many people had come to bid a fond farewell. Even Dr. and Mrs. Schwartz and their elder son, Robert, had come to pay respect. They, along with other Englishers, including Henry and Lorraine's neighbor, Mrs. Ferguson; Mrs. Kraybill, who'd taken Hannah and Mary Ruth to the Georgetown School in her car all those years; and Mrs. Esbenshade, a frequent customer of their roadside stand.

Such a time to bury someone . . . in the cold and miserable ground, he thought, lamenting that his wife had to pass away so near Christmas. *Too near . . .*

For all his remaining days on the earth, Abram would regret not having insisted on calling for the Hexedokder. Any hex doctor would have known what to do to turn the baby within Ida; the awful bleeding could have been stopped, no matter how far his wife had slipped away. But Ida had made her most holy choice, her final stand—she who had rejected the powwow practices all their married life. Even unto death, he'd wrongly let her have her say.

Chapter Twenty-Three

Piercing cold temperatures lingered through January. Roads became miserably icy and snow-packed as one blizzard followed another, with grooves from horse-drawn sleighs and the occasional buggy becoming deeper and harder to avoid as the days wore on. Power lines up and down White Oak Road were weighed down by thick ice, causing power outages for Englishers in a radius of several miles. But the lack of electricity did not affect Leah and her family, nor their surrounding Amish neighbors.

Leah was thankful for Dat's unexpected willingness to allow Mary Ruth a weekly visit on Saturday mornings, since it gave her opportunity to continue working at Dr. Schwartz's clinic once a week. The doctor reacted kindly when Leah shared her predicament, wholeheartedly approving the hours best suited for her. "We don't want to lose you," he told her, to which Lorraine agreed emphatically.

"If you're ever in a jam, you can always bring the little ones here," she'd said. "I'll gladly entertain them."

Harder than juggling her life with its added responsibilities was the gnawing within—the intense knowing that it was imperative for her to find some sensible resolution to the problem of her promise to Mamma . . . and her betrothal to Gid. She had been somewhat relieved that he had seemed to understand how important her vow to Mamma was—how critical it would be day to day and year by year.

With that in mind, she agreed to talk privately with him when Gid knocked on the kitchen door one afternoon. Cordially they talked things out every which way in the stillness of the barn, only for Gid to conclude they must go their separate ways, releasing her from her betrothal promise.

Such a hopeless situation. *Gid's right about this*, Leah thought, dread filling her soul. Yet she knew for sure her husband would have felt terribly trapped, surrounded by an extended family he had no say about and having to kowtow to Dat on a daily basis.

In the very place where they had spent so many hours working together, tending to the farm animals' needs, Gid removed his black hat and reached for her hand. Struggling to speak, he said softly, "'Tis such a hard thing . . . I'm ever so sorry. Truly, I am." His eyes were intent on hers. "One thing's sure." His voice grew stronger. "You have my truest friendship, Leah—for as long as ya live."

"And you have mine, too. For always." She choked back tears. "We'll . . . see each . . . other, jah?" she sputtered, realizing how awkward it would be to occasionally bump into him.

"As good friends . . . you can count on that."

She felt ever so blue as they parted, and then again a few hours later, when the finality of his decision and their good-byes struck her anew as she stood at the window and saw him crossing the barnyard, heading for home. He caught her eye and waved to her, but she couldn't mistake the look of despair on his face.

Then and there, she believed the best thing to ward off further misery for them both was not to interact at all, though it wouldn't be easy, since Gid was still working part-time for Dat. The winter season while the ground was resting would be the simplest time to maintain a distance. The spring and summer plowing and planting, along with the fall harvest, would be much more awkward, since Gid would be quite visible on the property.

So the dismal expression on Gid's usually cheerful face made Leah want to turn away. Yet it wasn't anyone's fault what had become of them, really. After all, she couldn't help that she had been the one Mamma asked to raise her babies; it was for Leah to accept her lot with a smile. Truly, she couldn't imagine otherwise . . . for the sake of the children.

◆

Gid kept his hands busy every day except the Lord's Day so his loss of Leah wouldn't overtake him. He spent each waking minute shoeing horses or clearing out the fencerow of small trees. Diligently tending to another new litter of German shepherd pups also took plenty of time, as did pruning his father's grapevines, keeping up with chores for Abram, and doing whatever Dawdi Mathias needed done over at his place.

He could not be angry with Abram for wanting to raise

his own children. It just wasn't in him. Leah was doing the right thing by her little sister and brother . . . the right thing by Ida, too. Under God, Gid couldn't fault her or Abram, neither one, although he suspected Abram no longer felt an urgency for Leah to marry, not with a healthy baby boy growing up under the Ebersol roof. Once Abe reached the age of five, he would be out helping his father. Wouldn't be but a few short years and Abram's little boy would find the fieldwork he was meant for.

Still, Leah was the kind of girl Gid had always wanted to marry—someone who loved the soil and didn't mind getting her fingernails dirty, who even helped with plowing and planting some if need be. If he hadn't had his heart so set on her since youth, this setback wouldn't be as devastating. He suspected Leah had never quite committed herself to him—not as she had to Jonas so long ago.

He was in love with a girl he could never have. Quite stuck, he had marked time for much too long and was now nearing the limit on age for attending Sunday night singings—too late to ever hope to find a Leah replacement, if that were even possible.

So Gid toiled long and hard, hoping to lose himself in his labor, burying his lifelong wish to take Leah as his beloved wife.

❖

Now and again Abram insisted on helping with some of the baby-related chores, things he knew Leah was altogether surprised about, such as holding out the towel and drying off his baby son after a warm bath. Once Abe was dressed for the night in his miniature white nightclothes, Abram put his face down right close and talked to him. He told his infant boy all about his deceased mamma as the sleepy bundle lay quietly in his arms, whispering, too, what Abe's new mamma had given up to care for him and Lydiann. He figured since Ida was gone, the least he could do was spend plenty of after-supper time with Lydiann and Abe, which was a most pleasant task. Fact was, he wished now he'd done the same with his older daughters when they were small.

One such evening following a meal of pork chops and savory rice, he took Abe from Leah while she and Hannah did the dishes. Dawdi John and Lizzie were with him around the wood stove while he balanced both youngsters on his lap.

Lydiann giggled when he tickled her nose with the length of his soft beard.

"Do it to Abe," Lydiann said playfully.

When he did, his beard made Abe, who was lying in the length of his lap, sneeze.

"Do it again!" Lydiann said, her eyes bright, even mischievous. For a fleeting moment he seemed to be looking into Sadie's little-girl eyes. "Dat . . . will ya?"

Sighing, he was more careful to be gentle this time and held the back of his infant son's hand up to his own face. Then, moving his head slightly, he tickled Abe, much to Lydiann's delight—and to his own.

It was as Abram chuckled and played with his wee ones that he caught Leah's eye across the kitchen. For the first time in many weeks, his heart was full, gladdened beyond words.

◆

As the winter days wore on, Leah and Hannah took turns caring for the babies, trading off working outside with Dat to grease and mend the harnesses. Smithy Gid and Thomas Ebersol were out slaughtering meat animals at both the Peachey and Jesse Ebersol farms, which meant Leah felt more at ease to go about her chores. Knowing she wouldn't run into Gid made her feel at once relieved and as blue as could be.

The occasional sound of red-winged blackbirds reminded her of previous rambles to visit her "piece of earth" and the rare thornless honey locust tree growing deep in the forest behind Aunt Lizzie's log house. But she dared not return there lest she be reminded of her first love and the many letters written to him.

The excitement of upcoming March farm sales brought plenty of chatter from Dat and Dawdi John, especially at mealtime. Even Hannah seemed happy about going along this year, one of the first times Leah remembered her younger sister being interested in such community events. Leah would miss seeing what machinery, cattle, household items, and odds and ends were up for sale, as well as the occasional entire farm on the auction block. Men, women, and children attended, and sometimes the schools closed for the day. It was a wonderful-good time to see dozens of cousins and lifelong friends and anticipate the coming spring, but this year Leah knew her place was snug at home with Lydiann and Abe. Truth be known, she much preferred to be with them than spending all day at a farm sale, anyway.

How things had changed. She contemplated the fact

while peeling potatoes on a Wednesday afternoon at the end of February, recalling the many years she'd rushed out to milk the cows each day at four o'clock, before suppertime. Today she glanced at the day clock, thinking ahead to Dat bringing the cows home. What a cozy, even warm spot the barn was with the animals all inside, waiting for their supper of silage and grain. Even on a bitter cold day like today, Leah missed tending to the animals, their breath warming the air. The Lord God had certainly handpicked a pleasant place for His Son to be born.

On a Saturday in mid-March Leah went on foot to the clinic, having arranged for Mary Ruth to spend a full day baby-sitting Abe and Lydiann. Walking up the sidewalk to the front entrance, she noticed a small white handkerchief. When she stooped to pick it up, she was surprised to see Sadie's butterfly handkerchief, the one with the embroidered cutwork. "What on earth?" she muttered, carrying it inside.

Dr. Schwartz was shuffling through paper work when she arrived at eight-thirty that morning, so she set to work sweeping and washing the floors, dusting, and then shaking out all the rugs, deciding not to bother him just yet. But around nine-fifteen, before the few Saturday patients were scheduled to arrive, she knocked on his open office door.

He looked up, smiled, and waved her inside. "Pull up a chair, Leah."

She removed the handkerchief from her pocket. "I found this lying on the walk. It belonged to my older sister."

His smile faded quickly, and he was silent for a long awkward moment. When he spoke, his voice sounded low and somewhat strained. "Are you sure of this?"

"Completely," she replied. "This is the hankie my sister placed over her dead baby's face the night you delivered him." She paused a moment to breathe. Then she added, "I'm sure you remember, Dr. Schwartz, because, if you don't mind my sayin' so, it was *your* grandson born—and died—that April night, ain't?" She found his expression odd—so peculiar, in fact, that she felt queasy. "It's the *only* handkerchief Hannah ever made like this. A special one indeed."

"Well, if it's Sadie's, as you say, I wonder how it found its way to the ground," he said rather defensively.

"I thought you might've tucked it in with the dead . . . baby—whatever it is a doctor does with a blue baby born too early." Right then, in a rush of memory, Sadie's heartbreaking labor and delivery came to her and caught her off guard. Leah couldn't go on—not this close to Mamma's death. Her heart felt suddenly cold, her nerves shot. She didn't know how she would manage the cleaning tasks ahead of her. "I'm sorry," she said at last. "That awful night still pains me so."

Dr. Schwartz reached out his hand, as though attempting to comfort her from where he sat. "Leah, you are correct about your sister's baby being mine and Lorraine's grandson, though my wife knows nothing of it."

She stared at him in disbelief. "You . . . never told her?"

He shook his head, hands now firmly clasped on the desk. "The news would have caused her tremendous sadness . . . even embarrassment. I saw no need for that."

The thought came to her. *He trusts me not to tell.* "You

must have kept my sister's special handkerchief, then . . . somewhere safe, in case she returned from Ohio?"

"No doubt, I *should* have given it back," he confessed, sighing loudly. "Now you have it in your possession. I suppose it's too late to send it off to Sadie."

"We have no way of contacting her." Then she found herself opening up, sharing her deep sense of loss over both Sadie's severe shunning and Mamma's death.

The doctor listened, removing his glasses and seeming to pay exceptionally close attention. When she was nearly spent, he admitted to her, "I did not keep the handkerchief in a safe place, as you suppose. I guess that's of little consolation to you, and I'm sorry."

Leah's mind was in a whirl. How *could* a warm and caring doctor overlook such a sensitive thing?

At home later—with the lovely hankie in her safe-keeping—Leah realized she could neither show Hannah nor tell her, as Hannah might ask questions about the night Sadie had birthed her baby. While Mamma had told both Hannah and Mary Ruth of Sadie's wild running-around days, making the twins privy to everything, the fact remained that Leah did not care to reveal the story from her viewpoint. Besides, it wasn't necessary for Hannah to know all Sadie had experienced that night.

In the privacy of her room, she caressed the emerald-and-gold butterfly hankie and noticed not a single bloodstain. Dr. Schwartz must have washed it thoroughly in cold water following the birth. Folding it carefully, she placed the delicate item deep in her hope chest, deciding that was the best place for it.

Moved to tears, she knelt beside the bed and asked the Lord to calm her nerves, then offered thanksgiving for the discovery of the handkerchief—the one truly important item of Sadie's she had in her care. She also prayed for God's protection and grace on her wayward sister, "Wherever she might be."

That done, she headed downstairs and turned her attention to Lydiann and Abe, who were in the kitchen being supervised by Mary Ruth. *I must put on a cheerful face*, she thought. *Please, Lord, help me.*

"Did it go well at the clinic?" asked Mary Ruth, warming a bottle for Abe while Lydiann sat at the table trying to string up a dozen or more empty spools.

"Jah, just fine."

Mary Ruth seemed anxious to talk about her schooling— what subjects she enjoyed most and how she'd dillydallied about joining the glee club, missing the auditions by a single day. Leah listened halfheartedly, her mind on Sadie and the little one, gone to heaven.

Mamma is tending now to her own precious grandson! she realized suddenly. This thought comforted her greatly as Mary Ruth chattered on.

During a lull in conversation, Leah went and took Abe from Mary Ruth and held him close. She looked into the tiny face of Mamma's handsome little boy—hair the color of sheaves of grain and those shining blue eyes—and battled both her own quivering lip and the tears that threatened to spill.

Chapter Twenty-four

Almost before Leah could comprehend it, a full year had passed, taking flight on wings of love. Her hands found plenty to do, and she did it with all her might—kneading and baking daily loaves of bread, scrubbing floors, washing diapers, and helping with the canning. When the after-supper hours rolled around, she often spent time playing with Mamma's babies.

Gradually her keen affection for Smithy Gid began to fade as she became more and more caught up in the routine of caring for a now four-year-old and an eighteen-month-old. Busier days she had never known.

Aunt Lizzie helped some, regularly looking in on Dawdi John due to his age. Dawdi was slowing down quite a lot and hadn't shown any interest in getting out in the fields for plowing or planting this year. Still more telling, he no longer cared for sitting outdoors once the warm days crept up. Truth was, he had become almost as much a homebody as Leah, and she enjoyed his company, taking the little ones next door quite often.

Dawdi had quit his fussing about wanting to return to

Hickory Hollow to live there, what with Mary Ruth's frequent visits. Since Aunt Lizzie continued to dote on him like he was a child, Dawdi John had himself a right nice setup. There were even times when Gid and the smithy came over to chew the fat with him, especially now that warmer weather was upon them. All around, the Ebersol Cottage had somehow managed to get back on an even keel without Mamma's pleasant disposition and her wonderful-good pies, though Leah was mighty glad to have caught up on nearly all of both Mamma's and Aunt Lizzie's recipe files. Gid and his family often benefited from this, as well, since Hannah liked to take an extra pie or two over to the Peachey farm from time to time; a blessing from Leah's hand to her former beau and his kin is the way she thought of it—the least she could do to bring a smile to Smithy Gid's kind face.

Abram asked Leah if she thought Lydiann was old enough to go with him to market and was right surprised to be given the go-ahead. All the way to Strasburg, Lydiann chattered beside him, sitting with her little hands folded in her lap. "I wanna be a gut cook like Mamma Leah," she said, eyes alight as she shared a list of recipes she wanted to learn.

He had to chuckle, but not so loudly she might mistakenly think he was making fun. "You follow your big sister round, and not only will ya be a fine cook but also a careful gardener, plower, sower, and harvester."

"Mamma can do *all* them things?"

He nodded. "All that and more."

Lydiann ducked her chin a bit, like she was taking it all in and rather amazed at the talents of her mother figure.

"Someday I'm sure Leah will teach you how to milk a cow," he volunteered.

Lydiann looked up at him, eyes blinking. "She already did. Just the other morning she sat me down on a stool, smack-dab under Ol' Rosie."

"Did she, now?"

"Jah, and it was the funniest thing." Lydiann sighed, unfolding her hands and adjusting her small bonnet. "Mamma Leah says I'll be out milking every mornin' once I turn six."

"Is that so?" He smiled more to himself than to his young daughter. Seemed Leah was bound and determined to create another outdoor girl, which was right fine with him. The world could definitely benefit from more than one Leah Ebersol, he decided then and there. Reaching around Lydiann, he pulled her into a bear hug to a stream of giggles.

◆

Gid was more than willing to help move Ivan and Mary Etta Troyer and their brood of ten children—newly transplanted from Sugarcreek, Ohio—into the farmhouse down the road from the Kauffmans' spread. Glad for a mild and sunny day, he carried heavy boxes into the large farmhouse, as well as the trestle table and kitchen benches. All the while he thought of Leah, wondering how to approach her with his news. After all, they had enjoyed a long-standing friendship nearly their whole lives, one that had even weathered the sad yet necessary end of their engagement. While he and three other young men from the church district got the new family settled, he considered stopping by the Ebersol home to visit with Leah after a bit. *Out of courtesy to such a dear friend.*

When he was free to leave, he headed up Georgetown Road in his open buggy, turning a sharp right into Abram's long drive. He noticed young Abe toddling about in the side yard, doing his best to chase after a red squirrel. The boy pointed a curious finger at the tree branch where the small creature had decided to perch. Abram came around the corner and scooped his son up into his arms, standing there with Abe still pointing and jabbering.

"Hullo!" Abram called to him.

Getting out of the carriage, Gid waved and hurried across the yard. "Catch any squirrels yet, Abe?" He tousled the towheaded youngster's thick hair.

"He's most interested in things that move," Abram explained. "Leah has her hands full watching *this* young'un."

"I see that."

"Well, let's go, Abe," Abram said as he carried him out toward the barn. Abram turned to look over his shoulder. "You here to see—?"

"Leah," Gid said quickly, making his way to the back door.

"Don't bother to knock," Abram called back to him. "Just give a holler. She's inside makin' supper."

He crept in the door furtively, quite aware of his own breathing. He called out her name. "Leah . . . it's Gid."

Turning, she looked at him from where she stood at the counter. She offered that warm and lovely smile of hers, and he wondered if it might disappear once she heard his confession. "Got a minute?" he asked.

She nodded. "What's on your mind?"

He knew full well that Hannah and Lydiann were out on the mule road together, for he'd seen them rolling a big ball on the ground, back and forth, as he'd come up the lane. He must not waste any time before sharing his heart. "I've been meaning to talk with ya."

She wore a slight look of worry on her face.

"I think it best you hear directly from me. Not through the grapevine . . ." He was conscious of the heat of his long-sleeved shirt for the first time today, and he tugged on the cuff absentmindedly. "You see, I've become quite fond of your sister Hannah," he started again. "I plan to speak to Abram 'bout the possibility of courting her. If, well . . . if it seems all right with you."

Her eyes were suddenly brighter than before. "All right? Oh, Gid, of course, it is. Really 'tis!" Then she surprised him by reaching for his hand. "This is wonderful-gut news, truly."

For a moment he thought he might hug her. But he refrained from doing so, squeezing only her hand. "Denki, Leah. This means a lot to me."

Pulling back, he stood there, gazing at her, his former love. His first and only sweetheart . . . till now. What an unexpected surprise that his heart should be reawakened with love for another when he hadn't thought such a thing possible. He was glad to have taken time to talk with Leah, just as Abram had encouraged him to do. Thoughtful as always, Leah had given him a most precious gift—reassurance that all was well.

Lizzie's nose was but a few inches from the damp earth. She'd gone tramping through the woods, needing a chance to clear her head, what with being cooped up too much these days in the Dawdi Haus with her ailing father. Bent nearly double, she laughed at herself, glad she was still as spry as ever. She pulled herself up from the barely visible trail and brushed off her long dress and apron. *Goodness me,* she thought, cracking a twig underfoot as she rose to stand. How she'd ever gotten her foot tangled in the underbrush, she didn't know. After all, she knew these vast woods like the back of her hand and wasn't any too shy about saying so.

They were, after all, her woods—hers and God's. Smiling, she turned and headed back east toward Abram's house. Springtime humidity hung in the air, making the moss grow faster on tree trunks around her. Creepers adorned the spruce and maples, leaving a welcome impression in her mind. Breathing deeply, she found herself thinking of her brother-in-law. He *had* begun to soften toward Mary Ruth, and this made Lizzie sit up and take notice. Ida's widower was also noticeably less gruff in general. Lizzie didn't know what to make of it, but she knew she liked working alongside him in the barn and elsewhere a whole lot more than ever before. Deciding right then she would not let up on her talk of the Lord, nearly daily now it seemed, she pushed on and made her way toward the clearing.

There she spotted Smithy Gid in the distance, climbing into his open buggy. *Same courting buggy he's had all these years, poor fella.* Seeing his carriage parked in Abram's lane set her mind to racing. While she had long suspected Gid of being sweet on Hannah, she wondered why he was showing up here in broad daylight.

Making her way down the mule road, she happened to see

Leah waving through the kitchen window at him. *A dearer boy there never was*, she thought, happy for Hannah but a little sad for Leah, who would never fully know Gid's love. Or any man's, for that matter.

Dear Lord, bless Leah today, she prayed. *Bless our faithful girl with your tender grace.*

———◆———

With another summer came opportunities for getting Lydiann and Abe outdoors, and Leah was glad of it. She liked to spread an old blanket out on the back lawn and sit and play with the children, sometimes feeding them small pieces of apple and orange. King, Blackie, and Sassy wandered over to investigate the fruity treats amid squeals of delight from the children, especially from Lydiann, who was nearly as fond of the dogs as she was her baby brother. Now and then Dat would stop what he was doing and make over the tots, paying closest attention to Abe.

It was late morning and Abe was fussy, ready for a nap. Hannah had just returned from the barn and came running over and plopped down on the blanket. "'Tis a right nice day, ain't?"

"One of the best times of year," Leah replied. "Wild roses are awful perty, farmers are makin' hay, and honeysuckle never smelt sweeter."

"And . . . young scholars can say, 'no more papers, no more books . . . no more teacher's tetchy looks,'" Hannah chanted the familiar verse. "Sure am glad *I'm* not in school anymore."

"Your thoughts must be with Mary Ruth today," said Leah.

"S'pose they are." She skimmed the palm of her hand across the blades of grass, and Sassy came and playfully nipped at Hannah's fingers. "The house seems so quiet sometimes, is all."

"How can that be, with the children growin' up under our noses?"

Hannah sighed. "You know what I mean."

Leah nodded; she knew, all right.

They sat there enjoying the warm weather and a hint of a breeze every so often, the scents of summer all around. The big leaves of the linden tree quaked gently outside the window.

"What's *really* on your mind, sister?" Leah said at last.

Hannah twitched her nose, looking at Lydiann. "How long before our little sister understands certain things?"

"Whatever do you mean?"

She leaned over and whispered in Leah's ear. "I need to talk to you . . . in private sometime."

"Well, why not say what's on your mind in English 'stead of Dutch? That'll keep Lydiann in the dark, if that's what you want." Leah rose and carried Abe to the back door while Hannah took Lydiann's hand and led her inside.

"I'll put Abe down for his nap," said Hannah while Leah sent Lydiann upstairs to find her dolly and a cradle.

When Hannah returned, her face was flushed. "Ach, but this might seem strange to you"—here she guided Leah through the kitchen to the screened-in back porch. "I don't know how you'll feel 'bout this. . . ."

"What is it, Hannah?" She studied her sister's eyes. Big

and brown, they were, and dancing like she'd never seen them.

"What I'm tryin' to say is, what would ya think if I told ya I like Smithy Gid? Not as just a friend, I mean."

Leah couldn't help herself. So . . . Gid had already talked to Hannah about the possibility of going for steady. She smiled and clapped her hands. "Well, it's clearly all over your face. I couldn't be happier for you—both of you."

"You mean it?"

"I can't think of a better match for Gid than my own precious sister."

Hannah kissed her good-bye. "I best not be gone too long, or Dat will wonder what's become of me." She turned and hurried away.

"Jah, go on now. But be back for dinner at straight-up noon," Leah called after her. She headed to the kitchen. Hannah deserved to have an attentive beau like Smithy Gid, dear soul that she was. No need to think twice on it. And she was the perfect choice for Gid, as well. To think Dat just might get his son-in-law of choice, after all!

As for Hannah, she'd been through a wringer of sorts, what with Ezra Stoltzfus's leaving the Amish church behind, getting himself shunned so soon after baptism. The grapevine had it that he'd upped and gone *ferhoodled* or worse after the death of Elias, as wild as if he'd never knelt his knee in baptism. So Hannah was better off, his dropping her like a hot potato and all, making it possible for Gid to have his chance.

Leah found Lydiann talking Dutch to her little faceless doll. She was saying it might not be so long and they'd all be going fishing with Dat and "Smitty Gid" over at Blackbird Pond . . . and wouldn't that be such fun?

Lydiann would enjoy the benefits of growing up with a brother; something Leah had always felt she'd missed. *She* had been the boy of the family, so to speak, but those days were gone for good. She was truly the woman of the house, not only Mamma to Lydiann and Abe, but the matriarch in charge of seeing that the household ran smoothly, including the Dawdi Haus. She no longer felt she'd missed out on certain joy by not marrying, as her friend Adah and most every other girl her age in the church community had. Goodness, Naomi Bontrager was already expecting her second baby.

In all of this, Leah did not feel she was fooling herself; after all, being a maidel was evidently her lot in life, and her role in helping raise Abe and Lydiann was a good one. She had dealt with her resentment toward Sadie and moved forward with life, ever so glad to be a mother to her youngest siblings. Truly it was God who had seen fit to bless her with these two adorable children.

After the noon meal, Abram was right pleased to see Leah outdoors with Abe and Lydiann in tow. He stopped to pump some well water, quenching his thirst while he fanned himself with his beat-up straw hat. He sure could use a new one. His father-in-law hadn't minced words about it, complaining to high heavens about how "awful ratty that old hat looks." John seemed to pick at near everything Abram did or didn't do these days. He'd become a rather cantankerous sort, living alone without his wife of many decades and losing his daughter Ida, all in the space of a few years. Still, Abram could relate all too keenly to John's hopelessness. In other ways, though, John had mellowed some recently, especially when it came time for Mary Ruth's visits.

With that in mind, he thought he ought to pay John a visit himself before too long.

Chatter from Abe brought his attention back to the present. "Thirsty?" he asked Leah.

Lydiann spoke up before Leah could, asking for a nice cold drink herself. Leah looked right pleased, watching Lydiann hold the dipper and sipper, the excess water dripping down her plump cheeks. Of course, now Abe was grousing for equal treatment.

Once the little ones were satisfied, they wandered about the lawn barefooted and laughing, soaking up the afternoon sunshine. His heart swelled with pride, glad for this moment to pause and reflect on the good thing his Leah had done . . . was *doing.* "Denki, Leah . . . for bein' such a gut mamma to the children." He wished he'd said this a long time ago.

"Dat . . . that's all right." Leah gave him a warm smile. "I love seein' them grow up like this."

"You've given up everything for my little ones." They both knew he was talking about Smithy Gid in particular.

"I'm happy with my life. Honestly." She paused, turning to check where Abe and Lydiann had disappeared to. Then she continued, "I prob'ly shouldn't say this, but you surely know Gid's sweet on Hannah." She said it nearly in a whisper.

"Oh, jah." He was careful not to react too cheerfully, wanting to be sensitive to any open wounds remaining from Leah and Gid's breakup. He looked her over but good. "Well, now . . . how do *you* feel 'bout it?"

She smiled again. "It's 'bout time you got the son-in-law you've been waitin' for!"

He studied her mighty hard at this instant, wondering . . . hoping . . . then, beyond all doubt, he knew she was quite sincere. Eagerly so, it seemed by the look of delight on her pretty face.

He called to Abe, who came running and jumped high into his arms. "Come along," he said, offering a hand to help up Leah. "Let's ride over to Georgetown and have us all some ice cream."

This brought an even bigger smile to Leah's face. To the words *ice cream*, Lydiann and Abe clapped with delight, which made Abram feel right pleased with himself. The Good Lord was surely shining down His blessings. *In spite of myself,* thought Abram.

Chapter Twenty-five

Leah was anxious to attend the July Sisters Day at Adah's house, two miles away. Thanks to Aunt Lizzie volunteering to baby-sit Lydiann and Abe, Leah was freed up to go with Hannah. Lizzie had been insisting all week long that it was high time for Leah to be around other adults. "You're in the house too much," she kept saying.

Leah had laughed, recognizing what her aunt said was true and looking forward to the outing. The women folk did share a gift of close friendship, even though she'd never much cared for their work frolics growing up.

"Friendships are the core of our lives, ain't so?" she said, enjoying the carriage ride.

Hannah nodded. "And sisters are always the best of friends."

"I should say." Leah wondered if Hannah was maudlin about her twin again, although Mary Ruth had been coming to see them three or four times a week lately. Aunt Lizzie, Dawdi John, and even Dat enjoyed seeing her, as well, and yearned for the delicious dishes Mary Ruth sometimes brought to share with the family, though she was reluctant to stay and eat, out of respect for Dat.

"We're mirrors to the past, in a way," Hannah said softly. "We look into each other's faces and remember what we know. . . ."

"Well, now, you're sounding like a dreamer today."

Hannah laughed. "Guess maybe Mary Ruth's rubbin' off on me some."

"But what you say is true. There *is* such deep understanding between sisters."

Hannah nodded and fell silent. Leah was thankful for this time alone, just the two of them. Scarcely did they ever have the opportunity to go out riding or to a work frolic like this. The sky seemed a prettier blue today and little robin red breast sang stronger because Hannah was here to share the day.

Once they arrived at Adah's house, Leah was happy to see Adah's younger sister, Dorcas, as well as Adah's five sisters-in-law, Ebersol cousins all. The kitchen was full up with sisters of every shape and size, peeling tomatoes at the sink, boiling water in large pots, preparing to stew the red fruit, as well as make soup and spaghetti sauce—an all-day affair. Several were expecting babies, including Adah herself. Leah found this sight, here in Adah's cozy kitchen, not only joyful on behalf of her dear friend, but she was excited for Adah to join yet again the maternal realm. "We're sharing the joys of motherhood after all, you and I," she whispered to her.

Adah flashed a quick sad look, but Leah squeezed her hand to reassure her all was well. Truly, it was.

Hannah helped mash a mountain of cooked tomatoes. After a time the mushy red color and strong odor made her feel queasy, and she wondered how she'd ever manage attending such canning frolics as Smithy Gid's wife someday. His mother's side of the family was tomato crazy, putting up anything and everything with the fruit in it. Far as she could tell, though, that was the one and only drawback to her marrying into the Peachey family one fine day.

She tried holding her breath as she crushed the nasty red fruits, but that didn't work, either, because when it came time for her to breathe again, she had to fill her lungs even more deeply with the fragrant aroma.

"Is Leah doin' okay, really?" Adah asked her, unaware Hannah was the one struggling at the moment, though not emotionally.

"She seems fine to me," she replied, glad to raise her head and her nose out of the immediate vicinity of the tomatoes. "Leah's the sweetest mother to Lydiann and Abe," she offered. "You should see her with them."

"I've seen her all right; I just can never tell for sure if Leah's all right *inside*," Adah persisted.

"Jah, I believe she is." Hannah wanted to put Adah's fears to rest. After all, she and Adah were soon to be sisters by marriage. She'd told no one just yet, but, short time that it had been since he'd declared his feelings for her, darling Gid had not only begun to court her but had already proposed marriage. He wasn't wasting any time, which was right fine with her, being she'd known him her entire life and Dat, Dawdi John, and Aunt Lizzie were all for it. "Long as it won't hurt Leah further," Lizzie had been quick to say.

"If there's ever any doubt, Hannah, you'll let me know 'bout Leah, jah?" asked Adah, clearly still devoted after all these years.

Adah, precious friend to Leah—always thinking of others, just as Leah was known to. *And that nearly to a fault,* Hannah thought. *Sometimes my sister is better to others than to herself.*

While Gid waited to shoe his next horse, he set about redding up. Suddenly thirsty, he finished sweeping the floor and ran to the house for some cold lemonade. Oddly enough, the kitchen, fragrant with the scent of freshly baked muffins, was empty. He walked to the window and stood watching for his customer, glad for the solitude. Gulping down a tall glass, he returned to the icebox and poured another. He then went and perched himself on the long bench next to the table, sitting there with his glass in hand.

All the while he daydreamed of pretty Hannah. There was something about the way she looked at him that made him think she was not just pretty but truly lovely. *She's very young,* he thought, realizing anew how peculiar it had seemed—but only at first—to meet up with fair Hannah Ebersol at a Sunday singing, though he'd seen and talked to her plenty of times out in Abram's barn. More than hesitant that particular night, he soon found his voice and discovered her to be nearly as easy to talk to as Leah, if not more so. Attentive and sweet, Hannah had won his heart in a matter of a few buggy rides home.

Right this minute he wondered if the Lord God might've had all this planned from the foundations of the earth, giving back the years he'd lost while waiting for Leah. Was it heresy to think about the heavenly Father that way? Gid had no intention of deliberating the notion, but it was true that Hannah, at only eighteen, had a good many childbearing years ahead of her as his loving wife. They would have themselves a wonderful-good time raising their brood, and if their babies looked anything like Hannah, he would be a very blessed and happy man.

He removed his straw hat and scratched his head. The Almighty certainly worked in extraordinary ways, seemed to him. Downright mystifying it was.

The clatter of carriage wheels brought him to his feet, and he left his glass half full on the table as he hurried outside to greet both horse and client.

It was on the ride home from Adah's that Leah and Hannah got to talking heart to heart. Weary from being on her feet for much of the day, Leah was content to sit back and relax, let Hannah rein down the horse to a slow walk, and, of all things, do much of the talking. She was getting to be nearly as chatty as Mary Ruth. *Nice to see her coming out of her shell little by little*, Leah thought, listening to her prattle about this and that.

They were coming up on the corner where a left-hand turnoff would lead to Naomi's parents' farmhouse when Hannah stopped talking and began humming a hymn from the Ausbund.

Smithy Gid came to mind and Leah said, "I think you and Gid are a right nice match."

"Oh?"

"Both of you enjoy music so."

"Jah, he plays his harmonica all the time." She paused, blushing a little.

"Not *all* the time, I hope."

"Oh, Leah ... you know what I mean." At this they began to giggle.

Just then two old codgers rode toward them, their white beards as long as any Leah had ever seen. They were leaning back against the seat, downright relaxed, just taking their sweet time. "Like there's no tomorrow," she whispered to Hannah.

The presence of another carriage made them quickly gather their wits and stop the tittering, since the men were within earshot. Once they'd passed, Hannah resumed their conversation. "If you feel comfortable 'bout it, I'd like you to be one of my bridesmaids, Leah."

"That's awful nice of you," Leah replied, meaning it.

"So you'll stand up with me?"

" 'Course I will."

" 'Tis awful sad Mary Ruth has no chance of being my bridesmaid."

Leah felt sorry, too. "Jah, but I wouldn't think of askin' Dat's permission on that. I can imagine what he'd say."

"Ain't that the truth."

"Be glad Mary Ruth will at least be in attendance," Leah reminded Hannah.

"Jah, that I am."

Leah, eager to cheer her sister, continued on a positive note. "Just think how happy Mamma would be over your upcoming marriage," she said. "She always liked Gid, ya know."

Hannah sighed. "We'll all miss her at the wedding, ain't so?"

Leah agreed and closed her eyes, thinking of dear Mamma.

Hannah stirred her back to the present. "I wish with all of my heart one certain sister could be on hand to witness my marriage, too."

Drowsily Leah reached over and patted Hannah's hand. "I know, dear sister. I know."

They rode quietly now, surrounded by the twitter of birds and the scent of new-mown hay and early harvest apples ripening in orchards. Leah found herself wondering how many more times she might be asked to be a bridesmaid. Naturally, as time went on, she would be passed over; no bride in her right mind would invite an old maidel to stand up with her. Maybe this *would* be the last time, which was quite all right. What with both Sadie and Mary Ruth having flown the nest, she could be Hannah's supportive and gentle right hand. Knowing her, dear Hannah would need a close sister-friend on her wedding day.

Evident in Hannah's eyes was her deep fondness for Smithy Gid. Leah was fully aware how much in love her sister and Gid were. *The love they share is the kind Jonas and I had together,* she thought. *The kind both Gid and Hannah deserve.*

While she had cared a great deal for Gid, lately she had come to the realization her love for him had not been the same as her love for Jonas. She had made this conscious discovery simply by watching Hannah's face when she spoke of

Gid, and, on one occasion, by observing them from afar as they held hands and walked together, Hannah leaning her head against Gid's strong arm. The adoring way they seemed to bend toward each other, even as they walked and talked, brought back a rush of memories. *So like the way Jonas and I always did. . . .*

Upon their return home, Leah let Hannah unhitch the horse and lead him to water in the barn, as she had so kindly offered to do. Leah tried to swallow the lump in her throat but did not succeed. Hastily she headed to the house, more eager than ever to hold Lydiann and Abe—*her* little ones—close to her heart.

Part Two

· · · ·

There is no greatness where there is
no simplicity, goodness and truth.

—Leo Tolstoy

· · · ·

Truth, crushed to earth, shall rise again.

—William Cullen Bryant

Chapter Twenty-Six

Spring 1956

The month of May arrived in misty splendor. Yellow daffo-
dils, along with purple and red tulips, raised their radiant
heads to the sky. Creeks were swollen and burbling, and it
seemed to Leah every song sparrow, robin, and meadowlark
must be joining in the springtime chorus.

She stood out near the hen house, watching Lydiann scatter feed, talking soft and low to the chickens and the solitary
rooster. *The way I always did*, she thought, smiling. Leah was
glad school doors were closed for summer vacation, the last
day having been Friday, the eighteenth, one day following
Lydiann's ninth birthday.

Tall for her age, Lydiann reminded Leah of Sadie as a
child. Though rather lanky like Leah, the energetic youngster
had outgrown her topsy-turvy tendency to fall over not only
herself but also occasional buckets of fresh milk, half-gallon
pails of shelled peas, and whatnot. Both Dat and Leah were
thankful for Lydiann's zeal for assisting with outdoor chores,
what with Hannah busy mothering two small girls—Ida Mae,
named for Mamma, and baby Katie Ann. Smithy Gid and

Hannah lived snug and contented in Aunt Lizzie's former log house, while Lizzie had moved down to the Dawdi Haus to care for Dawdi John after Gid and Hannah had tied the knot at a late autumn wedding four and a half years ago.

Cheerful and hardworking, Abe was almost six and a half and his father's shadow. Leah felt truly blessed to witness the close father-son relationship unfolding daily.

"That rooster's poutin', ain't so, Mamma Leah?" Lydiann said, frowning.

"I daresay you could be right 'bout that."

"He's mighty pushy, too . . . whatever's botherin' him?"

She went to stand near Lydiann. "Seems to me he wants some attention."

"From one of the hens . . . or from me?" Lydiann's sweet voice still retained its childlike appeal.

Leah smiled. "*All* the hens, prob'ly."

Laughing, Lydiann grinned at her. "Ach, Mamma, you're pullin' my leg. He don't want *all* them hens a-lookin' at him preenin', does he?"

"Well, maybe not." She put her hand on Lydiann's slender shoulder. They stood rooted to the spot, watching the chickens peck and scrap over their dinner, amused at their antics.

Abe came hollering out of the barn, running toward them. "Mamma! Lydiann! You's must come have a look-see!"

"What on earth?" Leah hurried to follow him back to the barn, with Lydiann close behind.

Abe made haste, climbing as fast as his short legs would take him, up the ladder to the hayloft. Getting to the top, he set about catching one of many cats. When he'd done so, he held it up by the nape of its neck and pointed to its hind end. "See, she's missin' her tail!"

Leah didn't know whether to laugh or cry at such a sorry sight.

Lydiann spoke up first. "She got it cut off during the harvest last year's my guess."

"Either that or the fellas got her on a lark—durin' a pest hunt," volunteered Abe.

Leah flinched. Abe was much too young to be aware of such things; he was just out of first grade, for goodness' sake! Truth was, some of the young men in the community were a bit too rowdy for her liking. They chose up sides nearly every night during harvest, giving themselves points for snuffing out the life of farm pests, a practice that kept teenage boys in the midst of rumschpringe busy in Gobbler's Knob instead of out smoking or chasing after worldly girls in Lancaster. Each side collected heads and tails for points, everything from rats and sparrows, to hawks and starlings. The group with the most points was rewarded with a baked-ham dinner.

"Does it hurt anything for a cat not to have a tail?" asked Lydiann.

"Makes it hard to keep the flies off her, I'd think," Abe spoke up, his dark blue eyes twinkling, framed by long thick lashes.

"Why did a cat get picked as a pest, I wonder?" Lydiann peered closely at the spot where the tail had been severed.

"Too many kitties can be looked on as a problem by some folk," Leah answered, wishing to switch to another subject. She'd known of farmers who drowned or shot their excess feline population, but if she had her way, there'd be a house cat or two living *inside* the Ebersol Cottage. Mamma never cared much for indoor pets, though, and neither did most of the women folk in the community, for that matter. These days, Dat had better things to do than argue for or against having a favorite cat, and Leah had decided not to pursue the matter.

"This one must've wandered over to the Peachey farm last fall, ain't?" Abe said, eyes still wide.

"Sad to say." Leah turned to head toward the ladder, hoping the children would follow and leave the subject of the poor cat be.

"I heard from brother Gid that Smitty asked for a pest hunt." Abe put the cat down and shuffled across the haymow. "Too many sparrows were diggin' holes in the straw stacks and roostin' in there. Them boys sewed some big ol' blankets together and trapped the birds inside the stacks. Once they got too hot or stopped breathing, the fellas just went in and cut off their heads."

Lydiann shrieked. "Mamma, make him stop talkin' 'bout that!"

Leah waited for Abe to bound down from the ladder, then placed a firm but gentle hand on his head. She stroked his blond hair, the color of the straw stacks he'd just described. "Best not be wishin' your youth away, young man," she said. "There's plenty of time for goin' on a lark with the boys."

"I s'pose" was all he said, and they headed back outside.

Lydiann tugged on her brother's black suspenders. "Lookee up there," she said, pointing at the sky. "Now *that's* a sight worth talking 'bout."

And it surely was. Leah noticed sunbeams threading a

pathway through a wispy patch of clouds, thankful for Lydiann's keen interest in the more pleasant side of nature. Abe, of course, was all boy with an ongoing appetite for food and otherwise and far louder than any of Abram's daughters had ever been, full of pep and broad grins. He was always mighty eager to find the first bumblebees come spring, which meant it was finally time to shed shoes and run barefoot. He also loved to take his fishing pole to the nearby creek or Blackbird Pond, sometimes joined by both Gid and Dat, but mostly—Leah knew this all too well—taking off to his favorite fishing hole without ever telling a soul where he was headed.

Just now he looked downright ornery with his front tooth missing—a true disheveled schoolboy with cropped hair. Scarcely, though, did Abe ever wear the straw hat expected to be worn by all men and boys starting at age two. *Hat or not, he's ever so dear,* she thought, wishing Mamma might have lived to see this day. These precious beautiful children were having the best time of their young lives, soaking up summertime.

God doeth all things well. . . .

She and Lydiann headed into the house. Without being told, Lydiann scrubbed her hands, and then set the table while Leah took the roasted chicken, stuffed with bread dressing, out of the oven.

Thinking again of Mamma, she asked Lydiann if she'd like to take a long walk after dinner. Bobbing her blond head, Lydiann said she would. Abe would be going over to Smithy Gid's grandfather's place with Dat this afternoon because Mathias Byler, Miriam Peachey's father, needed a hand with transplanting young tobacco plants into the field. Abe especially liked to go to "Dawdi Byler's," as Gid encouraged him to address the older gentleman, since young Abe got a kick out of hearing both Gid and Gid's grandfather play their harmonicas together.

After dishes were washed and dried, she and Lydiann made their way down the long lane toward the road, heading past the Peachey farm, clear out to the turnoff to the Kauffmans'.

Down the road a ways, they turned and climbed over a vine-filled ditch and then up a slight embankment, heading to the Amish cemetery protected by giant shade trees.

"Dat's parents are buried here somewhere," Leah said softly.

"They passed on before I was born, ain't?"

She nodded, looking down at Lydiann. "You would've loved Dawdi and Mammi Ebersol . . . a lot."

"What were they like?"

"Dawdi was kind and fun loving, yet he had his own ideas, I guess you could say."

"Bullheaded, ya mean?" Lydiann surprised her by saying.

"Ach, that doesn't become you, child."

"Es dutt mir leed." Lydiann hung her head.

"You best be sorry," Leah was quick to say, reminding herself of Mamma, who had never approved of her daughters speaking out of turn, calling folk names.

"Mammi Ebersol was sweet as cherry pie . . . never said an unkind word 'bout anyone. Not her whole life."

"I could be that sweet—even as honey," Lydiann said, looking up at her with innocent, yet spirited eyes.

"Jah, that you can certainly be." *When you want to*, she thought.

With that Lydiann reached for her hand, and they walked for a while amidst the headstones and trees. Leah was aware, once again, of the birds' exhilarating song. "Did you ever hear this verse from the Good Book? 'The flowers appear on the earth; the time of the singing of birds is come . . .'?"

"Can't say I have. Where'd *you* hear it?"

"Mamma told it to me once. She loved to listen to the birds, 'specially early in the morning."

Lydiann's eyes suddenly looked bluer. "What else did Mamma love?"

"That's easy." She turned and knelt down in the soft woodland grass. "She loved *you*. I wish you could remember her carryin' you here and there, talkin' to you in Dutch and English both, hopin' you'd grow up to respect the land and listen for the song of nature all round you."

"Aunt Lizzie does that, too, ain't so?"

"Maybe more than all of us."

"Even more than Mamma did?"

She hugged Lydiann close. "Each sister had certain things she enjoyed about God's green earth. For Mamma it was the birds and the way the sky could paint itself all kinds of colors. She saw the Lord God clearly in all of His creation, just as Aunt Lizzie does. Lizzie especially likes trampin' through the hillock up behind the house where Hannah and Gid live now."

"That's awful gut of Aunt Lizzie, givin' up her house and moving in with Dawdi."

"I should say, but it's the way of the People, ya know." She

277

rose and looked around, wishing she could walk straight to Mamma's grave, without getting lost as she had the previous time. It had been months since her last visit, as she had rejected the inclination to visit the graveyard during the frost and cold of winter—such a severe time to think of dearest Mamma lying cold in the ground. She was ever so glad that six feet under wasn't the end of things. According to Aunt Lizzie, Mamma's spirit was with the Lord Jesus. Her body was simply the unique shell of her, housing her spirit.

Leah located the small white marker with the few words etched in its stone:

Ida Brenneman Ebersol
B. September 2, 1904
D. December 27, 1949

"Will we ever see Mamma again?" Lydiann asked.

Leah was a bit taken aback by Lydiann's question. Truly, she did not wish to step on Dat's toes, because Lydiann was *his* daughter. "Jah, I happen to believe we will someday," she said hesitantly, longing to share the eternal truth as she understood it.

"But Dat says it's up to the Lord God on Judgment Day whether we go to heaven or to the *bad* place," Lydiann spoke up. "He says we can't know if we're saved just yet."

For sure, just as all the brethren were, Dat was adamant about that Day of Days being the first and only time a person would know where he or she was to spend eternity. Still, she knew there were some who believed differently amongst the People, as she did. Silent believers, Aunt Lizzie liked to call them.

"Always remember this, Lydiann—the Lord Jesus came as a baby to give us life. And not only while we're alive here on earth. In heaven, too."

"For certain, Mamma?" Lydiann asked, eyes wide with the hearing.

"Sure as God's love . . . that's the honest truth."

Lydiann seemed satisfied and turned to scamper around the cemetery, peering down at the small markers, reading the names and dates aloud in Pennsylvania Dutch.

Meanwhile, Leah sat beside her mother's grave. *We all miss you, Mamma*, she thought. *Except for Dat, I daresay I miss you most of all.*

———◆———

The wild ferns growing close to the road were nearly ankle-deep as Leah and Lydiann walked leisurely home from the cemetery. Leah pointed out one bird after another and yellow buttercups growing in clusters with no rhyme or reason.

"Why do ya think the Lord God made such perty colors every place?" asked Lydiann.

"Well, just think of all the different colors of people there are—red and yellow, black and white . . . we're all precious in His sight."

"That's the song Mary Ruth sings to me, ain't so?"

Leah nodded. She'd heard Mamma singing "Jesus Loves the Little Children," too, but Lydiann couldn't have remembered since she was only two when Mamma died. Mary Ruth, on the other hand, had sung it all the time to Lydiann and

Carl Nolt when he was little. Here lately Mary Ruth had been saying she thought it was a shame young Carl and Lydiann hadn't gotten acquainted as playmates, since they were neighbors and all, but truth was, Dat had no interest in either Lydiann or Abe rubbing shoulders much with Englishers. When all was said and done, Mennonites surely were Englishers, at least in Dat's book. Preacher Yoder's, too.

Thinking about the highly revered minister, she recalled he hadn't been able to attend Preaching service several times in a row. Word had it he was suffering from a bad heart—that, and some serious problems with asthma, which she guessed only worsened his heart ailment.

She and Lydiann had been walking for a while, working up a sweat, when Lydiann began to count the tiny white moths that fluttered here and there. Enjoying the sun and warm breeze, Leah happened to look off to the north and, lo and behold, if she didn't spy Dr. Schwartz's automobile parked in the field just down from Peacheys' property.

Curious, she strained to see, but what she saw startled her so much she stopped in her tracks. *Why's he kneeling in the grass . . . near that little mound of dirt?* she wondered, recalling the day she and Jonas had stumbled upon the peculiar plot.

"What're we stoppin' for?" asked Lydiann.

Promptly Leah started walking again, lest her young charge continue to ask questions or, worse, realize who was over there tending a grave with hand clippers and ask to go and talk to her *Dokder.*

"Come along, now." She picked up the pace. "You and I best be getting home for milkin'." She pointed out the Kauffmans' farm on the left side of the road, hoping to distract

Lydiann from *whatever* was going on over on the right. She succeeded, or thought she had, saying they ought to go visit Naomi and Luke here before too long, down near Ninepoints, where the couple had built themselves a nice new house with plenty of room for their growing family of young sons.

Thankfully they were nearing home when Lydiann piped up. "That was our doctor in the field, *jah*?"

Leah didn't say it was or wasn't; she simply hurried up the lane leading to the barnyard.

When they approached the house, Lydiann asked again.

"Dr. Schwartz owns that field" was all Leah cared to say.

Chapter Twenty-Seven

Hannah must've wanted to talk to Leah in the worst way, because she followed her up to the outhouse. "I know something 'bout Mary Ruth, but you can't tell a soul," she said, hurrying to keep step.

Leah had made several promises in her life that had cost her dearly, so she was rather hesitant for Hannah to say more. "Happy news, I hope?"

Hannah's face shone with the secret. "You'll be so surprised, I'm thinkin' . . . and jah, it's right happy. Wanna guess?"

"I'm afraid I'm too tired for that."

"Ach, don't go spoilin' my fun." Hannah looked hurt.

Leah couldn't have that. "I *do* want to hear what's on your mind. It's just, well . . . I'm not so interested in hearsay, ya know."

With a most sincere smile on her face, Hannah said, "This came straight from the horse's mouth, so ya don't have to worry none." She stopped to bend down and pull a weed out from between her toes. "Mary Ruth must've forgiven the English driver."

"*Who?*"

"You know . . . the young man who hit and killed Elias Stoltzfus."

Robert Schwartz? Leah suddenly felt tense.

"She's seein' the doctor's son, that young minister she and I heard preach in Quarryville years back, remember?"

"Are you certain of this?" She knew she must sound like a mother hen talking so straight, but, if true, this *was* interesting news!

"Mary Ruth told me . . . and agreed only you could know, too. Ya know, if Robert Schwartz should end up marryin' our sister, well, she could be a schoolteacher *and* a preacher's wife someday. Now, don't that beat all?"

Actually, Leah was somewhat startled at Hannah's apparent enthusiasm. "I didn't think you cared two cents 'bout Mennonite beliefs. So . . . why are *you* happy?"

"After Elias died so young and all, I'm awful glad Mary Ruth's not grieving anymore," Hannah said. "She's lookin' ahead to her future."

"The doctor and his wife are fine folk," Leah said. "I would hope their older son is just as nice, 'specially if he's a preacher. But can you imagine him falling for an Amish girl?"

"Well, she ain't so Amish anymore."

"Jah, 'tis true." Leah couldn't help but think how odd it was that another one of the doctor's sons had fallen for a Plain girl.

"Mary Ruth says Robert's completed his Bible studies in Virginia and has been offered a part-time job at the Quarryville church. I guess he'll fill in for the head pastor at times and teach Sunday school some, too. Mary Ruth will see him plenty . . . gut enough reason to attend services." To this Hannah laughed softly.

"I wonder if she realizes what might be required of her if they were to, well . . . marry," Leah said.

"I s'pose that remains to be seen. But for now she's all smiles. For sure and for certain."

Leah pondered the news. If Mary Ruth continued to see Robert, more than likely she'd never return to join the Amish church. Dat would be awful disappointed over that. Mamma, on the other hand, wouldn't care one bit up in heaven. But then again, a crush wasn't much to worry about, was it?

Robert sat behind the wheel, waiting for the gas station attendant to wash and dry the car's front and rear windows. He made some quick notes for his upcoming sermon, and when the time came to pay the bill for the gasoline, he dug into his pants pocket for the required cash while the tall attendant stood patiently.

On the ride home, his thoughts turned to Mary Ruth Ebersol, the young lady he was presently dating. It was she who had once loved and lost Elias Stoltzfus, the boy he had accidentally struck and killed nearly seven years ago. Though trusting the Lord for victory over his intense struggle, in all truth, recurring nightmares of the accident continued to haunt him. To think he had fallen hard for young Elias's intended, a homegrown Old Order Amish girl who'd converted to the Mennonite church of her own volition. Yet his association with her, pleasant and even exciting as it was, caused him to have to face the catastrophe yet again.

Redirecting his thoughts to his sermon outline, Robert pondered the Lord's own Sermon on the Mount, taking comfort in its promises. *Blessed are the meek: for they shall inherit the earth.*

Leah's bare feet took her across the cornfield to the Peacheys' house. Dat, Lydiann, and Abe had all gone fishing, and with some unexpected hours to herself, she had a hankering to see Miriam today. She felt nearly carefree enough to skip across the way.

When Miriam saw her from the porch swing, she called out, "Hullo, Leah!"

"Wie geht's?" she asked, happy to see Miriam looking so well.

"Oh, I'm fair to middlin'. Come sit with me here on the swing." Miriam slid over to make room. "It's awful pleasant today, but this weather won't last. The heat of June is just round the bend. We'll be tryin' to escape the sun in a few weeks."

"And the mosquitoes will be out in full force."

"How are your little ones, Leah?"

She smiled. "They're sweet as strawberry jam." Seemed everyone considered Lydiann and Abe *hers* now. Too soon, though, they'd be itching to try out their wings and fly, to create their own families; it was the way God set things in motion for humankind. Leah wasn't sure where she'd live or what she'd do once that time came, though it could be she'd end up living in the Dawdi Haus with Aunt Lizzie once Dawdi John passed on. But since no one but the Lord God knew the end from the beginning, there was no need to worry over the future.

She remembered, quite unexpectedly, Mamma saying the same thing to Hannah, especially when the twins were younger. Even Aunt Lizzie liked to point out that "Worryin' 'stead of trustin' just ain't the way of God's children." Leah sometimes wished she could be consistently cheerful, more like happy-go-lucky Lizzie. *Someday I will be . . . if I live long enough.*

"What can I do for ya?" Miriam asked.

"I'm curious 'bout one of Mamma's old recipes. It's not written down anywhere, since Mamma knew it by heart, but she's not here and . . ."

Miriam glanced at her and gripped her hand. "Aw, honey. You miss her, of course ya do. We *all* miss Ida so."

She hadn't come here just to ask about a recipe, nor to get sympathy—neither one. Truth was, she enjoyed talking to Miriam, and though she saw her several times a week from afar and at church twice a month, there were certain times when Leah felt she simply needed to look into Miriam's eyes and see and know the understanding Mamma had always found there.

"Which recipe are ya thinkin' of?" asked Miriam.

"Mamma's pineapple upside-down cake. I can't seem to remember how much of the shortening, baking powder, or vanilla. All the pinches of this and that tend to get stuck in my head."

"Seems to me that happens to all of us at one time or 'nother. Come inside. I'll try 'n' write it down so you'll have it."

"Denki." She followed her into the big spotless kitchen. Waiting for her to get a pad of paper and pen, Leah felt suddenly warm inside, most pleasantly so. Having this special recipe in her possession would be yet another connection to Mamma.

At precisely that moment she realized why Mamma might've risked disobeying, keeping back the forbidden letter from Sadie. *It's about losing and trying desperately to hold on*, she thought.

Even all these years later, she felt almost too glad to have destroyed the evidence, lest Dat, the preachers, or the bishop had gotten wind of it and thought less of Mamma than she deserved. Truly, coming to visit Miriam this day was one of the best things Leah could've done for both herself and her memory of Mamma.

Even the meadowlarks sang more sweetly as she accepted the cake recipe from Miriam and hugged her good-bye, heading back across the cornfield toward home.

Chapter Twenty-Eight

Mary Ruth insisted on helping Robert's mother set the table for the evening meal. "You mustn't treat me like a guest," she told Lorraine as they moved about the table, placing linen napkins and silverware in their proper places.

"Since you're Robert's steady girlfriend, you're nearly family," Lorraine replied, smiling across the table.

Robert strolled into the dining room. "What's this whispering I hear?" Mary Ruth caught his flirtatious wink.

Dr. Schwartz came in and stood behind his chair at the head of the table. "Are we ready for supper, dear?"

Lorraine's rosy cheeks seemed brighter than usual. "Please, be seated . . . and you, too, Mary Ruth. I can manage just fine."

Mary Ruth sat on one side of the table with Robert directly across from her. Having enjoyed one other fine spread at this grand old house, Mary Ruth knew what to expect. The lovely lace tablecloth reminded her once again that she had turned fancy rather quickly following Elias's death—so long ago now it seemed. Never had she questioned her chosen teaching profession, even though she knew it aggrieved her father no end; that, and the fact she'd abandoned the People. Surprisingly the tension had lessened somewhat over the years, and for this she was grateful. She could come and go as she pleased at the Ebersol Cottage, thanks in part to Leah and Aunt Lizzie. Maybe seeing Lydiann and Abe grow up, having little ones around again, had prompted Dat to be more flexible. Maybe, too, God was at work in his heart. This, she prayed for daily.

"Here we are," Lorraine said, carrying a tray of roasted chicken surrounded by an array of cooked vegetables—onions, cauliflower, broccoli, and new potatoes. She disappeared again and returned with a Waldorf salad and homemade applesauce sprinkled generously with cinnamon.

Once his wife was seated, Henry looked to Robert for the blessing. "Son?"

Robert bowed his head, as did the others. "Thank you, Lord, for these bountiful blessings laid out here before us. Bless the hands that prepared the food, and make us ever mindful of your love and grace, and your suffering and death on the cross for our sins. In Jesus' precious name. Amen."

"Thank you, Robert," Lorraine said, looking at her son with obvious affection. Then she directed Henry to pass the large platter to Mary Ruth.

The matching silver candlesticks with twinkling white tapers graced the meal, as well as the evening, and by the time the dessert was served, Mary Ruth felt almost too full, but grateful for this time spent with Robert's parents.

Sadly Henry and Lorraine had slim hope of having good fellowship with their younger son. Robert had shared that they scarcely ever heard from Derek. Mary Ruth found this to be distressing, especially because it was clear how fond Robert was of his parents. Just then she wondered if the opportunity would ever present itself for her to tell Robert what she knew of Derek—his illicit relationship with Sadie. *Too soon yet,* she decided.

When it came time to say their good-byes, Robert offered to walk with her over to the Nolts' house. On the way, he asked, "What do you plan to do with yourself all summer?"

"Oh, I have a few ideas." She told him how she had been lending a hand in Leah's vegetable garden. "And on washday, I help her heat up the water and whatnot. Of course, I *do* enjoy my little sister and brother, as well, so spending time with them means Leah can rest once in a while."

"I like the sound of this," he said, reaching for her hand. "Have yourself a good time with Leah . . . dear sister of yours."

"Do you pity her, Robert?"

"I didn't say that."

"I just thought . . . well, maybe I heard it in your voice."

He paused. "Your sister's an example for us all. A measure of a person's character is what's done in run-of-the-mill daily life, when no one is watching."

"Sounds like you could write that into one of your sermons."

"I just might."

She was aware of the sound of their shoes on the road but said no more.

At last Robert spoke again. "In your opinion, how did it happen that Jonas Mast left Leah behind, jewel that she is?"

"He was a fool, that's how." The words flew from her lips.

"I mean . . ." She caught herself. *I mustn't say such things. It's not becoming of me*, she thought. "I guess when it comes to my sisters and Abe, I have to say I have a tendency to be outspoken. I'm very sorry."

It wasn't until later, after she'd said good night and was nestled into bed, that it dawned on her how she must have come across to Robert. Still, she felt he must surely know her well enough to understand she wasn't as docile as some young women, though she *was* trying to mellow . . . on a day-by-day basis, with the Lord's help.

Her biggest struggle was thinking ahead to how things might work out if Robert kept looking at her the way he did . . . if he happened to ask her to marry him someday. Just how would such a thing affect her relationship with her family? Would they turn their backs on her, the way they had Sadie? She knew they would never shun her, but she was almost sure the wedge between her and Dat would grow.

On top of that, sometimes she had second thoughts about Robert because of his younger brother, Derek, and what she knew of *his* loose morals. What kind of boy would do such a thing to an innocent girl—that is, if Sadie had been innocent. Only the Lord knew such things. Even so, the more time she spent with Robert and the Schwartz family, the more Mary Ruth found herself pondering these things.

◆

The day after her evening with the Schwartzes, Mary Ruth was delighted to see Hannah standing at the front door of the Nolts' house. Before her sister could knock, Mary Ruth scurried to the screen door and opened it wide. "Aw, where are the little ones?" she asked, faintly disappointed Hannah hadn't brought her children.

Hannah smiled a bit wearily and stepped inside. "I took Aunt Lizzie up on her offer to stay with the girls awhile."

"Some grown-up talk should help some." Mary Ruth understood the amount of energy it took keeping up with youngsters. "It's draining being round children all day, although I must say I enjoy being a teacher as much as I thought I would."

Hannah smiled as they sat at Dottie's kitchen table. "You look awful gut, sister. I didn't want to come over too soon, not with school just out 'n' all. Thought you might need a week or so to catch your breath, prob'ly."

"That's considerate of you, but I'm always glad to see you."

Mary Ruth poured lemonade for them both and settled into their contented chitchat. "How's Lizzie's cottage in the woods working out for the four of you?" she asked.

"Just fine for now, but"—and here Hannah paused—"there's gonna be *five* of us in a little while."

"Another baby to love! How wonderful."

Hannah's face clouded over. "Come December," she said. "My next baby's due at Christmas, same as young Abe's birthday."

Mary Ruth reached over and squeezed her hand. "Now, you mustn't worry. You're *many* years younger than Mamma was with Abe, and the circumstances of his birth were highly unusual."

"Poor Mamma," Hannah whispered, sniffling. "She loved Abe ever so much."

"She loved us all." Mary Ruth observed Hannah, wondering if this was the right time to say more. They fell silent for a moment, and then she said, "And . . . Mamma loved the Lord Jesus, too. She opened her heart wide to His love and forgiveness."

Waiting to continue, she hoped Hannah might not turn away. Thankfully this time she did not get up and leave the table as she often did when Mary Ruth spoke either of Mamma's or her own spiritual perspective. "The decision to walk with Jesus is not so much a mental one as it is a yielding of the heart . . . to God's plan for our lives." She thought she might break down with emotion, so strongly she felt about this.

Hannah bobbed her head and fought her own tears. "I wish to goodness I'd asked Mamma certain things before she died," she admitted. "I waited much too long."

Mary Ruth's heart was tender toward her. "I had a private talk with Mamma not too long before she died . . . after Dat kicked me out of the house. She said she, too, was a believer, though a silent one, following Jesus and living out her days as best she could, considering the Ordnung . . . and Dat."

"Mamma?"

"Jah, and it's easy to see, too, isn't it? She had such a long-suffering, joyful way 'bout her, ya know. Mamma could forgive at the drop of a hat; a sure sign of her deep faith, I'd have to say."

"I miss her terribly." Hannah looked across the table and out the window beyond. For the longest time she sat there still as could be; then she whispered, "I've always been frightened of death. . . . Always."

"Oh, sister. Truly, there's no need to be." She rose and hurried to Hannah's side. Stroking her back, she said, "When she was nearing the end, Mamma wasn't afraid to pass over Jordan's banks to Glory. Leah said as much."

"Jah, I remember hearing that." Hannah sighed. "But when Mammi Ebersol died and we were just thirteen, honestly that was 'bout all I could think of—day in, day out. Such a worrywart I was then."

"And not *now*?"

Hannah smiled through tears, hugging her hard. "Sure, I worry too much. Gid, bless his heart; he's tryin' to help me with that."

"Smithy Gid's a fine man. I see it clearly in his eyes when he looks at you and your girls."

Hannah nodded in agreement. "You just don't know how wonderful-gut he is to me. Being his wife, I've experienced a lightness, an odd sort of peace."

"Then we're both happy, seems to me."

"Very happy," Hannah echoed.

"Who would have guessed I'd end up being courted by a Mennonite preacher—a doctor's son, at that."

"Your eyes sparkle with this path you've chosen, Mary Ruth. Truly, I'd always hoped you'd come back and be Amish with me, but it seems you've found something more befittin' you."

She smiled, thinking how dear it was of Hannah to say such a thing; despite their very different lives, her twin's heart was still warm toward her. "It's a good thing I *didn't* join church with you and then left, or we wouldn't be enjoying such close fellowship today." She got up and poured more lemonade for them.

"Do you ever think of our big sister?" Hannah asked.

"Oh, every day."

"Honestly, I worry 'bout Leah, having lost her close-in-age sister for life."

Mary Ruth sipped her lemonade. "I can't imagine us growing old and not knowing something about her. It's painful to consider."

"I wonder if she has more than the one child we'd heard she was expecting . . . back years ago."

Mary Ruth often wondered the same. "Let's hope she has a houseful by now. For our sister's sake—Jonas's too—being cut off from family as they are."

"Speakin' of wee ones, I best be thinkin' of returning home here perty soon. Lizzie's got her hands full."

"So does Leah," Mary Ruth said. "I'm going to help her as much as I can this summer. Such a cute little sister and brother we have. God was so good to Dat, don't you agree?"

Hannah wore a brighter smile now. "Such joy they bring to our wounded sister, too."

"The children do seem to comfort her. Leah's been known to keep things bottled up inside her, ya know."

She followed Hannah through the back door and outside, at once missing her horse-and-buggy days as Hannah got herself situated into Gid's fine gray family carriage. "The Lord be with you," she called.

"And with you!" came the familiar reply.

Mary Ruth was grateful for her sister's unexpected receptiveness to her words today. She would continue sowing seeds of the gospel into Hannah's precious heart. "Fertile soil," as Robert liked to say.

Robert. He had secretly admired her long before they'd ever actually gone on a real date. Then he had patiently waited to court her while she finished up her teaching certificate. Because he had been so patient, she had been able to focus on her studies, made possible, in the long run, by Hannah, who'd helped her out of a financial bind, surprising her with a secret hankie savings fund—a humbling gift, to say the least. Because of this gesture of kindness, Mary Ruth had been able to complete her college education with nary a debt, boarding with the Nolts and working for them several evenings a week, as well as waiting on tables at a Strasburg restaurant on the weekend. Hannah, in the end, had refused any talk of repayment.

The Lord had worked all things together for good, giving Mary Ruth the desire of her heart, teaching young children— the *passion* of her heart, really. She hoped to continue at the rural elementary school for English children. Her first calling, for now.

She stood in the yard, giving Hannah one long wave as the horse pulled the buggy out of their lane and onto the narrow road.

◆

. Hannah's fingertips felt numb from picking, shelling, and canning peas the day following her visit to Mary Ruth. She, Leah, and Lydiann would be doing the same again tomorrow while Aunt Lizzie again kept a watchful eye on Hannah's daughters. Peas took time and tallied up ever so slowly, but the work, though tedious, meant time spent with her sisters.

Now that evening had come, she and Gid stood alone on the back porch, looking up at the stars. "'Tis the best time of the day . . . right now," he whispered in her ear.

"Jah, just the two of us. The way it all started out, ain't?"

With the girls sound asleep, she was eager for his warm embrace and fervent kisses. But he seemed to want to talk, and she was willing to listen. "Just so ya know, our horse has the strangles, and we'll have to borrow one of Abram's for a while."

She breathed in the smell of the night as she leaned against the porch rail, Gid's arm around her waist. "Hope you and Dat can cure it soon enough."

"The disease is right contagious, so we'll have to isolate this one horse, for sure. 'Tis best to let the infection run its course, though."

"Isn't there something you can do?" she asked.

"Penicillin shots will only lengthen the disease, but Abram's goin' to give his drivin' horses shots to prevent it." Gid continued, talking of making hay all day and how he, Dat, and Sam Ebersol would be working together tomorrow. "Pop is best stayin' with shodding horses, I'm a-thinkin'. It gets harder and harder for him to make hay or fill silo every year that goes by. I'm just glad to be able to help him. Sam is, too."

"I'm afraid the same goes for Dat."

Gid nodded. "'Cept the difference 'tween my father and yours is Abram's battlin' hard growing old . . . wants to stay as young as he can for Lydiann and Abe's sake, prob'ly."

"I see the fight in him, too."

"On the other hand, my pop's back keeps goin' out on him. Don't know how much longer he'll be able to do his blacksmithing duties, really."

"What'll happen then?" She'd worried some about this off and on the past year.

"Right now, Sam is gut 'bout helping, so let's not cross that bridge 'fore we have to, dear."

Her concerns had run away with her yet again. No need to get Gid thinking too hard on that—the People took care of their own. Mamma would have said that when the time came, the Lord God heavenly Father would give them the strength and the grace they needed—just as it had been for Aunt Lizzie tending to Dawdi John and Leah caring so lovingly for Lydiann and Abe. She hoped it was true.

"You all right, Hannah?"

"Just thinkin', is all." She leaned against Gid's sturdy arm.

"Counting your blessings, jah?"

She nodded, not wanting her husband to wonder if her fears were taking her over once again. "Ever so many blessings," she managed to say.

Chapter Twenty-Nine

Sure is wet for July," Dawdi John said at midday. Leah, along with Lydiann and Abe, sat taking a quick breather in Dawdi's front room.

"It's July the *twelfth*," insisted Abe.

"What's the date matter?" Lydiann piped up.

"Matters to *me*," said Abe.

"Goodness," said Leah. "Aren't you lippy today."

Her boy nodded. "I'm getting myself ready for school here 'fore too long, fixin' to surprise my teacher."

"How's that?" Dawdi asked.

" 'Cause I can make heads 'n' tails of the calendar," Abe replied.

Leah ruffled his hair, taken once again by Abe's clever remarks. "That's not all she'll be pleased 'bout, I daresay. You've been workin' your arithmetic this summer . . . with some help from Lydiann and Dat."

Dawdi nodded his head, twitching his nose. "Right smart ya both are. Take after your mamma."

Abe's eyes lit up. "Mamma *Leah?*"

Dawdi leaned back with laughter. "Well, now, she's a bright one, too."

Lydiann was too quiet, Leah happened to notice. "Everything all right, Lyddie?"

She shook her head, her eyes filling with tears.

"Well, now, honey, what's wrong?" Dawdi asked.

"I . . . can't remember what my first mamma looked like no more."

Abe was quick to speak. "Me neither, Lyddie. But that don't mean I have to go 'n' cry 'bout it."

"Aw, now, Abe . . . don't act so," Dawdi John said. "Come here and sit on my knee." He put down his cane and Abe hopped up on his lap. "Let me tell you 'bout your mother who birthed ya."

"Your daughter, ain't?" Abe said.

Dawdi nodded. "She had the pertiest blue eyes I ever did see. Just look at your sister over there; she has your mother's eyes."

"What did *I* get of Mamma's?"

Somewhat comically, Dawdi scrutinized Abe. "Let me see . . ." He pulled on his long beard, frowning; then a smile spread across his wrinkled face. "I know. You have her spunk. I see it in your eyes—awful mischievous they are. And—"

"It's in his voice, too." Lydiann smiled at her brother.

"And what else?" Abe asked.

Leah felt compelled to speak up. "If ya ask me, you both have Mamma's pretty hair. Light as the color of wheat . . . even blonder than your aunt—" She almost said "Sadie" but stopped herself.

"What were you gonna say?" asked Abe.

Dawdi must have surmised her thoughts and intervened. "There are plenty-a light-headed relatives in the family, young man."

"So Abe's got Mamma's hair and eyes and her spunk," Lydiann said, looking right at her brother. "That oughta keep ya quiet for now."

Leah had to smile. *Ach, how they love to bicker.* Just as she and Sadie had as girls; same as Hannah and Mary Ruth, too. *They'll grow out of it one day,* she thought.

Dawdi began to tell a humorous story from his boyhood, quickly getting the children's attention by describing how rainy and muddy it had been one long-ago summer. "My boot got stuck on the mule road over in Hickory Hollow, where I lived in an old farmhouse with my parents, your young mamma, Aunt Lizzie, and a whole bunch of your great-aunts and great-uncles. Well, I pulled and pulled and could not get my boot out."

Lydiann grinned from ear to ear. "What'd ya do, Dawdi?"

"I decided I'd best just pull my foot out and leave my boot stuck there."

"You did, really?" Abe said.

"Jah, and I walked all the way down the road in the mud to the well, pumped out some water, and rinsed off my sock and foot. And that was that."

"What happened to your boot?" asked Lydiann.

"It stayed right there overnight till we got more rain, which turned the mud into stew . . . and I lugged the boot out."

This brought a round of giggles, egging Dawdi on but good.

Leah's mind wandered while the storytelling continued, back to early days when she, Sadie, Hannah, and Mary Ruth would sit at their father's knee, listening to him read *The Budget*. Aunt Lizzie and Mamma, ever near, would sit inches away doing their knitting or crocheting. Now and then, Mamma would make a little sound, and Dat would look her way, smile, and return to reading. It was as if they were connected by a fine and loving thread that wove the family together, night after night, day after day.

How she missed those times! Still, she wouldn't think of going back, even if she could—not with the children needing her so. Yet if she had to live her youthful days over again, she might choose to return to autumn hayrides and the snipe hunts she and Jonas, along with all their siblings, enjoyed so much. Back then she had been the age Lydiann was now; such an innocent, happy time.

The best part of those autumns had been the bright blue weather, warm and wistful during the days with a nip to the night air. Once she'd sat all alone out behind the barn in the high meadow just staring at the night sky, gazing at the big harvest moon, counting the stars, and wondering about her future—whom she might marry when she grew up . . . and how many little ones she and her husband would have one day.

The children's laughter, mingled with Dawdi John's, brought her back to the business at hand. "Best finish cookin' supper," she said, getting up.

Lydiann and Abe followed, giving Dawdi a hug before

they left. "We'll see ya at the table soon," Lydiann said with a mischievous smile. "Mamma and I are makin' a surprise for everyone."

Leah lifted her finger to her lips. "Now, Lydiann, don't spoil things by sayin' too much."

"Ach, girls can't keep no secrets," Abe spouted off.

Dawdi chuckled and Leah shooed the children toward the connecting door, back to the main house.

Leah glanced out the window, making note of the fine summer day as she and the family, except for Aunt Lizzie and Dawdi John, all sat down to breakfast.

Immediately following the silent prayer, Abe announced too loudly, "Today's Friday the thirteenth!"

Dat quickly linked the date to superstition. "So 'tis best to be extra alert and careful, 'least till sundown."

Mamma would not have approved of Dat saying such a thing, yet he joked about it anyway, though he surely knew better. Good thing Aunt Lizzie hadn't joined them for eggs and pancakes. She would've spoken up but quick, putting an end to the nonsense talk. Lizzie had been cut from the same mold as Mamma, and for this Leah was glad.

Once Dat was finished eating, he left the table for the barn. It was then Leah told Lydiann and Abe both there was nothing to worry about. "Don't worry yourself about the date. We're not so superstitious, really—never have been."

Abe looked puzzled, glancing over his shoulder toward the back door. "But Dat said—"

303

"I know what your father said." She was struggling, not sure how to preserve respect for Dat while teaching the children what she knew to be true—what she knew her mamma and Aunt Lizzie would have said. She didn't want to out-and-out discredit her father, but she felt troubled deep in her soul each time Dat talked about such dark things.

Just last week he had suggested the hex doctor come take a look at Lydiann when she'd gotten bit up by mosquitoes and welts had come out all over her legs. Had it not been for Aunt Lizzie prevailing, Leah would have been at a loss to handle things. Dat, after all, was Lydiann's father. She, on the other hand, was merely a substitute mother with little say—at least it seemed so at times like this.

"Do you remember where we're goin' today?" she asked Lydiann and Abe, changing the subject as gracefully as possible.

"To see the doctor!" Lydiann said merrily. She liked having her "ticker checked," as Dr. Schwartz called it when he listened to the children's hearts with his stethoscope.

"In one hour we must leave," she told them, pointing for Lydiann to clear the dirty dishes from the table, and then directing Abe toward the back door to go and offer Dat some help in the barn.

"Dawdi John was mighty happy with our supper surprise last night," Lydiann said, getting up from the table.

Abe smacked his lips. "So was I. Dawdi and Dat both liked your pineapple upside-down cake, Mamma."

"There's some left for dinner today," Lydiann told him. "Now, how 'bout that?"

To this Abe went running outside, hollering the happy

news to Dat. Leah stood at the back door and watched him go, glad all the talk of Friday the thirteenth was past for now.

❖

"Hose off your feet; it's time to go," Leah called to Abe. She didn't want Abe dragging mud into the clean clinic when the children arrived for their checkups. Dr. Schwartz had said there was no sense waiting till closer to the start of the school to have their appointments—"Things get hectic then," he'd told her two weeks ago. Besides that, with news of several youngsters in the area having contracted the dreaded polio, Dr. Schwartz had urged her to bring Abe and Lydiann in for their first dose of the new vaccine. Although it was still midsummer, they would get their clean bill of health from a medical doctor, as well as prevention against the contagious disease, before Dat got any more ideas about calling for the powwow doctor.

The horse hitched up to the carriage easily, and in no time at all they were headed down the one-mile stretch to the clinic. "I wonder how much I weigh *this* year," Abe said, sitting to the left of Leah in the front seat.

Leah waited for Lydiann to say something either funny or snooty, but she was silent in the second seat. Glad for the peace, Leah focused on the steady rhythm of the *clip-clopping* of the horse.

Soon Lydiann began to hum rather forcefully "Jesus Loves Me," the song Mary Ruth had often sung to the children.

"For the Bible tells me so . . ." Abe joined in, his voice cracking.

When they came to the part, "Little ones to Him belong . . . they are weak . . ." Leah winced, recalling how tiny Sadie's baby had been at his birth. She hummed along with the children, hoping to dispel her momentary gloom.

Arriving well before the appointment, Leah noticed another horse and buggy waiting ahead of them in the lane. Not knowing who was parked there, she decided, since it was so pretty out, she and the children would just sit in the carriage till closer to time to go inside.

Promptly, though, Abe jumped down from the carriage and moseyed over to the other gray buggy. Relaxing in the front seat, she decided not to hinder him from being sociable, since it came so naturally to him. She closed her eyes for a moment.

Next thing she knew, Lydiann had climbed out and run over to join Abe. With both children standing there chattering away, she reluctantly got out and tied the horse to the post, then walked slowly to the other buggy.

"Mamma, this here's Mandie and Jake Mast," Lydiann said quickly when she saw her coming.

"Well, hullo . . . children." She was flabbergasted to see Fannie's twins sitting there by themselves.

Mandie explained. "Our mamma's inside . . . has a nasty flu."

"Jah, she's been terrible sick." Jake nodded his head as he spoke.

Mandie's blond hair was pure contrast to Jake's dark head and eyes. "We're goin' straight home once Mamma gets herself some medicine," she said.

"She needs to feel better and right quick," Jake added.

They don't know of their parents' stand against us Ebersols, thought Leah, finding it rather curious to be here talking so freely with Jonas's baby sister and brother. She savored the special moment; these twins would have been her brother- and sister-in-law had she and Jonas married.

"What's *your* name?" Mandie asked her, blue eyes twinkling.

"I'm Cousin Leah," she said, not revealing her last name. "And this is Lydiann and Abe."

"Abe already told us his name." Jake smiled broadly, showing his white teeth. A wider grin she'd never seen.

"Leah's a right perty name," Mandie said. "And . . . you're our cousin?"

She straightened, repeating that she was indeed. *They've never heard tell of their eldest brother's first love.*

Suddenly Jake jumped down out of the carriage. "Let's see how tall I am next to you, Lydiann."

"Jake, what on earth are ya doin'?" Mandie scowled from the carriage. "She's a girl, for pity's sake."

"She's our *cousin*, for pity's sake!" Jake hollered over his shoulder.

"No need to yell, children," Leah found herself chiding them, watching in disbelief as Jake and Lydiann simultaneously turned themselves around and stood back to back, head to head.

"I'm taller, ain't so, Mamma?" asked Lydiann, staring straight ahead, holding still as could be.

Observing the childish scene play out before her eyes, she was intent on the irony of the unexpected meeting—Cousin Fannie inside paying a visit to the doctor for a summer flu;

307

the twins out here. "Well, it's hard to say, really . . . but jah, I s'pose you are. But only by a hair."

To this Lydiann giggled. Jake, on the other hand, looked terribly concerned, if not upset.

"See, Jake? I *am* taller than you!" Lydiann said a bit too gleefully.

"That can't be," Jake insisted, his hands on his slender hips.

"Come along, now," Leah said, turning to go while Abe and Lydiann said good-bye to their newfound cousins.

"Won'tcha come to Grasshopper Level 'n' visit us?" Jake asked.

"That'd be fun," Lydiann said, waving.

"See ya later!" called Mandie.

Obviously Abe and Lydiann were quite taken with the cute twins. When at last they joined Leah, they hurried up the long walk toward the clinic.

Glancing over her shoulder at Cousin Fannie's youngsters, Leah had mixed feelings about the encounter. For as obstinate as the Masts were toward the Ebersols, there was little or no hope they would ever see hide nor hair of Jake and Mandie again.

Chapter Thirty

Leah quickened her pace to keep up with Lydiann and Abe, delighting in their chatter as the three of them walked down the road to the schoolhouse this second week of school. Abe was in second grade this year, looking splendid in his lavender shirt, black broadfall trousers, and suspenders. Today, for a nice change, he wore his straw hat firmly on his head. Lydiann was pretty as a picture in her green dress and crisp black apron, her small hair bun hidden beneath her white prayer veiling.

Leah had been mighty busy sewing several new sets of clothes for each child during the final weeks of August, and she had volunteered to help clean up the schoolhouse with other parents in preparation for the start of school, as well.

"Won'tcha come back for our school picnic today?" Lydiann asked her.

"*Please*, Mamma," Abe begged, hopping up and down.

"Do ya really want me to?" she said, knowing full well the answer.

"'Course we do!" Abe shouted.

309

"The pupils from the school over on Esbenshade Road are joinin' us today, too," Lydiann said.

"A *wunderbaar Picknick!*" said Abe.

In her busyness, she'd completely forgotten the combined school event. Mandie and Jake Mast attended the other school that served the conservative Mennonite and Amish children in the Grasshopper Level area. What fun it would be for Lydiann and Abe to see their Mast cousins again. "Sure, I'll return at eleven-thirty with the horse and buggy," she said.

"Will ya stay for story time after lunch recess?" Abe asked, swinging his lunch pail.

"We'll see." She wanted them to enjoy their classmates, feel at liberty to make friends, not be too dependent on her.

"Aw, won'tcha, Mamma?" she whined.

"None of the other mothers stay, do they?"

Abe shook his head. "But you ain't like them," he said. "You're younger than most."

"Pertier too." Lydiann reached for her hand and held it tight.

Quickly Leah directed their attention to the various trees, different kinds of birds, and other familiar landmarks along the road. It was a good long walk, but it was a fine way to extend her day with them. They never seemed to tire of her presence, as if they required her more than some children needed their mammas.

◆

Back home again, Leah canned seven quarts of peaches, then made up a large batch of catsup, with help from Lizzie.

While making a sandwich to take back with her to the children's school, a decisive knock came at the back door. The smithy had "sorrowful news to bear" of Preacher Yoder's passing. "Happened just hours ago." Their longtime minister had died of a heart attack.

"We're in need of a new preacher," Aunt Lizzie said as the two women watched smithy Peachey scurry out to the barn to tell the news to Abram and Gid.

"I 'spect we'll be having an ordination service 'fore too long," Leah said.

"We best start prayin' for God's will in the selection of a new minister," Aunt Lizzie said reverently.

"Does Dat ever pray thataway?" asked Leah.

"What do ya mean?"

"Does Dat beseech the Lord God heavenly Father for divine will in all things the way you do?" *The way Mamma always did,* she thought.

Aunt Lizzie's face brightened at Leah's question. "I believe the Lord is definitely at work in Abram's heart," she replied softly, yet confidently. "You wait 'n' see. He'll come round to the saving grace."

Lizzie's remarks wondered Leah. "I hope you're right 'bout that," she found herself saying. "Maybe then there won't be so much talk of hex doctors anymore."

"Oh jah . . . all that white witchcraft talk will fly out the window. You'll see."

Lizzie's words went round and round in Leah's head. Even as she hitched up the horse and headed back to the little one-room school for lunch, the words "you'll see" continued to echo in her brain.

Actually, she was glad for a reason to be gone over the noon hour, what with plans for the minister's wake no doubt taking shape. *Lizzie's far better at such things,* she thought as she rode down Georgetown Road.

When she arrived, the school yard was bustling with children, girls eating their sack lunches on the grass, boys eating theirs on the merry-go-round.

Lydiann looked awful sad when Leah found her. "Our Mast cousins didn't come," she said. "All the other pupils did . . .'cept not them."

They must've told their mamma about meeting Lydiann and Abe, Leah decided. *Cousin Fannie's shunning the youngest Ebersols through her twins!*

Leah had to offer some sort of explanation to distract poor Lydiann, though in all truth, a mere girl didn't need to know such spiteful things. "Maybe Jake and Mandie are under the weather," she offered as a possible excuse.

"That can't be it," Lydiann piped up. "The teacher said their mamma kept them home today."

On purpose . . . in case they might have themselves another good time with Abe and Lydiann, thought Leah. *Will this never end?* She was tempted to ride over to the Masts' orchard house and storm up to the back door to give Cousin Fannie a good tongue-lashing. It was one thing to punish the Ebersol grown-ups, but this!

Following the news of Preacher Yoder's death, Lizzie promptly hurried across the field to visit Miriam Peachey. They spent a few minutes at the kitchen table making a list of food items necessary for supplying the grieving family; then she and Miriam said good-bye and Lizzie ambled back to the house to prepare roast-beef sandwiches for her father and Abram.

At the noon meal she was mindful to stay out of their table conversation as the two men discussed the Yoder family wake and the subsequent funeral and burial services.

When they were finished eating, Abram bowed his head for the silent prayer; then she cleared the table and washed and dried the dishes. That done, she swept the kitchen floor, and then the back porch and sidewalk. All the while, she contemplated her earlier exchange with Leah. Was it possible Abram would indeed embrace the Lord as Savior? Lizzie *had* seen strong indications he was softening, little cracks of light slowly penetrating his gritty soul.

Privately she continued to share with him what she'd learned over the years through time spent on her knees in prayer and by reading Scripture. *Faith cometh by hearing, and hearing by the word of God.* Tenaciously she clung to this passage in Romans whenever Abram became resistant. Yet she felt sure the frequency and the fervency of her witness was getting through to him, touching the deep of his heart.

◆

"Mamma? Are you upset?" Abe asked hours after the picnic, sitting next to Leah in the front seat of the carriage as she drove them home.

Leah hadn't realized it, but here she was groaning, disturbing the children.

She gathered her wits. "I'm all right."

Lydiann began to rehash the day. "S'posin' *I* should be upset, too, since our own cousins didn't come to the picnic."

Abe shook his little head. "When will we see them again, Mamma?"

Before Leah could answer, Lydiann suggested they invite Jake and Mandie to Abe's birthday, "come December."

Abe's eyes shone. "Jah, and maybe Christmas dinner, too!"

◆

Late that night, Leah was too fidgety to sleep. So . . . the Mast twins *had* told their mother of meeting Cousin Leah. Oh, to have been a fly on the backseat of the buggy!

She struggled to put into practice what the Scriptures taught about forgiveness, for the Masts surely needed to be forgiven, didn't they?

Sitting up in bed, she stared into the darkness of her room. She wished she could be at peace with all men—*and* women—including kinfolk like Peter and Fannie and their children.

Dear Lord, drive my anger far from me, she prayed.

Chapter Thirty-One

The letter from Sadie to the bishop was a single page long, and Abram's first reaction was to walk away and ignore it.

Bishop Bontrager, large man that he was, stood near the hay baler in Abram's own barn, blocking the setting sun's horizontal rays from coming through the door. "Go ahead, Abram, have a look-see." The bishop pushed the letter into his hands, apparently eager to hear what Abram made of it.

Fairly torn, Abram felt pressured to read his long-lost daughter's letter. At the same time he was curious to know why she'd written in the first place. Walking toward the doorway, he held the page up to the last vestiges of daylight.

Friday, September 14, 1956
Dear Bishop Bontrager,

Greetings from Nappanee, Indiana, where I have been living for eight years.

I am writing to ask your kind permission to return to my family. This would be ever so helpful to me, even necessary at this distressing time. You see, I am a widow as of two weeks ago, due to a silo-building accident in Goshen.

Since I am under the Bann in my home church, I thought it best to contact you directly. I hope you might pave the way for this request. It has been a long time since my baptism and my leaving, and since then I have been a God-fearing woman and made my peace with the Lord God and with a church here in Nappanee, as well as the Millersburg, Ohio, district, where first I confessed my sins privately to the ministers.

Will you allow me to make things right with this letter? I want to return home to look into the faces of my dear father, mother, and sisters with the shunning lifted from me.

> *Respectfully,*
> *Sadie (Ebersol)*

Abram scarcely knew what to say. Sadie wanted to come home, wanted to repent. "So much she doesn't know 'bout us," he said. "She has no knowledge of Ida's passing . . . is unaware of her little brother."

My firstborn . . . a young widow, he thought, pained.

Before Abram was fully ready to relinquish the letter, the bishop reached for it and quickly stuffed it back into the envelope. "I have half a mind to say she ought not return. Simply puttin' words on a page is not enough for me to give a shunned woman the go-ahead to come home."

Abram's heart sank. "Then, ya must not believe she's sincere?"

"Sincerely *wrong*, she is. Your eldest ain't above the Ordnung, though she might think so. If she wants to live with you and Leah and the rest of the family, she'll have to offer a kneeling repentance before the entire membership. Nothin' less." The bishop tapped the envelope on the palm of his callused hand. "If she should be stupid enough to make an attempt at returning without takin' the proper steps, you and Leah will be shunned, too."

Caught coming and going, Abram thought, realizing he was contemplating the same things Ida used to say—and Lizzie would now. It made little sense to slap the Bann on a family just because they had a shunned relative, and one obviously in need. But he kept his opinion to himself, not wanting to jeopardize an opportunity to see his daughter and possibly young grandchildren. What an awful long time had passed since Sadie had left home, and now she was living in Indiana. Evidently Jonas couldn't make it as a carpenter in Ohio. Abram wasn't too surprised at that; not with the bishops out there and here frowning hard on young men who thumbed their noses at farming. *Seems mighty English to do otherwise*, he thought.

But now Jonas had been killed building a silo. Such risky, even dangerous work—anybody knew that. *Especially for a scrawny carpenter!*

Poor Sadie lived with the same familiar pain of loss as he did. The realization swept over him, and he felt sorry for his ambivalent feelings toward his own flesh and blood . . . even after all these years of her absence and her defiant refusal to make recompense here at home, where it most mattered.

"Will ya write and remind her of what she must do?" he asked the bishop.

The burly man leaned on the baler and looked him straight in the face. "I'm sure you miss her and I can't blame ya for it. I'll write her what's expected. If she's yielded and agreeable, I'll let you know."

Stunned at the change in the bishop's attitude, Abram nodded. "I'll wait to hear from you. Denki!"

The older man headed out toward the sinking sun. Then, almost as if he'd forgotten to say what was still on his mind, he turned and asked, "How will this affect Leah, do ya think? And your young children, too?"

Abram inhaled sharply. "Once you hear back from my eldest, I'll speak with Leah, break it to her . . . somehow. Then she and I will decide what to tell Lydiann and Abe."

"I'll drop by again. I 'spect it'll be soon."

Sadie needs us now, he thought. *Surely she'll abide by the Ordnung this time.*

He watched as the bishop made his way toward his buggy, wondering how to go about telling Leah, when it was time. *I have some fences to mend,* he thought ruefully.

Leah sat down in the kitchen with Dat, who had come in from the barn midafternoon, removed his straw hat, and placed it slowly on the table. "I have some news for ya, Leah." Breathing deeply, he sat next to her on the wooden bench. "Your sister's comin' home with the bishop's blessing. She says she wants to repent."

"My sister?" Her heart leaped up. *Sadie's returning to us!*

Dat continued, explaining the letter and visit of a week ago, the bishop's follow-up—all of it. Leah hung on every word, yet wondered why her father's somber face did not match his joyful words. "What's wrong, Dat? Why are ya sad?"

He faltered just then, staring long at the floor. When he

looked up, the color had drained from his face. "Truth is, she's comin' back a widow."

The thorny words narrowly stuck in her mind. *My sister, a widow?*

She studied Dat, struggling with the meaning of this. *So Jonas must be dead.*

Dat was talking again, but she scarcely heard a word. Something that had been buried so long ago broke free within her. Years of innocent pretense, of hoping and striving . . . wanting to forgive Sadie and praying it was so. All of it simmered to the surface in that moment, and no longer could she hold back the tide. She put her head down and sobbed on her arm.

Dat reached out to comfort her. "There, there, my lamb," he said, the way Mamma always had. "This, too, shall pass."

Powerless to think of anything but her own loss of Jonas, she raised her head, eyes clouded with tears. "*Nee*—no!" she sobbed. "My sister took my beau . . . *my* beloved. Don't you see? She stole the years that were meant for me—for Jonas and me! Now he's dead, gone forever!"

Dat's face fell, plainly dumbfounded at her outburst. "Leah. . . ?" His eyes were intent on her, a concerned frown on his face.

Beneath his gaze, she felt as foolish as a young child. Yet she was crushed to near despair.

Abram, taken aback by Leah's outburst, had never seen her so distraught, neither so outspoken. Promptly he stopped trying to calm her, feeling inadequate to do so. *I should've asked Lizzie to be on hand,* he thought.

319

Never had he felt comfortable when it came to a weeping woman. Here Leah was, unable to dry her tears, beside herself with fresh grief over Sadie's betrayal. Just when he had been so sure she was long past her anger and sadness.

He wondered how to make things better, how to place the ultimate blame where it belonged. He contemplated telling her of his conversation with Jonas, the two of them hidden away in the cornfield the day of Leah's and Jonas's baptisms. Such a confession might redirect Leah's resentment—and rightly so.

He rose to stretch his legs and move about the kitchen, to give himself a chance to think how he ought to reveal his deception, beginning with his furtive phone call to David Mellinger clear back when Jonas first began courting Leah, when she was merely sixteen. And . . . ending with Peter Mast's visit over a year later, when Abram had spoken half-truths, not putting to rest the rumor that there was something more than innocent friendship between Gid and Leah. All of his subtle scheming to keep Jonas away—far removed from Leah. For what purpose? So Smithy Gid could have his chance, nothing more. Clearly from Leah's apparent anguish, he had been decidedly wrong on all counts.

Inhaling slowly, he felt he must open up to her, to confess at least in part. "There's something you oughta know. I should've told ya, oh, so long ago."

She looked at him, visibly puzzled, eyes red.

"I'm mighty sorry," he began again. "From the deep of my heart, I am."

She remained silent.

"Jonas marrying your sister was partly my fault," he said.

"Your fault? How can that be?"

He was pacing now. *I regret the day I ever meddled with her future*, he thought. *Leah's a maidel now because of me.*

"Dat? What is it?" Leah asked, her pretty brow lined with deep concern.

"*Narr*," he began. "I was a fool. . . ."

A bewildered look crossed her face, yet it was evident she wanted to understand, to hear him out. "Whatever do ya mean, Dat?"

He stood near the wood stove, feeling mighty chilled; he didn't dare consider sitting at the table any longer, so far from the slow fire in the belly of the stove. No, he needed the warmth. As it was, he could barely relax the muscles in his jaw enough to speak, to make his mouth form the words that must finally be said.

Chapter Thirty-Two

Not only was Leah perplexed at the idea of Sadie's returning home, she was dismayed to think Dat had created feelings of doubt in Jonas regarding her faithfulness to him, shedding more than a little suspicion on Leah's companionable association with Gid!

She recalled the alarming letter Jonas had sent so long ago, asking her pointed questions about Smithy Gid. Poor Jonas had gotten his doubts about her from Dat, of all people. Still, what part had Sadie played in this? Leah had not fully understood the ins and outs of Peter Mast's visit here that autumn day as described by Dat, and she wondered if her father was holding back other things he'd rather not say; she could only imagine what they might be.

Nevertheless, Sadie was soon to be traveling home, and Leah needed to make some necessary sleeping arrangements. She asked Dat if he'd mind moving downstairs to the spare bedroom off the front room, and he agreed immediately, giving up the largest of the bedrooms to Leah and Lydiann, who didn't mind sharing the room over the kitchen, the warmest in the house. Even if Sadie had more than one or two children to bed down, in no way did Leah feel comfortable handing over Dat and Mamma's bedroom to their disobedient daughter and her offspring. *Jonas and Sadie's little ones . . .*

Hannah and Mary Ruth's former bedroom would become Sadie and her children's, since it was the farthest removed from Leah's new bedroom—*a good idea,* she thought. Abe, bless his heart, would have Leah's old room, with its lovely view of the barnyard and the woods.

So it was decided, and she was glad Dat never questioned her one iota. Each of them would have a place to call his or her own, and Leah would still be near enough to Lydiann and Abe, to look after them a bit.

Lizzie helped her wash down the walls and redd up the spare room for Dat, and he promptly moved his clothing and personal items the next day. When all the changes had been made and the rooms were ready on Saturday, Leah put a pot of chicken corn soup on the stove for supper, then asked Lydiann to watch and stir it every so often.

She noticed a whole flock of wild turkeys—two dozen or more—strutting around the barnyard and even more of them in the cornfield, finding leftovers from the harvest, as she headed up to the woods to visit Hannah. Once there, she was happy to see petite and sweet Ida Mae who, at almost three, was as chatty and fair as Mary Ruth had always been. "She even looks like your twin when she was tiny!" Leah said, to which Hannah agreed.

Katie Ann, the other wee dishwasher in the making, was said to be napping. "She does so twice a day now, which is right nice," Hannah said, pushing back a loose strand of strawberry blond hair.

Leah got down on the floor and played with Ida Mae, who was talking to the knitted-sock hand puppet Hannah had made. It was one Leah had used through the years to soothe hurt or ailing children at Dr. Schwartz's medical clinic.

"Should we plan something special for our lost sister when she returns?" Hannah asked.

She would not share with Hannah how despairing she felt about Sadie. "Maybe so" was all she said.

"Wouldn't it be fun? A right nice welcome home."

Leah rose and headed for the door, struggling with the lump in her throat.

"You just got here," Hannah called to her. "What's your hurry?"

"I thought of walking in the woods, that's all." She didn't say she needed some time alone, that she felt all this pressure in her chest might cause her to suffocate.

"Aw, Leah, come back. Are ya sad over Preacher Yoder's passing?"

"I . . . I'll see ya later." Right then she felt sorry about being short with Hannah, but she couldn't stay a minute longer, not if she didn't want to be seen weeping.

Hurrying out the back door, she rushed past the stone wall and gardens, noticing that the recent killing frost had put an end to Hannah's late-summer flowers. But Leah didn't dare stop to sit there and try to calm herself. She hastened on, trying in vain to locate her cherished honey locust tree, but too many years had come and gone since the bliss-filled hours spent beneath its trunk.

She pressed on, looking anxiously for her favorite tree, aware of geese overhead, honking their way south for the winter. Eventually unable to find her way to her former piece of earth, she headed up a ways to the crest of the hillock, to the old hunter's shanty, surprised it was still standing—though barely that.

Deciding against going inside, she wandered around and looked for a place to sit where she could be alone with the towering trees and the dense foliage, soaking up the peace here. She found a cluster of boulders, recalling this to be the spot where Smithy Gid had found her the day she'd wandered here and gotten herself lost. Not worried that such a thing would occur again, she sat herself down. *So Hannah wants to have a party, but Sadie deserves no such thing.*

A scampering squirrel stopped to look at her, his tiny head slightly cocked as if to say, *Hullo, lonely Leah. What're you doing here in my woods?*

She realized she still had an imagination, probably thanks to the strong influence of the children—her children. How she loved them! Cheerful yet outspoken Lydiann . . . and Abe, who was always caring, eager, and confident. Both seemed mighty glad to have her as a mamma and often said so.

But she best not think on such prideful things; she didn't need the children's reassurance. She just needed to simmer down like the kettle full of soup at home.

I've lost Jonas twice. She let the harsh truth seep into her bones. *Once to Sadie and now to death, both in the space of nine years.*

She felt she'd aged in just a few days of grieving Jonas's

death. Holding her slender hands out before her, she peered at small veins protruding through pale skin. *It's a good thing Smithy Gid woke up and married Hannah,* she thought, feeling at once sorry for herself, yet knowing what a happy couple Gid and Hannah were.

Looking up, she tried to see the sky, but only the tiniest dots of light shone through the canopy. She was taken anew by the quietude and suddenly missed her youth, gone with the years.

When she heard whistling, she turned to see where the sound hailed from, and there was Aunt Lizzie tramping toward her. "Hullo, honey-girl!"

"Out for an afternoon walk?" she asked, glad to see her.

"Been trampin' through these woods for a gut many years now; don't 'spect I'll quit anytime soon." Lizzie came and sat next to her on the boulder. "I daresay *you* aren't walkin' so much as thinkin'."

She knows me through and through.

"Your sister's comin' home and you're beside yourself, ain't?"

"That'd be one way of puttin' it."

"Well, best get it out of your system before she arrives." Lizzie mopped her brow with the palm of her hand.

"How would ya say I oughta go 'bout that?"

Lizzie straightened a bit, pushing her work shoes down deep into the leaves and vines. "Lean hard on the Lord, honey-girl."

Wondering, she voiced the question aloud. "Does God truly know how I'm feelin' just now?"

Lizzie started a little and looked Leah full in the face. "He knows this time of suffering you're goin' through . . . that it's awful hard. But this must be His plan for you, as difficult as that is to understand. Life ain't a bed of roses; it's downright painful at times. But I 'spect if ya get your eyes off yourself and look at your sister, you'll see she's in need of our love now more than ever. A widow and not even thirty yet, for pity's sake."

"I *do* love her," Leah said softly. "I've prayed for her all these years. But now I just don't know how I can . . ." She stopped because she simply couldn't go on.

"Sooner or later, you'll have to forgive her, Leah. The path of unforgiveness is a thorny one." Aunt Lizzie had known all along what it was eating away at her.

"I wish I didn't have to go to the membership meeting, witness my sister kneelin' before the Lord God and the brethren, confessing aloud her past sins." All this time she'd yearned for this very thing for Sadie's sake; yet here it was nearly the eve of such a meeting, and all she wanted to do was run far from it. She didn't care to hear the words of repentance that would ultimately lift the Bann from Sadie. The shunned one would be welcomed back, profoundly so, into the warmth of Dat's home, *her* refuge.

"I see now I can't begin to think of voting to accept her back into the fellowship. I just can't, Lizzie." She wept sad tears in her birth mother's arms.

"There, there, you go 'n' cry it out. Then, when you're through, we'll head on home for supper. We'll see this through together, you 'n' me."

Leah wept good and long. When she'd had her cry, she wiped her face dry with the edge of Lizzie's apron, startlingly aware of the bitterness within—sorrowful remnants of the past.

Somewhere along the way, they had silently agreed not to talk while milking cows, which was exactly how it was Monday morning. Leah felt she had little to say to Dat.

They finished the milking, and while her father carried away the cans of fresh milk to the milk house, Leah headed back to her indoor chores. From now on, she decided, Abe, or Sadie—once she arrived—could help with the milking. She, on the other hand, was in charge of the house and by no means ready to give up her place of responsibility and authority, under God and Dat, to her elder sister. Sadie did not deserve that place of honor. She'd abandoned this family to have her own will and way with her life. And now, if she was to come home, Leah felt strongly about making sure Sadie knew where things stood—certainly no longer could she hold the honored place of Abram's eldest daughter. No, Sadie had forfeited that standing, no two ways about it.

Late in the afternoon Adah surprised Leah by stopping by, once all her wash had been dried and folded. She came alone, all smiles, with a "wonderful-gut idea. Let's have a card shower for your sister." Her eyes were bright with the suggestion. "If ya want, I could help out with some cold cuts and whatnot, turn it into a coming-home party and invite as many of the women folk who'd wanna come." She offered, as well, to spread the news.

"Well, since we don't know exactly *when* she's comin', why not wait to see if she actually does."

Adah frowned quickly. "Do ya mean to say she might change her mind?"

Leah shrugged her shoulders. "How should I know? It's been a long time. . . ."

Nodding, Adah patted her arm. "We'll bide our time, if that's what you want to do."

Leah didn't have the heart to say much more, and she couldn't help but wonder how Mamma would expect her to treat Sadie after all this time. Sooner or later, like Aunt Lizzie had said, Leah knew she would have to unearth the merciless and bitter root deep within and look at it for what it was. *Whatever pain may come of this, for Mamma's sake, I must choose to be kind.*

Chapter Thirty-Three

Leah spied her first—Sadie plodding up the long lane, carrying only a tan suitcase. She looked smaller somehow, weighed down by the cares of life and her bulky luggage. Her dress hung too loosely, as if she'd lost weight suddenly, and her hair was blonder than Leah remembered, the gleam of it peeking out from beneath her prayer veiling. But then again, maybe it was simply the light cast by the sun at high noon.

Leah paused where she was, standing nearly like a statue, bewildered to witness this moment alone. *Where's Dat?* she wondered, thinking she ought to call for him and Dawdi John or Aunt Lizzie—all of them, really.

But she felt the sound of her own voice would have heightened the peculiarity of the moment, making her feel weak, even powerless. She battled against her own reluctance but could not call out even a welcome to her sister; instead, she managed to raise a hand in a feeble wave. Here was the sister she had thought she'd forgiven. Good thing Sadie hadn't looked up right then, noticed her standing there in her old brown choring dress and apron, wearing a pair of

Mamma's worn-out shoes. Good thing, because she'd probably be wondering why Leah wasn't tearing down the path, throwing her arms around her, saying over and again, "Oh, I missed ya ever so much, I did. Wonderful-gut to have you home. . . ."

She swallowed the lump in her throat and wondered where Sadie's children were, or at least the one. Had she left them behind in Indiana with close church friends or Jonas's family, maybe? If so, did this mean she was merely coming for a visit, nothing more? Surprised at the sense of calm that came over her at the latter thought, Leah inhaled deeply and willed herself to move forward.

One step at a time, she made her way down the lane, her legs as stiff as solid planks.

Sadie, seeing her now for the first time, hesitated, then dropped her suitcase and hurried forward. Her arms were outstretched like those of a doll, and her eyes glistened as her embrace found Leah. The bittersweet moment nearly overtook her, so fervently did Sadie enfold her.

"I missed ya so, Leah . . . oh, you just don't know."

"It's been . . . a long . . . time" was the best Leah could muster. To mimic the tender words that came from Sadie's lips would have been false and ever so wrong.

Sadie stepped back and, drying her tears, asked, "Where's Smithy Gid?"

A bit surprised, Leah said, "Oh, he's fillin' silo with Sam Ebersol—you remember our uncle Jesse's youngest boy? Sam and Adah Peachey are married now."

Sadie nodded, seemingly a bit dazed.

"Didja have to travel long?" asked Leah, bending to pick up the suitcase.

"First by bus, then by train; then from Lancaster I rode the trolley back to Strasburg." She stopped and caught her breath. "After that, I hired a taxi driver to bring me on home."

Leah said nothing as Sadie took in the house, the grounds, the barn, and milk house. "So you and Gid, are ya livin' in the main house now? Are Dat and Mamma snug in the Dawdi Haus?"

She felt the air go out of her. "What do ya mean Gid and me?"

"You and your *husband*, Smithy Gid."

"Why, no. He's married to Hannah."

"Hannah?" A quick frown crossed Sadie's brow and she stumbled.

"Watch your step," Leah offered, reaching out a hand.

Sadie grasped it and they walked hand in hand.

"Where are your children?" Leah asked. "We heard you were expecting a baby back some time ago."

Sadie was quiet as they made their way toward the house. "Stillborn babies were all I ever birthed, Leah . . . same as my first wee son, so long ago."

As sorrowful as Sadie appeared just now, Leah thought she best be thinking how she should tell her sister of Mamma's passing. Sadie must hear the heartrending news before ever encountering either Dat or Aunt Lizzie. It was the compassionate thing to do.

When they approached the back door, Leah knew she must speak up. She paused on the sidewalk and turned to look at Sadie. "There's something you oughta know . . . in case you didn't hear. Believe me, I tried to get word to you."

Sadie's countenance turned nearly gray.

As upset as Leah was, her heart went out to her sister. "I'm awful sorry to be the one to tell ya, but someone ever so dear passed away a while back. Someone we all loved very much."

Sadie's eyes welled up with tears, and she shook her head. "Not Mamma. Please, say it's not my mamma."

Leah breathed in some air for courage. "Jah, Mamma's gone to Jesus."

Sadie collapsed on the back stoop, her hands over her eyes, head down, sobbing, knees up close to her face. She began to rock back and forth. "Dear, dear Mamma."

Leah felt compelled to explain further, wanting to comfort her sister in this moment; yet she stood without moving, arms held stiffly behind her back. "Mamma's been gone for many years now. She passed away giving birth to Abe."

Looking up, Sadie blinked her eyes, tears staining her face. "Ya mean to say, Mamma had another child after Lydiann?" Sadie frowned with wonder. "I have a baby brother?"

Leah honestly wished there was a better way to catch her up on things than standing here on the back stoop. "Well . . . Abe's not such a baby anymore. He's nearly seven—will be, come Christmas." She wished to say more, wanted to set the record straight. Abe wasn't just Sadie's baby brother. In all truth, he was Leah's son, only not by birth, just as she had been Mamma's daughter in every way that truly mattered.

But hadn't Sadie, travel weary, taken in enough information in the past few minutes? Maybe too much for having just arrived home. That the gaunt young woman before her had suffered more than her share of pain was clearly etched on her face, beautiful as it still was.

"Come in and rest. I'll make you some sweet tea." Leah opened the door and held it, then led the way into the kitchen.

"That'll hit the spot. Goodness knows, I need something to pick me up." Sadie dried her tears and, sighing loudly, sat down on the bench beside the table.

"Once you've had a sip or two, you'll want to go next door and say hello to Dawdi John and Aunt Lizzie. Dawdi's up in years and doesn't go out much, but he still tells us some mighty interesting stories. He and Lizzie both are excited to see you, of course. Dat, too, but he must be over at the smithy's, or he would've shown his face by now."

"That's all right. I'll take my tea quietly." Sadie accepted the warm cup and held it between her hands, staring at Leah. "Didja . . . well, I mean, should I ask . . . if you ever married?"

Please don't ask this, she thought, unsure how to share any more of the essential things. Leaning her head back, she began. "Long after we heard you were married, nearly two years later, Smithy Gid did court me, but only for a time. When Mamma was dying, she asked me to raise Lydiann and Abe. Honestly, maybe you'd rather not—"

"No, no . . . I want to know about you, sister. It's been the hardest thing, me bein' separated from my own family for all these years."

Leah continued on, telling how she had made the promise to care for Mamma's little ones and how that promise had sealed her future as a maidel due to Dat's eagerness to raise his own son and daughter, instead of allowing Gid and Leah to do so. But she didn't care to say much more. It was enough . . . almost, to have Sadie sitting here in the kitchen, sipping brewed tea with her, like old times. Enough to have those sad blue eyes staring and searching hungrily, as if looking for meaning in Leah's gaze, longing to know what she had missed here in her own family's home.

Leah didn't have the heart to go on, though she wished she might tell Sadie how sorry she was Jonas had died so terribly young, leaving her a widow. *Awful sorry . . .*

———◆———

Leah felt nearly too ill to attend the required membership meeting the Sunday following Sadie's arrival, but she went anyway, sitting clear in the back, thus allowing herself no *visual* memory of repentant Sadie kneeling before the People. But her ears surely witnessed Sadie's embarrassing, even frank words of confession—the repeated meetings in the hunter's shack in the woods, the loss of her illegitimate son. . . . She cringed, wishing to stop up her ears, as well, but surely . . . *surely*, Sadie's heart was pure before God and the People. Surely Sadie hadn't come home to repent just because she was a widow and all alone in the world.

Leah, nevertheless, had become quite ill with an early autumn flu. The stress of having to vote to receive her shunned sister back into the fold had made her absolutely green round the gills, but she did her duty as a church member in good standing. *Good thing the ministers can't see into my heart,* she thought, despising her own reluctance to forgive and forget.

After the common meal at Uncle Jesse Ebersol's place, where house church had been held, several couples and their

335

families followed Dat's carriage back home for a visit. Naomi and Luke Bontrager came with their little boys, as well as Hannah and Gid and their girls.

Mary Ruth joined all of them after church, as well, just as she'd quickly come to visit on the first evening of Sadie's arrival.

Leah felt some better later in the afternoon and joined the cheerful group, though she kept to herself, not stepping into her usual role as hostess. No doubt sensing her difficulty, dear Lizzie filled her shoes instead, and Leah pulled up a chair, relieved to simply sit and not lift a finger.

Abe hovered near, evidently not interested in playing with his cousins. Leah was glad for his company and that he stood protectively beside her chair for the longest time. Lydiann, however, was her outgoing self, readily engaging the laughter and attention of the big sister she'd never known. Because of the severity of the shunning, neither Lydiann nor Abe could remember hearing Sadie's name uttered in their lifetime. So there was much catching up to be done, and everyone, especially Sadie, seemed to enjoy the spontaneous get-together. They all stayed and talked till milking time, and then disbanded outdoors with Naomi and Sadie weeping in each other's arms, best friends reuniting under the canopy of heaven.

Dear Lord, please give me the grace I need, Leah pleaded. But the tearful scene was too much for her, and she slipped back into the house to soothe herself yet again.

Chapter Thirty-four

Soon the daily routine—Monday washday, Tuesday ironing and cleaning—took precedence as the newness of Sadie's return began to wear off, at least for Leah. Lydiann, on the other hand, was rather taken with Sadie and followed her around the house incessantly, Leah noticed.

Early Wednesday morning, while Leah was still making the bed in her room, a firm knock came at the door. "Who's there?" she called, reckoning who it might be.

"It's Sadie."

Stopping what she was doing, Leah moved toward the door and opened it slowly.

Before her stood her sister, the blue gone from her eyes, washed away by tears. "May I come in?" she asked.

"If it's important enough for you to be cryin', then I 'spect we ought to go outside," she surprised herself by saying. Honestly, she didn't much care to hear Sadie tell of her widowed sorrow, not in the privacy of Leah's bedroom. Not this near-sacred place where Mamma had given up her life for Abe . . . and where Leah had made her important promise.

337

"I'm not meanin' to box your ears," Sadie said suddenly. "But the way ya talk, you'd think we were gonna have it out between us."

Leah hadn't meant to be reckless with her words. "I'll meet you out front, where we can speak plainly without bein' overheard."

Sadie frowned, seemingly surprised. "All right, then."

Leah closed her door. She took her time finishing up the bed making, even set the green shades straight, eyeing them carefully so they each matched in length across the three windows on the side facing the woods. All this before ever leaving the house to meet Sadie.

"Truth be told, you act like you wish I'd stayed away forever," Sadie said when they were alone amidst the trees on the rolling front lawn. "And don't be sayin' otherwise."

There was nothing to add, really. Leah felt if she couldn't say anything nice, she ought not to say anything at all.

"What's wrong, Leah? Why do you seem to detest me?"

She filled her lungs with air. "Best not talk 'bout it, I'm thinkin'."

"Why? Does it annoy you that I assumed you were married to Smithy Gid? If so, I was only saying what Jonas told me years back."

"He told you *that?*" She was as bewildered now as she had been the day his strange letter arrived, followed by total silence once she promptly responded, writing him the truth.

"Several times, jah."

"But there was nothing tender between Gid and me, 'least not while I was engaged to Jonas." She paused. "Are you rememberin' things correctly—did Jonas really say that?"

"Why, sure he did. Even his father confirmed to Jonas that Gid was sweet on you, that Dat had given his blessing for him to court you. All this while you were betrothed to Jonas—just as he was completing his carpentry apprenticeship and preparing to travel home for your wedding."

So this was what Peter Mast and Dat had secretly discussed—the two of them had destroyed her future with Jonas!

"Frankly," Sadie went on, "at the time, I found it downright surprisin', but I assumed you'd decided to follow Dat's wishes in the end and marry Gid instead."

"That's ridiculous. You of all people knew how much I loved Jonas!"

"Jah, I thought I knew that, but I was altogether befuddled when I saw you and Gid holdin' hands in the woods that day you got yourself lost up there. Remember?"

"You saw *what?*" She couldn't believe her ears. Sadie was off in the head!

Her sister went on, describing the day Gid had gone in search of Leah, at Mamma's urging. Sadie told how she herself had gone into the forest, up to the low stone wall rimming Aunt Lizzie's log house. "Smithy Gid and you were holding hands and laughin' together. I saw it with my own eyes, so you can't deny it."

"You must've told this to Jonas," Leah said, not recalling the hand-holding incident whatsoever. "You made me look unfaithful . . . was that what you did?"

Sadie shook her head, blinking back tears. "I simply told

him once he asked what I knew 'bout Gid, and only after that. You must believe me, Leah. He'd heard, but not from me, that you'd gone to a summertime singing in our barn where you'd linked up with Gid, then walked home with him through the cornfield."

Again, she was wholly baffled. "I believe I recall that evening, but Adah and I went *together* to the singing. She and I, along with Gid—the three of us—walked over to the Peacheys' afterward . . . innocent as the day is long."

Sadie touched her elbow. "Ach, Leah, I don't care to bring up the past. That's not why I say these things. I only wondered why you hadn't married Smithy Gid after Jonas and I had believed it so strongly."

They were still for a moment as the sun rose higher through the trees from its dawning place. "I s'pose there's nothin' to be gained by rehashing all this," Leah said, grappling with her own words. "We oughta be thinking of *you* now, sister. Your needs . . . your great loss." She looked at her brokenhearted sister, sharing the intense sorrow. "How sad to have lost Jonas that way—in the silo accident. I feel right sorry for you . . . him so young and all."

A shadow swept over Sadie's face. "Didja say . . . Jonas?"

Leah nodded, unable to go on, wishing not to visualize the fatal fall from such a height.

Sadie shook her head slowly. "Oh, Leah . . . no wonder. You're sadly mistaken. I haven't seen Jonas in years."

Leah's breath bounded out of her lungs. *What on earth . . . how can this be?* "You mean you didn't . . . you never married Jonas at all?" She held herself around the middle, thinking she might be sick then and there.

Shaking her head, Sadie appeared as flabbergasted as Leah felt. "Why, no. I married Harvey Hochstetler . . . from Indiana." Sadie began to explain how Jonas had taken care to befriend her after she'd shared with him the tale of her wild rumschpringe. He had gone so far as to begin to date her, "solely out of a sense of duty, not love. He and I went our separate ways the following spring, after I met a boy named John Graber, who introduced me to Harvey."

"And what of Jonas? Where is he?"

Sadie shook her head sadly. "I don't know."

"When was the last you heard of him? Where was he then?" She felt nearly panic-stricken, suddenly aware of the horrid string of deceit coupled with misunderstandings. Unspeakable, for sure and for certain.

"I last saw Jonas in Millersburg. He was preparing to move, though he never said just where. I assumed he was hoping to set up his own carpentry shop somewhere in Ohio, but I can't be sure." Sadie went on. "Bein' shunned ruined his life, he said. It changed everything . . . made it impossible for him to continue his ties with his family and friends. Jonas once told me he felt like a man without a country. I surely understood that."

"So he just disappeared . . . is that what you're sayin'?" Leah sat right down in the grass, her legs incapable of supporting her. She held her hands over her heart, no longer able to deny her tears. "Oh, Sadie, I can't bear to hear any more," she cried. "Please stop. I . . . loved him so."

Sadie knelt next to her, wrapping her arms around her. "I'm sorry for comin' between you and Jonas," she whispered, leaning her head against Leah's. "I should've known you and

Smithy Gid were merely good friends. I should've known. . . ."

Like a breeze blowing the memory of that day gently back, the treacherous hike out of the deepest part of the woods became clear in Leah's mind. She recalled well-meaning Gid reaching for her hand several times, steadying her when she felt nearly too weak to walk, having strayed through the immense tangle of the woods, wandering for hours. He had merely protected her as a big brother. Nothing more.

But there were no words now to speak the truth of it to Sadie. Instead, she wept in her big sister's arms—for the lost years, for her resentment toward Sadie, who had been caught in a maze of misconceptions. Her heart ached, as well, for the long-ago sweetheart she would never see again. Dear Jonas . . . gone forever. Leah felt as if her very life was being driven from her.

Whispering now, Sadie said, "Do you remember what Mamma used to tell us? 'God knows the end from the beginning.'"

How on earth could the Lord God know such a thing, as Mamma had ofttimes said, and yet allow what had happened to take place? The end from the beginning. Leah had missed being Jonas's loving wife by a series of errors. Nothing more.

After a time, when the sadness and disbelief had spilled forth in a great veil of tears—Sadie comforting her through it all—Leah dried her eyes and kissed her sister. "The grapevine had it all wrong 'bout you and Jonas," Leah said softly, still puzzled by the absolute certainty of the news they'd received over the years.

Sadie spoke up, attesting to the fickleness of gossip. "No

wonder you've despised tittle-tattle your whole life," she remarked, to which Leah could only nod her throbbing head.

Together, the two of them rose slowly and walked hand in hand toward the house. *Sadie's return is both an end and a beginning for us all,* Leah thought, hoping it would be so when all was said and done. She was mindful to breathe deeply, willing her headache away. The children would be hungry for breakfast soon, and she must wear a smile for them.

But it was Sadie who was smiling broadly now. "What do ya say if I help Dat and Lydiann with the milkin' from here on out?"

"Well, now, are ya sure, sister?"

"That's one chore you should never have to do again. After all these years."

Leah was surprised but pleased. "Sounds quite all right to me. I'll be glad to cook breakfast and pack the children's lunch pails." With Sadie's offer to do the milking chores, Leah realized they'd reversed roles from childhood. Not only that, but she and Sadie were both single women, without husbands or hope of any. *Together under the same roof,* she thought, finding the notion almost humorous in a strange sort of way, recalling the saying, "Too many cooks spoil the broth."

With that she carried stacked firewood for the cook stove into the kitchen, where she was met by the sound of Lydiann's expressive voice. Sitting at the table, Lydiann carefully practiced the poem she was expected to recite at school today.

" 'My Father, what am I that all Thy mercies sweet, like sunlight fall so constant o'er my way? That thy great love should shelter me, and guide my steps so tenderly through every changing day?'"

Leah could not simply stand there and overhear the truth of the rhymed verse, spoken so clearly by her young charge. Honestly, she couldn't help herself; she smiled. Quickly pushing the wood into the belly of the stove, she hurried to Lydiann's side. "God's mercies *are* new every morning, ain't so?" she found herself saying as she slipped her arm around her.

Looking up at her with shining eyes, Lydiann said, "You must've heard me sayin' my poem, Mamma."

"Indeed I did, and I hope you never forget those perty words, 'cause they're ever so true." Leah's heart was filled anew with love for her dear ones. She kissed her girl's forehead and rose to make pancakes, eager for this shining new day.

Epilogue

It's nearly Christmastide again, and Hannah continues to worry about her new little one coming so close to Abe's seventh birthday—Mamma's going-to-Glory date. I wish she would trust the Good Lord more. Fortunately Sadie's homecoming *has* seemed to help Hannah some. Actually, all of us are better in spirit since Sadie's return to Gobbler's Knob.

Dat and I had a much-needed talk following her return. Both hurt and befuddled, I expressed my disappointment over the role he had played in Jonas's and my breakup. His keen desire for Smithy Gid "to have his chance" was the culprit . . . the one and only motivation for my father's deception. Ever so adamant about my choice of a mate, he sadly shared with me that he had lost his head to dogged aspiration, and one wrong turn had simply led to another. In the end, Dat pleaded my pardon, and I surrendered to his open arms, with a clearer picture of the past. Some might say I have every right to carry a grudge, but an unforgiving spirit eventually destroys the soul, and I have better things to do.

This week Dat and Smithy Peachey are out chopping

wood with a group of other men, filling up the woodsheds round Gobbler's Knob while the women folk have been swapping dozens of cookies and recipes, everything from snowballs and coconut cookies to snickerdoodles and whoopie pies.

I try never to think of Jonas any longer. Knowing him, he's happily married and busy with his carpentry work, with plenty of little mouths to feed. I have to admit I'm glad he didn't end up with Sadie, because then, who knows, he might've been helping to build that silo, same as Harvey Hochstetler was the day he died. Who's to know really, except the Lord. *He* knows the end from the beginning and sees Jonas Mast and his dear ones wherever they are. 'Tis not for me to ponder.

The gray pallor of grief has flown away; I know this to be true. There was a spring in my step early this morning as I donned my boots and trudged through the snow to scatter feed for the small birds that stay with us during winter. While out in the crisp air, I noticed the hydrangea bushes bare against the side of the house. How Mamma loved their colorful summertime clusters! Yet each autumn they shed their pretty pink blossoms, and next year's buds lie dormant on the bough, waiting to burst forth and bloom again.

As for Aunt Lizzie's remark to me in the woods, I'm making a conscious effort to keep my eyes off myself and what I had viewed as a rather bleak future as a maidel, once Lydiann and Abe are grown, that is. I'm looking more compassionately on Sadie—helping her walk through yet another Proving because of our severe bishop. He's setting her up as an example for other young people, just as she always worried he would.

Preacher Yoder's death left a mighty big hole in our midst. We had ordination for the new minister back in October, a week following Sadie's kneeling confession. The divine selection—the lot—fell on Smithy Gid, so he's become Preacher Peachey now, which gets Lydiann's tongue tied up at times. I told her to simply call him Brother Gid, and she does.

Dat's standing up more and more to the bishop and beginning to talk to the Lord on his own, is what Aunt Lizzie tells me. She and Dat still go round and round sometimes, fussing over the least things. I guess she feels she must keep Mamma's beliefs alive with her own voice.

Yesterday Abe came bouncing home from school with a Scripture verse on his lips. " 'Be not conformed to this world,' " he said, eyes big as buttons. To which Sadie nodded her head, genuinely in agreement. *Her* motto these days, and she tells it to the children every other minute seems to me, is " 'For the wages of sin is death; but the gift of God is eternal life.' "

Come spring and the first song of the robin, I will go in search of the honey locust tree. I'll take Lydiann and Abe along and introduce them to the beauty and the tranquility of the deep forest—make some new memories. And when berrypicking time creeps up on us again, we'll go and pick a pail of juicy ripe strawberries and bake some strawberry-rhubarb pies for no other reason than that they taste so wonderful-gut. After all, desserts are supposed to be plenty sweet.

Lately I find myself staring far less at the night sky, contemplating the number of stars, than I do counting the smiles on Lydiann's and Abe's faces, the dear ones Mamma gave to me. Providence, some might say. I call it love, plain and simple.

Acknowledgments

I offer heartfelt thanks to each research assistant and prayer partner, for each helpful encounter, and for each wonderful person who gave expert advice in the thrilling journey-mission of writing this book.

Fondly I think of Eli and Vesta Hochstetler of Berlin, Ohio, who opened their hearts and delightful bookstore to me last fall, and who drove me to visit a working blacksmith shop deep in Amish country. Thank you! Great appreciation also goes to the young Amish smithy who gave a crash course in the art of shoeing horses.

Hank and Ruth Hershberger were a tremendous help, inviting me to their lovely Sugar Creek home and answering numerous questions, including Amish ins and outs of "going on a lark" and "pest hunts." I am truly grateful!

Monk and Marijane Troyer discovered information regarding the horse disease the "strangles," as well as other vital information. Thanks for inviting me to a joyful evening of food and fellowship with your newlywed son and daughter-in-law. I enjoyed every minute of Monk's storytelling, as well.

My thanks to Sandi Heisler, who graciously offered medical information regarding home births and midwives.

A big thank-you to Aleta Hirschberg and Iris Jones, my Kansas aunties, who shared their memories of Saturday-night baths in a large galvanized tub. And to Priscilla Stoltzfus, who helped with many Amish-related questions.

As always, to my devoted friends in Lancaster County Amish country who help with research but who wish to remain anonymous . . . I am forever indebted. May the Lord bless each of you abundantly!

I am so appreciative of my publisher, Gary Johnson, whose wit and wisdom brighten our days, and whose ongoing vision and prayers make books like this one possible.

Many thanks to my superb editors. To Carol Johnson, who knows my readers as well as anyone and who is a treasured friend indeed. To Rochelle Gloege, a remarkable editor who makes my writing sing. And to David Horton, whose astute perspective and attention to the nitty-gritty details are so vital.

To Steve Oates, Bethany's VP of Marketing, and his amazing team, an enormous thank you for the earnest prayers, the behind-the-scenes work that gets my books into the hands of readers, and for Steve's perpetual humor, a welcome relief from the stress of writing deadlines!

To my faithful (and affectionate) readers, who offer a wealth of encouragement. Every letter and email message is read with keen interest and appreciation.

My dear family is my underpinning of support. Much love and gratitude to my husband, Dave, for his tender encouragement and practical help. To Julie, Janie, Jonathan, and Ariel for their infectious smiles, energizing food, and solid editorial input. And I'm ever grateful to my wonderful parents, Herb and Jane Jones, whose life and ministry of faith are the heritage that has brought me this far. Thanks for your persistent prayers, Dad and Mother, so critical to my writing journey.

Finally I offer up my heart anew to my dear Lord Jesus, who has called me to walk with Him all the days of my life.

CB

---◆---

Watch for Book 4,

The Prodigal, in October 2004.

---◆---